Your Fussy Baby

Your Fussy Baby

HOW TO SOOTHE YOUR NEWBORN

MARC WEISSBLUTH, M.D.

BALLANTINE BOOKS

NEW YORK

A Ballantine Book
Published by The Random House Publishing Group

Copyright © 2003 Marc Weissbluth, M.D.

All rights reserved.

Published in the United States by Ballantine Books, an imprint of The
Random House Publishing Group, a division of Random House, Inc.,
New York, and simultaneously in Canada by Random House of Canada
Limited, Toronto.

www.ballantinebooks.com

The Cataloging-in-Publication Data for this title is available from the
Library of Congress.

ISBN 978-0-345-46300-5

Cover design by Richard Rossiter
Cover photograph by LWA-Dann Tardis/CORBIS

Printed in the United States of America

First Edition: August 2003

9 8 7 6 5

This book is dedicated to
Linda Weissbluth

Contents

ACKNOWLEDGMENTS   xv

INTRODUCTION   xvii

   HOW TO USE THIS BOOK IF YOU HAVE NOT YET
     DELIVERED YOUR BABY   xvii

   HOW TO USE THIS BOOK IF YOU HAVE ALREADY
     DELIVERED YOUR BABY   xvii

   WHAT IS "FUSSING"?   xvii

   MY FIRST EXPERIENCE WITH EXTREME FUSSINESS   xix

Chapter 1. Common Fussiness and Crying   1

   WHAT DOES CRYING MEAN?   2

   WHAT SHOULD PARENTS DO ABOUT CRYING?   3

     You Cannot Spoil Your Newborn   3

     Frequent and Infrequent Criers   5

   SIMILARITIES BETWEEN COMMON FUSSINESS/
     CRYING AND EXTREME FUSSINESS/COLIC   5

     1. All Babies Cry Some of the Time   6

     2. Some Crying Cannot Be Attributed
       to an Obvious Cause   6

     3. Two to Three Hours of Crying Per Day
       Is Average   8

     4. Many Babies Have Evening Crying
       Spells   9

     5. Crying Decreases at About Three Months   9

   EXTREME FUSSINESS/COLIC MAY JUST BE A LOT OF
     COMMON FUSSINESS   10

   WHICH BABIES CRY MORE?   14

Chapter 2. Extreme Fussiness/Colic   16

   CLINICAL DEFINITIONS OF EXTREME FUSSINESS/COLIC   20

IS EXTREME FUSSINESS/COLIC A DISEASE?   22

EXTREME FUSSINESS IS VERY COMMON   22

THE CURIOUS HISTORY OF EXTREME FUSSINESS/COLIC   24

    Extreme Fussiness/Colic Is Not the
      Sort of Problem Doctors Like   25

    The Nature of Extreme Fussiness/Colic
      in Behavioral Research   26

    A Bias Against Moms?   27

    What Can a Doctor Do About Extreme
      Fussiness/Colic?   27

    You and Your Pediatrician   28

ELEVEN MYTHS ABOUT EXTREME FUSSINESS/COLIC

(AND WHY YOU SHOULDN'T BELIEVE THEM)   29

    Fallacy No. 1: There Is No Such
      Thing as Extreme Fussiness/Colic   29

    Fallacy No. 2: Maternal Anxiety
      Causes Extreme Fussiness/Colic   30

    Fallacy No. 3: Extreme Fussiness/Colic
      Is a Gastrointestinal Problem   31

    Fallacy No. 4: Something the Baby
      Has Eaten Disagrees with Her   32

    Fallacy No. 5: The Nursing Mother's Diet   34

    Fallacy No. 6: Breast-fed Babies
      Have Less Extreme Fussiness/Colic   35

    Fallacy No. 7: Firstborn Children Have
      Extreme Fussiness/Colic More Often   36

    Fallacy No. 8: Fresh Air Causes
      Extreme Fussiness/Colic   37

    Fallacy No. 9: Boys Get It More than Girls   37

    Fallacy No. 10: Better-Educated Mothers
      Have More Extremely Fussy/
      Colicky Babies   38

    Fallacy No. 11: Extremely Fussy/Colicky
      Babies Are More Intelligent   38

    Why So Many Myths?   39

WHAT WE ACTUALLY KNOW ABOUT EXTREME

FUSSINESS/COLIC   40

    What Kind of Research?   40

    Dr. Illingworth: It's Not Allergy, Gas,
      or Spoiling   42

Dr. Wessel: It's Not Allergy and It's
Not the Family 45
Dr. Paradise: It's Not the Mother's
Personality 47
Dr. Stewart: It's Tension 50
Dr. Schnall and Dr. Shaver: It Is
Not Maternal Anxiety 52
Urinary Tract Infection? 54
Drugs During Labor? 54
Gastroesophageal Reflux 55
Naturally Occurring Substances
May Cause Extreme Fussiness/Colic 55
Exterogestation 59
Severe Physiological Disturbances 60
THE STATE OF THE ART OF EXTREME FUSSINESS/COLIC 61

Chapter 3. Birth to Four Months of Age: How to
Soothe and Help Your Baby to Sleep 63
INTRODUCTION AND ADVICE 63
YOUR RELATIONSHIP WITH YOUR EXTREMELY
FUSSY/COLICKY BABY 64
Take Care of Yourself 65
Creative Parenting 67
Hospitalization 68
Caring for a Family with an
Extremely Fussy/Colicky Newborn 69
Father Care: Our Secret Weapon
for Soothing 70
Sucking Is Soothing 72
Rhythmic Rocking Motions 75
Swaddling 76
Music 77
Voices 77
Sound Machines 77
Lullabies 78
Massage 80
Sleep Associations 81
Respect Your Baby's Need to Sleep:
The One- to Two-Hour Window
of Wakefulness 82

Drowsy Cues	83
Other Soothing Methods	84
Everything Works . . . for a While	85
Night-lights	86
WHAT IS BEST FOR YOU AND YOUR FAMILY?	86
Breast-feeding Versus Formula Feeding	86
Family Bed Versus Crib	88
Back Sleeping Versus Side Sleeping	89
New Mothers Versus Experienced Mothers	89
Older Mothers Versus Younger Mothers	90
Singletons Versus Multiples	91
Return to Work	91
"No Cry" Versus "Let Cry"	92
Sleep Training Does Not Mean "Let Cry"	92
Sleep Training: My Idea	93
Newborns	93
Babies a Few Weeks Old	94
Six-Week-Old and Older Babies	95
Problems in Older Babies	97
Mistaken Ideas About Sleep Training	98
DIFFERENT DECISIONS FOR DIFFERENT BABIES	98
Introduction	98
Common Fussiness	103
Extreme Fussiness/Colic	104
Breast-feeding the Fussy Baby *(Nancy Nelson, R.N., IBCLC)*	111
Chapter 4. Temperament at Four Months of Age	118
EXTREME FUSSINESS AND TEMPERAMENT	118
A STANDARDIZED TEMPERAMENT RATING	119
INFANT TEMPERAMENT CHARACTERISTICS	119
Activity (General Motion, Energy)	120
Rhythmicity (Regularity of Bodily Functions)	120
Approach/Withdrawal (First Reaction)	120
Adaptability (Flexibility)	121
Intensity	126
Mood	126
Persistence	126
Distractibility	127

Threshold (Sensitivity) 127

DIFFICULT TEMPERAMENT 128

LIMITATIONS OF TEMPERAMENT MEASURES 129

DIFFICULT TEMPERAMENT AND EXTREME

FUSSINESS/COLIC 131

Chapter 5. After Four Months of Age: How to Prevent Sleep Problems 133

INTRODUCTION: SLEEP BEFORE AND AFTER

FOUR MONTHS 133

Is Extreme Fussiness/Colic a Sleep Disorder? 133

Newborn Sleep Patterns 135

Sleeping Positions 136

Understanding Sleep: Sleep States 136

Newborns Have a Unique Sleep

Pattern for Three to Four Months 137

Day Sleep Versus Night Sleep 137

Possibility No. 1: Extreme Fussiness/Colic is

Connected with Disorganized Sleep 138

Sleep and Breathing Rhythms 139

Sleep, Temperature, and Endocrine Rhythms 140

Possibility No. 2: Extreme Fussiness/

Colic Is an "Acted-Out" REM Period 142

The Crying-Temperament-Sleep Connection 144

Extreme Fussiness/Colic May Be

Part of a Larger Problem 147

As Extreme Fussiness Ends 149

Time for a Change 149

MOTHERS' DESCRIPTIONS OF THEIR BABIES

AT AGE FOUR MONTHS 150

WHAT MOTHERS SAY ABOUT FIRST BABIES

AFTER EXTREME FUSSINESS/COLIC ENDS 154

SECOND-BORN INFANTS ARE LIKE FIRST-

BORNS AFTER EXTREME FUSSINESS/COLIC ENDS 157

EXPERIENCED MOTHERS AND EXTREMELY

FUSSY/COLICKY BABIES 158

SLEEP AFTER EXTREME FUSSINESS/COLIC ENDS 159

What Is a Good Night's Sleep? 160

Does Your Baby Have a Sleep Problem? 161

What's Enough Sleep for a Newborn? 161

Solid Foods   162

Night Wakings Are Normal   162

Parental Response   163

When Older Babies Wake at Night   164

Why Older Infants Awaken   164

The Wrong Sleep Schedule   164

Parental Reinforcement   165

Your Cranky Baby May Just Be Tired   165

BREAST-FEEDING VERSUS BOTTLE-FEEDING

AND FAMILY BED VERSUS CRIB   166

Introduction   166

"No Cry" Versus "Let Cry"   168

Common Fussiness (80 Percent):

Low Risk for Sleep Problems

After Four Months   170

"Check and Console" or Graduated

Extinction ("Controlled Crying")   171

Extreme Fussiness/Colic (20 Percent):

High Risk for Sleep Problems

After Four Months   174

Gradual Approach   177

Step 1: Do Not Pick Him Up   178

Step 2: Cut Back on Your Responses   178

Step 3: Spend Less Time   179

Step 4: Wait a While   179

Will It Work?   179

Focus on the Morning Nap   180

The One- to Two-Hour Window of

Wakefulness   181

"Do I Have to Put My Baby Down

While She Is Still Awake?"   182

Bottle-feeding and Crib   183

Breast-feeding and Family Bed   184

THE TREATMENT OF TRAINED NIGHT CRYING   184

Let the Baby Alone   184

Learn to Be Consistent   185

Reduce External Stimulation   185

Begin with Bedtime   186

PARENTS: NO EXCUSES!   187

Make the Decision   188

And Then Do It 189

If It Doesn't Work 190

Improvement 190

Drugs to Make Your Baby Sleep 190

Not All Night Waking Is a Problem 191

MOTHERS TALK ABOUT THEIR EXPERIENCES 191

WHAT SHOULD I DO? 212

Chapter 6. Love Your Baby 213

HUGS, KISSES, AND LOVE HELP YOUR BABY GROW 216

**Chapter 7. Summary and Action Plans
for Exhausted Parents** 217

Sleep Time Routines 221

Short Intervals of Wakefulness 222

WATCH FOR DROWSY SIGNS

SLEEP TRAINING SUMMARY 223

Four Months of Age 225

After Four Months of Age 228

INDEX 233

Acknowledgments

I am grateful to those parents who contributed their stories and to Mrs. Clare K. Rothschild for her editorial assistance.

Introduction

How to Use This Book if You Have Not Yet Delivered Your Baby

Are you a mother reading this book before you have delivered your baby? If so, I strongly suggest that you read Chapters 1, 2, and 3, which explain what we know about fussy babies, so that you will better understand how to soothe your baby after your baby is born.

How to Use This Book if You Have Already Delivered Your Baby

If you have already delivered your baby and are exhausted or worried or both, turn to Chapter 7 immediately for a quick summary of the background and plan of action. Then turn to Chapter 3 for more details.

If you are a father reading this book, you will not suffer from "baby brain"—the confused mental state caused by the fatigue, stress, and sleep deprivation from not sleeping well for many months before and after the baby is born. Therefore, read the entire book as quickly as you can to coach your wife through this wonderful, marvelous, and chaotic time.

What Is "Fussing"?

Giving birth to a new baby unleashes unique and powerful forces within both mother and baby. The experience of childbirth is an event unlike all others. Furthermore, the job of having a baby is different from the more ordinary pleasures women experience. Caressing her, holding her warm skin to your cheek, feeding her, gazing into her eyes . . . your heart melts. Could there be a more beautiful and graceful creation?

During the first few days, your child is so peaceful and calm, you may wonder if you have to wake her to feed her. You may notice that she does not suck with very much strength or interest before she snoozes off into deep slumber again. It is even normal for your baby to lose weight during these first few days. In fact, if your baby was born early, this quiet and sleepy state may last longer than a few days.

After a few days, or around the due date for babies born early, however, you may notice that things begin to change. Your baby becomes more wakeful and alert and sucks with more strength. She has a more wide-open-eyed look. It is as if her sleepy brain has begun to wake up—just in time to catch the breast milk if you are nursing your baby. The weight loss that is normal in babies during the few days after birth slows down, stops, and then reverses itself.

As your baby becomes more wakeful, she moves her arms and legs around more, and her eyes study and follow you about; sometimes she may even fuss for several minutes. To "fuss" is to become upset, to fret, to be less settled, or to get stirred up. During a fussy spell, your baby appears nervous, agitated, and unable to fall asleep or stay awake. Sometimes she appears irritable—excitable, easily upset, and unhappily sensitive to stimuli such as loud noises. She may melt down into a crying state easily if not soothed by her parents. It is not clear what is irritating, annoying, or exasperating her. This behavior may irritate a mother or father as well. Parents feel sympathy for their baby and might also feel displeasure that she requires so much attention. When extra soothing seems not to help, the baby may provoke in her parents feelings of impatience or even anger.

All babies have moments of fussiness and irritability. Some babies, however, have so much of this fussiness and irritability that if you added up all the minutes of fussiness and irritability, it would be equal to more than three hours per day. If your baby behaves this way for more than three days a week and for more than three weeks, it is often labeled "extreme fussiness." "Colic" has also been used to describe babies with extreme fussiness, but there is no reason to use this separate label. I prefer to use the term "extreme fussiness" because all babies fuss; some babies simply fuss more and all babies fuss much more than they cry. Unfortunately, some babies with extreme fussiness also have moments of inconsolable crying. This means that they might cry despite all efforts to comfort them. This book will explain how to soothe all babies during their fussy moments, whether it is low-level, common fussiness or intense, heart-rending, never-ending, extreme fussiness/colic.

Every new parent quickly discovers two facts: Though it is not always easy to soothe a baby, you cannot send a fussy baby back. My wife, Linda, liked to teasingly say that she looked for a return address on Elliot, our first son, during his spells of extreme fussiness. If your baby has extreme fussiness, he is undoubtedly putting you through a trying and confusing time. You may face hours of fussing or crying every day. You may feel that your baby is beyond your reach. You may not be getting much rest. You may feel guilty, angry, or just unlucky. You may not really understand what is happening or why. If so, I wrote this book for you.

Furthermore, fussiness often causes parents to go back on their initial decisions to breast-feed or sleep with a baby, because the baby is so disconcertingly fussy. Again, if you are facing this problem, I wrote this book for you.

My First Experience with Extreme Fussiness

I was a medical student at Stanford University when my first son was born. He fussed and cried for hours on end. Neither my wife nor I thought this was strange. We assumed that all babies behaved this way. No one told us (fortunately) that he had a "condition." We didn't know enough to worry that it might be because he was a boy, or a firstborn, or breast-fed, or because we were unwittingly making him miserable. The relative dearth of information on extreme fussiness in the sixties was a blessing for us.

I remember rocking my son for hours on end while memorizing neuroanatomy. I would close my eyes, hoping he would do the same, but when I peeked to see if he'd fallen asleep, his radar-beam gaze was solidly fixed on me. Calming him down usually required an hour or two of rocking. Once he began breathing deeply and regularly in my arms I would attempt to put him down in his crib. But if I was impatient and tried to put him down before true deep sleep developed, he would arch his back, open his eyes wide, and resume the dreaded fussing and crying.

My wife was studying Old Church Slavonic (which is, in my opinion, harder than neuroanatomy) at the time. So we took turns pacing, walking, and rocking. In our student apartment, my son's room was above our postage stamp–sized kitchen. I remember unwashed dinner dishes piling up because the slightest bang from a dish or cabinet might awaken our little angel. Looking back, I think we were too tired and preoccupied to worry about this behavior. But it was a very taxing time. (And I have never felt quite the same about neuroanatomy.)

If this routine sounds unhappily familiar to you, you might like to know that things settled down for us within a few months. In his fourth month, our son transitioned into a delightful and peaceful baby. Furthermore, our three subsequent children had no extreme fussiness or crying. I would even argue that if I were not a pediatrician and researcher on the problem of extreme fussiness, I would probably remember those first long months with Elliot as an entirely delightful time in our lives.

Though I did not label it at the time, Elliot had a classic case of extreme fussiness, also called colic. There is even some question as to whether labeling a pattern of behavior such as this one makes it seem better or worse. In any case, many parents are relieved to know that this kind of fussing is so common that traditional medicine gives it a name. Others, though, feel differently; as one mother told me, "Once you give it a name, it's a real problem." A father was perfectly willing to admit that his young daughter fussed and screamed for hours on end, but emphatically denied that she could have extreme fussiness/colic. If parents prefer to think they just have a fussy baby, this is fine. For, as we shall see, the line between normal fussing behaving and extreme fussiness/colic is arbitrary. When does sadness become depression? When does overweight become obesity? When does intelligence become genius? Fussing and crying becomes extreme fussiness/colic when doctors and medical researchers say it does. The question is, how do they come to their conclusions, and how do these pertain to you?

The fact is, all normal babies fuss some of the time, and most parents are not sure how to handle it. You may have seen child care books with charts that depicts extreme fussiness/colic behavior in one column and plain crying in another. The charts are meant as tools to help parents determine whether their child has extreme fussiness/colic or not. Of course, such charts are misleading. Extreme fussiness is not an absolute, all-or-nothing proposition. In fact, one researcher, Dr. Joseph Brennemann, wrote that fussiness is "an almost inevitable occurrence sometime in early infancy. Few infants escape it." He is right that **all** babies have periods of unexplained fussiness. The fussiness that drives parents to distraction and puzzles pediatricians, however, the condition that warrants the label "extreme fussiness," is the kind that lasts for several hours a day over the course of several weeks or months. Even this behavior, though, is simply on the extreme end of a spectrum of normal crying and fussing in infants. Extreme fussiness, therefore, is just an extreme form of what all normal healthy babies do. *Extreme fussiness/colic is not a disease.*

This book aims to teach you why babies fuss as a means of helping you cope with as well as soothe fussy babies. Because extreme fussiness/colic means different things to different people and because trustworthy information is scarce, enormous numbers of so-called solutions have been put forth over the years. Unfortunately, many treatments—even some suggested by doctors and nurses—are totally ineffectual. One of the purposes of this book is to separate these so-called facts from the truth. I examine the most common theories about extreme fussiness, many of which you have probably already heard from well-meaning relatives and friends. I will review what reliable modern research can actually claim to know about extreme fussiness, based on properly conducted scientific experiments reported in professional journals. For example, a number of studies have pointed to links connecting extreme fussiness/colic with a certain infant temperaments and/or sleep rhythms. Here I have brought together for you a sampling of the results of the most reliable and significant studies in hopes of shedding light on this rather common but forbidding topic. Finally, I offer suggestions on coping with extreme fussiness in light of this information. I will also discuss how to prevent extreme fussiness from turning into a long-term behavioral sleeping problem and how to solve that problem if it occurs.

Over time a predictable sleep-wake cycle will develop in your baby. This rhythm is the outward manifestation of an *internal timing system*. Imagine many little clocks ticking throughout the entire body, all under the control of a master clock in our brain. The master clock is like a conductor that sets the tempo so that all of the body clocks, like musicians, are in time with each other. It takes time, about three to four months or sometimes longer, for the internal timing system to develop. Babies fuss and/or cry a lot during the first three to four months, especially at six weeks of age. After six weeks, the clocks that control night sleep have developed and most babies are now more able to settle down and sleep better at night. Later, after twelve to sixteen weeks, the clocks that control daytime sleep, or naps, have developed, and most babies are now more able to take more predictable, longer, and fewer naps.

The development of this **internal timing system** is under genetic control, so there is a lot of individual variation. It is as if some children are doing the tango and others are doing the waltz! As parents, we have to learn to dance in sync with our children. But sometimes we may feel like we have two left feet.

The reason it is easy to trip or get out of sync is because our baby's rhythms shift around and take time to develop, so it can be hard to follow them. Please don't give up, even though it is sometimes hard to follow the beat or the dance is hard to learn.

This book is based on the belief that an informed parent is an effective parent. Parents are better able to soothe fussy babies when they understand why newborn babies fuss.

Your Fussy Baby

CHAPTER 1

Common Fussiness and Crying

Some of the things we know about ordinary, brief, or common fussing and crying shed light on extreme fussiness/colic. This information is often comforting to parents who are distressed by their child's fussing or crying. (If you have skipped the Introduction, you may want to go back and read it now. The Introduction explains how to use the book and describes what I mean by "fussiness.")

As a pediatrician, parents often ask me why their babies fuss or cry—and often during such inconvenient hours! While it is true that babies often "melt down" during the evening and sleeping hours, these behaviors also occur during the day. During the day, though, their fussing is less bothersome, making less of an impression. Step number one in understanding your baby's fussiness is to try to become sensitive to *all* of your child's fussy times and even to gradations between the best and worst fussing or crying. It might be worthwhile to keep a detailed diary so that you can separate your child's actual behavior from your perceptions, which can be affected by your own tiredness and frustration. And even the fussiest babies have good times, too, which may also be helpful to record.

I admit it can be hard to be objective about fussing and crying. Crying is an irritating sound. It seems to suggest misery and pain. It is virtually impossible to ignore. There is

1

something about it that, as one mother put it, "poisons the atmosphere." You cannot sleep, enjoy a meal, or concentrate on anything else when you can hear a baby crying. Crying might be a survival mechanism that developed in the process of human evolution. It certainly seems to be nature's way of making sure a baby gets the attention she needs.

What Does Crying Mean?

Tennyson wrote in "In Memoriam":

> *But what am I?*
> *An infant crying in the night;*
> *An infant crying for the light;*
> *And with no language but a cry.*

Of course, crying is one of the only ways a newborn infant can communicate. But the meaning of a baby's crying is open to interpretation. We think that a crying baby is hurting, frightened, or angry; this crying is taken as a form of criticism, loneliness, or tension.

There is something in each of us that identifies with a baby's crying. Who has not felt alone in a strange world, cold, confused, and unable to communicate? We project onto the sobbing child all the despair of the human condition. But it is important to recognize that we really do not know what a baby's crying means. Though babies do cry when they have been hurt or frightened, it is incorrect to assume that a crying infant is either hurt or scared. We cannot even be certain a crying baby is unhappy. Some researchers have observed that stress hormones do not increase during some spells of crying as they do during, for example, circumcision or the drawing of blood from an infant. On the basis of this they concluded that during extreme fussiness, babies were not experiencing pain. Perhaps there is some truth to the folk wisdom which claims that babies cry "to exercise their lungs" or because it's one of the few things they know how to do. Birds fly, babies cry.

Whatever the case (and we will return to the important problem of why babies cry), remember that a screaming infant is not "doing a number" on you. Infants do not cry to manipulate, influence, punish, control, or intentionally annoy you. Infants of one to four months do not realize that their crying can get results. They do not even know that they are a separate person from you. They are just crying. And they may not even realize that!

What Should Parents Do About Crying?

A well-known British pediatrician, Dr. Illingworth, once claimed that one cause of crying is fatigue. This might suggest that you should let a crying baby alone to sleep. But Illingworth also added, categorically, that during the first few weeks of life an infant should be consoled rather than left alone. He claimed that picking up a baby when he or she cries results in less crying later on. This claim was later verified in a direct observational study by American researchers Silvia Bell and Mary Ainsworth at John Hopkins University. They disproved the notion that continually responding to a newborn's cry encourages crying behavior.

You Cannot Spoil Your Newborn

Bell and Ainsworth focused on twenty-six middle-class infant-mother pairs. Data were gathered by observing these mothers and children at home. First, observers confirmed that *all* infants have some crying spells. They noted the number of crying episodes that a mother ignored, the number she responded to, the length of time it took her to respond, what kind of response she made, and the overall effectiveness of her response. Picking up the baby and holding him proved to be the most effective way to terminate crying. Talking to him or gesturing at him from a distance was the least effective.

Bell and Ainsworth observed that, during the first few months, some mothers were deliberately unresponsive when their babies cried because they feared they might spoil their babies.

Data over an entire year, however, showed that mothers who consistently and promptly responded to their infant's crying were rewarded at the age of one year with infants who cried less frequently, and for shorter durations, than those infants whose mothers ignored crying or delayed responding.

The authors of the study concluded, therefore, that infant crying is so disagreeable or "changeworthy" to adults that it probably serves a useful evolutionary function. They added that infant crying should be viewed as an "attachment" or "proximity-promoting" behavior because most often it served to bring a parent closer to a child. Furthermore, Bell and Ainsworth acknowledged the extreme difficulty of a mother or father ignoring a baby's crying. They recommended that a mother not struggle to overcome the natural impulse to comfort her crying child. An infant less than three months of age is, according to their study, at no risk of being spoiled.

The conclusion of this study is similar to others that suggest that conditioning or training an infant is extremely difficult even in a carefully controlled laboratory environment. Spoiling, after all, is simply encouraging an undesirable behavior. But babies under a few months of age cannot "learn" a crying habit because they are not neurologically mature enough (neurological maturity is a necessary precursor to what later becomes psychological development). After all, at three weeks of age a baby is not even neurologically mature enough to learn to smile specifically at her mother. This suggests that it takes time for a baby's brain to develop before it can recognize you and respond to this recognition (and melt your heart with her fantastic smile). Specific social smiling at parents normally develops at about six weeks (in premature deliveries, this occurs at about six weeks after the expected date of delivery). The logic follows: If you cannot teach a baby to smile before she is neurologically ready, why assume you can teach her to cry? Actually, during the first several weeks of life, babies do smile when they are asleep. But this is not a socially responsive smile. Interestingly, they can cry when they are asleep as well.

However, studies performed after the Bell and Ainsworth

study strongly suggest that you *can* teach a crying habit to children over six months of age by indiscriminately responding to all vocalizations—always picking them up and/or soothing them. These children—having reached a sufficient level of neurological maturity—learn to cry for attention. For infants over six months of age (in contrast to newborns), parents who respond only to cries that appear to be intense or related to hunger or soiling and do not respond to quiet whimpers, mild calls, and other types of low-level whining sounds have children who at one year of age cry less. By the way, many parents do not realize that even the best babies may exhibit quiet whimpers, mild calls, low-level whining, or whimpering sounds while they remain sound asleep!

Frequent and Infrequent Criers

Bell and Ainsworth also concluded that in children between nine and twelve months of age, frequency of crying (how often a crying spell occurred) was a sign of "individual stability." Babies under nine months of age displayed fewer patterns of crying, but after nine months a baby could be identified as a frequent/long or infrequent/brief crier, an identification that often held as the child grew older. Logical conclusions from this study are, then, that infrequent criers after nine months of age were those babies whose mothers responded promptly to crying during their early months, becoming increasingly discriminate as they matured. These conclusions may, however, be too simple. Might there be biological differences among certain groups of babies that cause some to cry less and others, more? To begin to investigate this question, more background is necessary.

Similarities Between Common Fussiness/ Crying and Extreme Fussiness/Colic

Several studies of common fussing/crying show that the line between normal fussiness and extreme fussiness/colic is indistinct.

Specifically, common fussiness mimics patterns associated with extreme fussiness/colic in five fundamental ways.

1. All Babies Cry Some of the Time

Crying in infants was studied intensively by a group of researchers at the Mayo Clinic. In their first study, they observed seventy-two babies in a newborn nursery. They worked in shifts so that each baby was observed twenty-four hours a day. The observers recorded start times of any and all crying as well as the duration. They attempted in each case to attribute a cause to the crying—wet or soiled diapers, hunger, cramped positions, chilling, and the like—if one was apparent. These researchers found that most of the newborns cried between one and eleven minutes per hour. The average daily total duration of crying was about two hours for these seventy-two babies.

Observation continued as the babies experienced normal postpartum life in the nursery for eight days—the recommended hospital stay at that time. Observing these babies around the clock during these eight days, researchers found that the minimum amount of crying time per day was 48 minutes. The maximum amount of crying time per day was 243 minutes (4 hours and 3 minutes). To clarify, **all** of the infants cried some of the time—at least 48 minutes per day. The average amount of crying was about two hours per day.

2. Some Crying Cannot Be Attributed to an Obvious Cause

The researchers then attempted to classify the causes of crying into the following categories: hunger, vomiting, wet or soiled diapers, being cold, being in an uncomfortable position, and unknown reasons. For example, if the baby was crying and sucking at common feeding intervals and was calmed by feeding, the crying was attributed to hunger. They found that hunger was the cause of crying 36 percent of the time spent crying. A wet diaper caused 21 percent of this group's crying, and soiled diapers about 8 percent. Interesting, however, is that a full 35 percent of all crying minutes were attributed, by this study, to "unknown reasons." The researchers were surprised that over one-third of all the minutes crying for these infants could not be explained by an apparent cause. In other words, if you cannot figure out why your baby is crying, you are in good company!

Next, these researchers evaluated their data from the perspective of frequency, the number of separate bouts of crying. Each spell of crying was recorded once, regardless of how long it lasted. In these tallies, they found that the number of bouts of crying for "unknown reasons" was greater than for any other cause, including hunger.

Their conclusions, then, were that the group's total amount of time spent crying caused by hunger was only slightly higher than the total amount of time spent crying caused by "unknown reasons," but that the number of bouts of crying caused by "unknown reasons" was greater than the number of bouts of crying caused by hunger. If these conclusions are accurate and pertain to the population at large, they make a rather important point. Babies have more separate crying spells for unknown reasons than they do for known reasons such as being hungry, wet, or soiled.

Furthermore, other research among babies of different cultural upbringings, including the !Kung San in southern Africa, has demonstrated that the number of individual crying spells per day does not vary. American, Dutch, and !Kung San babies tend to cry about the same number of times per day. This additional research suggests that how often a baby cries is biologically driven. !Kung San babies, though, have been shown to have crying spells of shorter duration. In addition to the fact that hunger is all but ruled out as a cause for their bouts of crying because they are breast-fed regularly and often, the !Kung San babies are held continually, enabling mothers to respond to even the weakest fret within seconds. It has not been determined whether these shorter crying spells among the !Kung San result from frequent breast-feeding, continual holding, prompt responding, or all three. Of course, decreasing the duration of the same number of spells results in less total time overall spent fussing. This suggests that breast-feeding, holding, and prompt attention may decrease ordinary fussing from escalating into extreme fussiness/colic. I'll discuss this more later, but now let's return to the Mayo study.

The findings of the Mayo study, then, are that **all** babies cry during the newborn period and that much of this crying cannot be attributed to any obvious cause. The authors made some guesses about nonobvious causes: bright lights, cramping movements or stomach contractions as a part of digestion, loud noises, or loss of equilibrium. They added, almost as an afterthought, that perhaps an infant's crying expressed a need to be touched or rocked in a rhythmic motion. This is somewhat striking because unlike mothers today, the researchers did not assume that all babies have a need to be gently caressed in a tender, loving, or lingering fashion.

The authors continued the study on forty-two of the infants from the original sample, using as data detailed diaries recorded by individual mothers in their own homes. This data covered about twenty-one days at home after a nine- or ten-day stay in the normal newborn nursery. **All** of these babies had some crying spells. They averaged four crying spells per day. Fifty-five percent of these spells were attributed to hunger. Crying for "unknown reasons" occurred in 20 percent of babies. Here again, unknown reasons was second only to hunger as a cause of crying. Crying associated with vomiting, stooling, urination, overheating, bathing, chilling, lights, or noises (attributions made by their mothers) were individually less common than crying "for unknown reasons." In conclusion, **all** babies cry during the first few weeks of life, and often we do not know why.

3. Two to Three Hours of Crying Per Day Is Average

The well-known Cambridge pediatrician T. Berry Brazelton also performed his own important study on crying. Using diaries completed by parents to study crying in eighty infants, he concluded that fussiness and spells of crying that are unrelated to hunger or to wet or soiled diapers occurred in virtually **all** of his babies. Furthermore, only twelve of the eighty babies fussed less than one and a half hours per day. About half cried for about two hours per day, but this crying increased to an average of about three hours per day at the age of six weeks. Thereafter the amount of crying declined to about one hour per day by the age of twelve weeks. Brazelton's research is significant for two reasons. Not only did he confirm that all babies have spells of fussing/crying, but he also made the important observation that these spells increase and peak at six weeks of age. Such a six-week peak of crying has been documented subsequently by numerous others. In fact, the pattern of more crying during the first twelve weeks with a pattern of peaking at six weeks has even been documented among the !Kung San infants. It seems, therefore, safe to conclude that the following phenomena are not related to parenting styles but are instead biologically determined: (1) some varying degree of fussiness occurs in all babies but is not attributable to a known cause; (2) the number of fussy/crying spells per day; (3) higher frequency of fussy/crying spells in the first twelve weeks of life; and (4) a peak of fussy/crying behavior at six weeks of age. How can this be so?

4. Many Babies Have Evening Crying Spells

Brazelton also concluded that crying spells became much more focused or concentrated in the evening when the infants were about six weeks of age. At this age, very little crying occurred during the day. The spells of crying in the evening proved to be predictable and their onset was sudden. Regarding this rapid shift in behavior in the evening from a calm/quiet state to a crying state, Brazelton offered no explanation. The Japanese have a specific term for this behavior. It is "night crying."

5. Crying Decreases at About Three Months

As mentioned above, Brazelton found that, on average, crying decreased to about one hour per day by the age of twelve weeks. Another study undertaken by researchers at Harvard University verified Dr. Brazelton's observations using tape recordings of infants crying in their homes. These researchers observed the same time course: an increase in crying at about six weeks that decreased by about twelve weeks. This means that the natural history of unexplained fussing and crying runs the same time course as that of extreme fussiness/colic behavior. In both cases, babies calmed down at about three months of age. Also at this time a stable individual pattern of crying behavior that will hold true for at least the next year seems to develop. Also, as mentioned before, more crying during the first three weeks and a general pattern of increasing fussiness and crying peaking at about six weeks of age and then decreasing occurs in all babies, in all cultures.

This point cannot be overemphasized, so I want to repeat it. Even among cultures where babies are constantly held, breast-fed very frequently, and always responded to, there still existed a peak pattern of fussing and crying at about six weeks and more fussing and crying during the first three months. Because the caretaking practices are so different between !Kung San and American mothers and the fussing and crying patterns are so similar, it is likely that fussing and crying behavior reflect mainly the maturation of the baby's brain, not parenting practices. On the other hand, parenting might affect the duration of each individual crying bout.

Extreme Fussiness/Colic May Just Be a Lot of Common Fussiness

In his study, Brazelton implies that those infants in his study who cried more than the others were indistinguishable from infants with extreme fussiness/colic—that there was no gulf between normal crying and extreme fussiness/colic, only that they were two points on a spectrum. Extremely fussy/colicky babies simply cry like other babies, only more so; or, if you prefer, most babies cry like extremely fussy babies, only less so. This difference between normal crying and extreme fussiness shows up clearly in graph form. Below are charts of three general patterns of infant crying. There are gradations among them, of course, and no baby fits any one pattern perfectly.

Figure 1 shows the common pattern of normal infant fussiness/crying, including unexplained fussiness. It should reassure mothers who, noticing that their infant's crying has abruptly increased to around three hours a day at six weeks, worry that this increase in crying will develop into extreme fussiness. This usually does not occur. On a related point, many nursing mothers report feeding problems around six weeks. This is because sucking is soothing for babies and mothers often confuse fussiness with hunger. Your baby may suck whether hungry or fussy, but your baby is less likely to suck with as strong a force or interest when fussy. When fussy but not hungry, your baby will not be soothed by nursing. The sucking pattern for a baby who is fussy is different from one who is hungry. When fussy, your baby sucks rapidly and repeatedly without much swallowing: suck-suck-suck-suck-swallow. The sucking pattern when your baby is hungry is a more rhythmic style: suck-swallow-suck-swallow. Remember that six weeks is

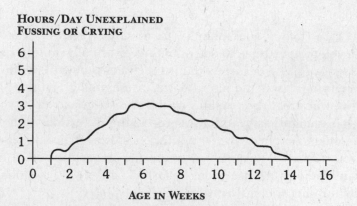

HOURS/DAY UNEXPLAINED
FUSSING OR CRYING

AGE IN WEEKS

Figure 1. Unexplained fussiness; little or none in first few days; about two hours/day at two weeks of age; three hours/day at six weeks of age; and one hour/day at twelve weeks of age.

usually the normal peak of unexplained fussiness. "Treatments" for this fussiness around six weeks of age appear to work because your baby was about ready to naturally calm down anyway. Figure 2 depicts fussiness/colic in babies from birth to three months of age. As you can see, the onset of prolonged crying occurs shortly after birth.

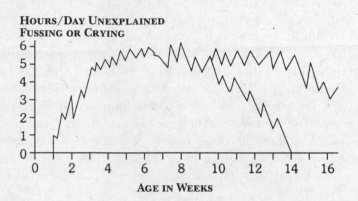

Figure 2. Extreme fussiness/colic rapidly increases to three or more hours a day with great variation day to day, and might last longer than three months.

Figure 3 describes infants who, for a few weeks, appear to be developing extreme fussiness but never actually do. After a few days or several days (less than three weeks) of extreme fussing or crying they settle into a pattern resembling Figure 1. Doctors who treat these babies in their initial weeks of fussiness/crying might claim to have cured extreme fussiness/colic, but the reduction in crying is spontaneous. Research shows it is inappropriate to diagnose extreme fussiness/colic before three weeks of age because about half of all babies will fuss and cry a lot for only one or two weeks.

When mothers describe their infants' behavior in their own words, descriptions of extreme fussiness are remarkably consistent. Detailed interviews with hundreds of mothers whose in-

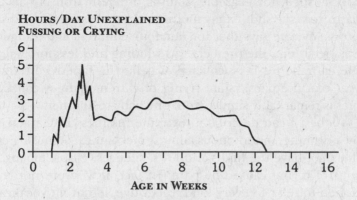

Figure 3. Burst of unexplained fussiness resembling colic, but lasting only a few weeks or only a few days.

fants had extreme fussiness/colic, and a study of diaries they kept of their infant's behavior clarifies, first, that it is impossible to detect differences based on the sex of the child, the social class or age of the mother, or birth order, and, second, that an important feature of extreme fussiness/colic crying is an erratic pattern from day to day. There are great days, good days, bad days, and nightmare days when you want to pull your hair out.

Furthermore, in terms of actual behavioral manifestations of fussiness, sometimes extreme fussiness or crying is rhythmical, and sometimes it is a persistent monotone. The crying infant may be consolable on one day and inconsolable the next. Sometimes infants are consolable in the morning and inconsolable at night. Days may occur without any bouts of extreme fussiness/colic. Also, the duration of spells may vary considerably from day to day or within a given day. Nearly all mothers describe rapid and unexplained changes in mood in their infants.

The message of this chapter is that extreme fussiness/colic is an unusual amount of normal common fussiness/crying. It is not qualitatively different from other kinds of crying, although it may sound slightly different. A baby in an extremely fussy/ colicky spell, for example, sounds different from a baby who has received a shot. Many mothers can make even finer distinctions. My wife says that for our four children, the hunger cry was persistent, the tired cry was whining and less forceful, and the extreme fussiness/colic cry was harsh. Tape recordings reveal that the paroxysmal crying of extremely fussy/colicky babies is remarkably similar from one baby to another.

As best I can describe it, extreme fussiness is characterized by a droning, monotonous, almost mechanical-sounding cry. It does not have the highs and lows, silences, gasps, moans, and sobs of crying caused by pain. In fact, if we were not conditioned to refer to every loud, repetitive, irritating vocalization made by a baby as "crying," the noise of extreme fussiness/colic might have its own name. Often the crying sounds of extreme fussiness are closer to wheezing or gasping.

Returning to the idea that, though audibly distinctive, extreme fussiness/colic is, in essence, only an abnormally large amount of normal fussiness/crying, the question remains: Why do certain babies persist in fussiness, while most only fuss or cry in brief stretches?

Which Babies Cry More?

Brazelton suggested that the fussy infants in his study—the ones whom we might say possessed extreme fussiness—have a distinct personality type. They seemed to Brazelton more active or sensitive. Much earlier, Illingworth came to a similar conclusion. In a paper entitled "Crying in Infants and Children," Illingworth concluded that the amount of crying for an individual baby is related to the personality of the baby—that placid and easy babies cry less than determined and difficult babies. (Temperament differences will be taken up in Chapter 4.) Illingworth surmised that during the first three months of life, crying is due to loneliness or a desire to be picked up. Perhaps, he thought, some babies feel this need more acutely or express it more persistently than others.

In my view, the question is valid as to whether the difference among babies is traceable to temperament: not all babies are able to calm themselves down at the same rate, and extremely fussy/colicky children may be unable to calm themselves down at all. It does seem that babies with extreme fussiness/colic tend to be more determined, sensitive, and difficult to soothe. Or maybe it is a question of sensitivity: Extremely fussy/colicky babies are continually disturbed by stimuli that other babies can ignore. Or, finally, perhaps these differences among children are traceable to some physical provocation—something that causes all babies a little distress bothers extremely fussy/colicky babies much more.

Remember that your infant with extreme fussiness/colic is not doing anything other babies do not do. She is just doing it a little more persistently.

IMPORTANT POINT

Fussiness will not continue forever.
Babies become much more settled and delightful after about three to four months.

CHAPTER 2

Extreme Fussiness/Colic

Extreme fussiness in healthy infants is usually characterized by spells (paroxysmal attacks) of irritability, fussing, or crying occurring in the evening hours. Older research focused on crying only because it was the major complaint of parents and the most dramatic observable feature. Modern research, however, focuses not on crying but on fussiness, for two reasons: Fussing occurs twice as often as crying, *and* it is possible that successful management of common fussiness may prevent fussing from escalating into extreme fussiness/colicky crying. Traditional views regarding extreme fussiness/colic have been based on data obtained almost exclusively from parents' reports. Obviously, parental anxiety, fatigue, and preconceptions may influence parents' descriptions of their infants' behavior. Contemporary views of extreme fussiness/colic attempt to include more objective data derived from voice-activated audio recordings and observations in the home. Results from these studies are compatible with traditional observations. But an interesting question is raised: *Can a baby who does not cry much have extreme fussiness/colic?*

To answer that question, let us look at older concepts of colic. The traditional view of colic was developed by the British pediatrician Dr. Illingworth, who defined colic as "violent rhythmical, screaming attacks which did not stop when the infants were picked up, and for which no cause, such as underfeeding, could be found." Further clarifying Illingworth's definition is the following description by the American pediatrician Dr. Wessel. Wessel diagnosed a colicky infant as "one who, otherwise healthy and well-fed, had paroxysms of irritability, fussing or crying lasting for a total of more than 3 hours a day and occurring on more than 3 days in one week . . . and that the paroxysms continued to recur for more than 3 weeks." Taking the two together, the definition of colic, or what we refer to as "extreme fussiness," is *long durations of irritability, fussing, or crying per day, occurring many days per week, and continuing for many weeks* in an otherwise healthy infant.

Both Illingworth's and Wessel's studies showed that the attacks do not usually occur during the first few days but are present in about 80 percent of affected infants by two weeks of age. All affected infants have the onset of their spells by three weeks of age. About 80 percent of extremely fussy infants begin their spells between 5 P.M. and 8 P.M., and their spells usually end by midnight. An additional 12 percent of infants experience their spells later in the evening, starting between 7 P.M. and 10 P.M. and ending by 2 A.M. At two months of age about 50 percent of extremely fussy infants no longer have these crying spells, and by three months of age an additional 30 percent of infants are free of fussiness. By about four months of age, an additional 10 percent, or 90 percent of all previously extremely fussy/colicky infants, are free of symptoms. The average duration of the fussy spells lasts almost four hours. The onset of extreme fussiness in premature infants is usually delayed and starts near the expected date of delivery regardless of the gestational age at birth.

Spells of extreme fussing/colic are not qualitatively different from common fussing or crying, differing only in intensity (accounting for the different vocalization many parents attest to), duration of spell, or persistence over time. Again, these are quantitative, not qualitative, differences. The documented natural history of common fussing/crying (onset, duration, and time of occurrence and cessation) parallels that of extreme fussiness/colic. Extreme fussiness/colic represents only an extreme form of normal infant behavior.

During spells of extreme fussiness/colic, the baby is often described as "hypertonic" because the entire body is stiffened, the fists are tightly clenched, and the legs are flexed rigidly over the abdomen. Babies sometimes display uncoordinated jerky movements of their limbs, which have been described as batting or flapping the arms or kicking the legs. At other times the movements are described as writhing, twisting, or turning. These movements are not present at other times, and these babies have normal neurological examinations.

Air swallowing may also occur with these agitated movements. During spells of crying, this swallowed air probably accounts for gassiness—another common feature of extremely fussy/colicky babies. There is no evidence to suggest that the gassiness in extremely fussy/colicky babies is caused by disease of the gastrointestinal system. There is also no strong evidence linking extreme fussiness/colic with method of feeding or food allergy.

Another feature of some, but not all, extremely fussy infants is stimulus-sensitivity. These babies appear to be either easily startled or easily awakened. Frequent awakenings at night often occur in these infants. A bothersome feature of colicky infants in general is extreme daytime wakefulness manifested in either brief naps or no napping.

Viewing fussiness from a modern viewpoint, it is important to remember that Wessel's research focused on paroxysmal *fussing*, not crying. Wessel's definition of extreme fussiness/colic did *not* require that a baby must cry a great deal. Our definition of extreme fussiness is compatible with Wessel's. In fact, recent research has established that fussing is a behavior that occurs more frequently and lasts longer than crying. Let us attempt to further clarify the distinction between fussing and crying.

Ian St. James-Roberts, Ph.D., defined *fussing* as periods during which a baby is unsettled and irritable and may be vocalizing, but not continuously crying. *Crying,* however, was defined as periods of intense distressed vocalization. *Colic* was defined as inconsolable crying in concert with other behaviors, such as those thought to result from stomach or bowel pain. St. James-Roberts collected data from parent diaries, twenty-four-hour voice-activated audio recordings, and home visits. Overall, he found that babies exhibited an average of about 171 minutes of fussing, crying, or colicky behavior each day, and the distribution was approximately 60 percent fussing, 30 percent crying, and 10 percent colic—that is, on any given day, *fussing occurred twice as much as crying*. The actual amount of time per day for colic was only about 14 minutes.

From his entire sample, St. James-Roberts isolated a subgroup whom he referred to as persistent criers based upon the occurrence of three or more hours of fussing or crying per day. In this group, 221 minutes of fussing, crying, or colicky behavior occurred every day, but again, only 11 percent, or 25 minutes, was colic, compared to 61 percent fussing and 28 percent crying behaviors. Again, in this smaller but more bothersome group, *babies fussed twice as often as they cried*.

In fact, among this subgroup that St. James-Roberts referred to as persistent criers, 63 percent never had a single episode of colic! In other words, 63 percent of infants were always consolable. Remember, they did fuss and cry a great deal throughout the day—many for three or more hours. The author concluded that low-intensity fussing was much more common than intense crying and that fussing, crying, and colic, though separable, are related behaviors on a single continuum spanning from lower to higher intensity.

St. James-Roberts also showed that as infants approach their six-week peak of fussing or crying, most of the increase in so-called colic is due not to more crying but to more fussing. Furthermore, he showed that fussing is a behavior that demonstrates more consistent patterns in individual babies over time than crying. It might be helpful to think about it this way: Fussing is a kind of pre-cry state, a state of distress or agitation that quickly becomes more intense or extreme and moves into crying unless parents make an effort to soothe the baby. Unfortunately, sometimes children slip into inconsolability despite their parents' efforts. Once they have reached this extreme state, nothing seems to help them to stop their crying.

Now you are familiar with the most relevant international research of the past hundred years on extreme fussiness/colic, you may have decided they accurately describe your baby. How do these observations of research translate into modern diagnoses at your pediatrician's office?

Clinical Definitions of Extreme Fussiness/Colic

Some doctors maintain that extreme fussiness, by definition, must involve spells of violent, rhythmic screaming. Other doctors say it is not extreme fussiness/colic unless the baby's legs are drawn up and he seems to expel gas. Some doctors use the timing of the condition—the way the spells usually start about two weeks of age, end around three months, and are worst in the evening—as an indication of extreme fussiness. Others claim that only babies who are ill-tempered and fussy in all of their waking hours should be labeled as extremely fussy/colicky. What all agree on, however, is that the extremely fussy baby is well and thriving with nothing wrong apart from these fussy spells.

Based on both laboratory research and clinical observations, we have agreed on a broader definition. By extreme fussiness/colic, we mean *irritability, fussiness, or crying for which no physical cause can be found, which lasts more than three hours a day, occurs more than three days a week, and continues for more than three weeks.* Often at least a portion of the crying is inconsolable. Babies who do not fit this profile have common fussiness.

Let's examine this definition point by point.

No physical cause. Extreme fussiness/colic occurs only among healthy infants. If there is a medical problem that might be causing the baby discomfort, her crying is not labeled extreme fussiness/colic and she needs medical attention. If something in a baby's environment—temperature, noise, or wetness or soiling—is causing her to cry, this environmental disturbance is correctable.

Inconsolable crying. This is probably the aspect of extreme fussiness/colic that distresses parents most. Most crying infants can be quieted with holding, walking, rocking, a pacifier, a car ride, a feeding, or quiet talking. Extremely fussy/colicky babies, by contrast, cannot. Parental attempts to soothe have either no effect or only a temporary one.

More than three hours a day. Three hours of fussing per day is normal. More than three hours (total) per day more than three days per week for more than three weeks, however, represents extreme fussiness.

More than three days a week. Most extremely fussy/colicky babies have good days when they hardly cry at all, sleep through the night, and seem to be "over it," but they also have bad days when their crying seems interminable. Parents become frustrated and upset when the process starts again. Further frustrating is that almost never does it follow the same pattern from day to day.

More than three weeks. Extreme fussiness is a persistent condition. This does not mean that you should endure three weeks of screaming before you seek help. It is always useful to check with your pediatrician to ensure that your baby's fussiness has no physical cause. Persistent fussiness lasting more than three weeks, however, in an otherwise healthy baby is extreme fussiness (see Table 1).

TABLE 1
DESCRIPTIONS OF EXTREME FUSSINESS

Extremely fussy infants have spells of:
Unexplained fussiness, fretfulness, irritability, crying
Piercing screaming attacks
Explosive or inconsolable crying

Noise and rumbling in the gut, excessive flatulence or gas
(and/or) apparent abdominal pain with legs drawn up onto
the abdomen
Fists clenched

Extremely fussy/colicky infants are:
Vigorous
Intense, wound-up
Energetic, excitable
Easily startled
Gassy
Grimacing, stiffening, twisting
Easily and frequently awakened
"Squirmy as a worm in hot ashes"

Is Extreme Fussiness/Colic a Disease?

Babies do fuss, but they don't "have" fussiness like you might
"have" a disease. Fussing is to infants what adolescence is to
teenagers. Fussy infants and rebellious adolescents are difficult
for parents to deal with, but their behaviors are related to stages
of development, not medical problems. Extreme fussiness/colic,
while a clinical definition, evades the definition of a medical
problem. Why? Primarily because, to the disappointment of all
parents with children who qualify, even extreme fussiness requires no treatment and has no cure. The fact is that all babies
outgrow fussiness naturally.

Extreme Fussiness/Colic Is Very Common

If your baby has extreme fussiness/colic, you are not alone.
Once you begin talking and asking about it, you will be
amazed at the company you are in. Ask your parents, in-laws,
aunts, and uncles. Is yours the first extremely fussy/colicky
baby in your family? Talk to your friends, and you will find that
your baby is not the only extremely fussy/colicky baby in your
city, town, or even neighborhood.

As the studies above suggest, one out of five babies has extreme fussiness/colic. Judging from the lack of information on extreme fussiness/colic, you would never guess that it affects about 20 percent of all babies. If your baby has extreme fussiness, you are not alone; over seven hundred thousand infants each year in the United States behave this way.

Furthermore, extreme fussiness cuts across nations and across cultures. Curiously, though, the Chinese call what we describe as extreme fussiness/colic "hundred days crying" and consider it a normal behavior pattern. The Vietnamese call it "three months plus ten days crying." These Asian views represent the belief that fussiness is a normal stage of development through which all children pass. This view was also common in the West before Western medicine began diagnosing problems involving the colon (from which the word *colic* is derived). While these medical diagnoses are relatively recent, the condition has been recorded for hundreds of years. Take, for example, Shakespeare's lines about the first of seven ages of man: "At first, the infant crying and puking in the nurse's arms."

The first pediatrics textbook in English, *The Boke of Chyldren,* published in 1553, refers to "colicke" as "rumbling in the gut." This book was written before the introduction of coffee and tobacco to England—so much for blaming the mother's bad habits for her child's distress! Indeed, a hectic lifestyle is not responsible for extreme fussiness. It has been with us as long as there have been babies.

I have consulted with many parents of extremely fussy/colicky infants. They have helped me to see that extreme fussiness/colic is one of the "dirty little secrets" of pediatrics. Often parents feel embarrassed about mentioning it. Often pediatricians do not want to hear about it. You may have heard your own pediatrician say, "Oh, that's just a touch of colic," leaving you to cope on your own. What is really true about extreme fussiness? Why does my baby have it?

FOUR IMPORTANT THINGS
TO REMEMBER ABOUT
EXTREME FUSSINESS

1. Your baby is healthy and will thrive.
2. You are not the cause of your baby's extreme fussiness; it is not your fault.
3. It will pass.
4. You can take steps to cope with extreme fussiness/colic and to make sure that there are no lasting ill effects.

The Curious History of Extreme Fussiness/Colic

Historically, extreme fussiness/colic has escaped medical understanding. While reliable scientific research, as above, documents the phenomenon in terms of its behavioral manifestations, no one has yet provided a persuasive explanation of why it happens. At various times researchers have blamed extreme fussiness/colic on overfeeding, underfeeding, food with too much carbohydrate, too much starch, too much protein, allergy (a reaction to horsehair, feathers, orange juice, or other substances), overly permissive parents, too much attention, too little attention, exposure to cold, and lack of oral satisfaction. These explanations are the result of an underlying belief that the condition is a medical problem instead of a stage of development.

To all of the above "medical diagnoses," "cures" were only wishful thinking. Some suggested older "cures" have included weaning the baby from the breast; adding goat's milk, olive oil, or banana powder to her diet; treatment with bicarbonate of soda, chlorohydrate, opium derivatives, peppermint, or dill water; giving an enema or suppository; offering a pacifier;

handling the baby more gently; and a drink of whiskey (which Illingworth specifies is to be "taken *by the parent!*").

Of course, a review of the literature on almost any medical condition provides an array of absurd notions taken seriously at one time or another. In the case of extreme fussiness/colic, however, because no cause has been isolated nor a definition agreed upon, mistaken—even absurd and irrational—ideas regarding the condition persist even today. Only in the last thirty or forty years have controlled experiments been conducted that compare groups of extreme fussy/colicky babies. Modern "cures"—familiar, I am sure, to many—include crib vibrators, recordings of heartbeat or womb sounds, antigas drugs, drugs to reduce gastroesophageal reflux, elimination of milk products from a nursing mother's diet, and the admonition to carry your baby more often.

Extreme Fussiness/Colic Is Not the Sort of Problem Doctors Like

Even today, little is taught about extreme fussiness/colic in medical schools. As we now know, it is not a disease and it has no definite cause. It does not even have an exact diagnostic set of symptoms. Nothing about extreme fussiness/colic shows up on X rays, stool analyses, or blood tests. Diagnoses strike many as arbitrary and subjective. There is no treatment of choice, which is why most doctors understandably shy away. They take comfort in the fact that extreme fussiness/colic does not kill or harm infants. They know that infants will outgrow the behavior. Often, however, they do not recognize the devastating effect extreme fussiness has on parents. A physician might say to a mother whose child suffers from extreme fussiness, "This is not serious. If only you would relax and take it easy, then your baby would calm down." Yet when I give talks on extreme fussiness to groups of physicians I play for them a tape of an extreme fussy/colicky baby at the height of paroxysmal crying. After no more than a minute the audience itself cries, "Enough! Turn it off!" I imagine if these pediatricians spent an entire evening with an extremely fussy/colicky baby, they would be more sympathetic.

The Nature of Extreme Fussiness/Colic in Behavioral Research

Another possible explanation for the neglect of extreme fussiness is traceable to methodological difficulties involved in medical research on human behavior. Some doctors and researchers prefer to observe children only when awake, while others like to study children asleep. Like larks and owls, these professions do not flock together—they rarely talk to one another, let alone share findings. Extreme fussiness/colic, a condition that actually resides somewhere between awake and asleep behaviors, falls in an academic no-man's-land.

There is also a species of researchers I call hawks. Rather than observe, they like to prod and provoke babies in order to measure their responses. They snap rubber bands against their heels, block airflow through their noses, and make them breathe a low-oxygen air-gas mixture. Some of these hawks are probably overly aggressive. Others, however, have contributed significantly to our knowledge of child development. Unfortunately, there is no reliable way to provoke an extreme fussy/colicky spell in the laboratory, and few researchers care to be out taking measurements in the evening, when most extreme fussiness occurs. Since every baby is different and no baby's extreme fussiness/colic is exactly the same from day to day, controlled experiments pose real challenges. This is why extreme fussiness/colic has been described by the larks but only recently really studied by owls and hawks.

Pressing the metaphor even further, in the academic aviary larks, owls, and hawks live in different trees. These various professions have their own schools, their own journals, and even their own distinctive songs. Specific kinds of behaviors are often separated from one another: Crying is studied separately from social smiling, and night awakening is studied separately from length of night sleep periods. Yet a thorough understanding of extreme fussiness involves comprehension of these other behaviors as well. My intention in the next section is to explain how these seemingly separate infant behaviors relate to each other: extreme fussiness, crying, temperament, and sleeping. Extreme fussiness/colic has not fallen successfully into the territory of any single discipline. Perhaps, as we will see, it comprises a territory of its own.

A Bias Against Moms?

There is certainly an element of condescension toward women originating from the time when most pediatricians were men. When a male physician meets the distraught, tearful, and exhausted mother of an extremely fussy child, he often assumes the problem lies with her. Even if he admits extreme fussiness/colic is a pediatric problem, he accepts an easy out: blame the mother, blame her diet, her breast milk, her choice of formula, her inexperience, her overly active imagination, and so on. A comparison might be drawn between extreme fussiness/colic and menstrual cramps: Male doctors who have never experienced them either trivialize their pain or, worse, doubt their validity at all.

Some doctors are so unwilling to talk seriously about extreme fussiness that a baby may continue to fuss or cry, but a mother will no longer bring it up. As far as the doctor knows, the condition has abated, confirming mistaken ideas about the condition such as that the mother is the cause.

What Can a Doctor Do About Extreme Fussiness/Colic?

As far as treatment goes, most pediatricians do not believe there is anything they can do. A typical approach is to stall and/or reassure the mother until the extreme fussiness/colic runs its natural course. Some try to treat extreme fussiness/colic with phenobarbital, herbal teas, or drugs intended to prevent gas formation in the stomach; even antacids have been used! Also, in the past drugs that decrease muscle tone in the intestines have been prescribed. The decision whether to prescribe a given drug usually depends on a given physician's training, whether the doctor has children of his or her own with extreme fussiness/colic, and the amount of pressure a doctor is under from the parents to help halt the screaming.

I am amused regularly by pediatricians who claim to "cure" extreme fussiness/colic. Usually the mother is exhorted to try a series of "treatments" over the course of several weeks. Between the child's twelfth to sixteenth weeks, one treatment magically has the prescribed effect, although that same treatment does not work on the next child, or the next, or the next. Of course, the lesson is that extreme fussiness/colic has "cured" itself and would have done so apart from any prescribed treatment. Attributing the cure of extreme fussiness/colic to a treatment, however, has led to a host of unhelpful ideas about "curing" extreme fussiness/colic. This is the case with any condition that clears up spontaneously. Your doctor suggests chicken soup for a cold, and after eating chicken soup for six days your cold is in fact gone, but the connection between the soup and the improvement of health is not causal.

In terms of any ailment that spontaneously corrects itself over time, medical doctors can still play an effective role. They can, for example, keep parents from exhausting themselves physically and emotionally over mythical causes and cures. Doctors can offer a sympathetic ear, calm understanding, and sincere interest. A follow-up telephone call to parents asking, "How did things go last night?" is often invaluable for boosting a parent's morale. Moreover, doctors should see mothers in person often enough to look for and detect signs of exhaustion, despair, or family stress, and should be prepared to recommend help.

You and Your Pediatrician

In despair over your pediatrician's inability to treat extreme fussiness/colic, you should not lose faith in your doctor's ability to monitor and treat other aspects of your child's health and development. You may need to find someone else, though—a sympathetic relative, a friend who has been through extreme fussiness/colic herself, a clinic nurse—to help you through this time. If your baby's extreme fussiness/colic makes your pediatrician impatient, patronizing, or unwilling to spend time with you, this may be a good time to find a more sympathetic doctor. Do not simply accept erroneous advice, such as the suggestion to switch formulas. If such advice is given, ask your baby's doctor what he or she expects to accomplish by this treatment.

Eleven Myths About Extreme Fussiness/Colic (and Why You Shouldn't Believe Them)

Once friends and relatives hear (or decide) that you have a baby with extreme fussiness/colic, the advice will start. You will hear all sorts of theories about the causes of extreme fussiness. People will offer their own pet remedies, and if you aren't already overwhelmed and confused, you certainly will be now.

Here are eleven popular fallacies about extreme fussiness. They have gained widespread acceptance because, as we have shown, extreme fussiness/colic means different things to different people. Because there is no universally accepted definition of extreme fussiness/colic, the field is wide open. Some of these fallacies are based on observed relationships, one-time coincidences, or what *seems* logical. None of them stands up to scientific scrutiny. I will explain why you should not believe any of them. Then I hope you will put them out of your mind and devote your energy to coping with your noisy little bundle.

Fallacy No. 1: There Is No Such Thing as Extreme Fussiness/Colic

Some doctors say they have never seen an extremely fussy/colicky baby. They believe the problem is with overanxious, inexperienced mothers who exaggerate normal fussing and crying out of proportion. I would remind these doctors that they seldom see babies in the evening, when extreme fussiness/colic is usually at its worst. They do not have to listen to hours of crying day after day. Too many mothers—experienced, calm third- and fourth-time mothers—have reported similar crying patterns for extreme fussiness/colic to be a fiction. Researchers have documented spells of extreme fussiness/colic on home videotapes, and these tapes clearly show that the mothers are no different from mothers of babies with common fussiness/crying.

Fallacy No. 2: Maternal Anxiety Causes Extreme Fussiness/Colic

There can be no more destructive a belief than this one. Imagine telling a mother who is already worried about her child's crying that she is responsible! The guilt, resentment, anger, and frustration produced by this fallacy is unconscionable. It can incite others in the household to blame the mother for the extreme fussiness/colic. It often persuades mothers themselves that they are at fault. Believing that extreme fussiness is her own fault can keep a mother from getting the help she needs. Once she decides that she is inadequate at mothering, discussing the infant's behavior with her pediatrician or anybody else becomes a threatening and painful prospect.

When a parent believes it is her or his fault that a baby is fussy, every cry becomes an accusation. For this reason, extreme fussiness/colic—and the fallacy that parental inadequacy has caused it—sometimes can be connected to child abuse or other domestic violence. One abusive father I know was untroubled by what he felt was "hunger crying" but became violent at the sound of extreme fussiness/colicky crying, which he interpreted as disapproval. "The baby was angry at me," he said, and he reacted by striking the infant. Sadly, there is a coincidental peak of homicides of infants between six and eight weeks of age, which some speculate may be brought on by adults losing control in the face of extreme fussiness.

Furthermore, responsible studies including home videotapes have clarified that mothers of extreme fussy babies are no more anxious, high-strung, or emotionally unstable than mothers of quiet babies. In no way are the parents responsible for extreme fussiness/colic.

Fallacy No. 3: Extreme Fussiness/Colic Is a Gastrointestinal Problem

This fallacy may be the most deeply entrenched myth about extreme fussiness. As previously stated, the term *colic* itself comes from *colon*, implying a connection with the digestive system. As noted above, the first English-language book on pediatrics, *The Boke of Chyldren,* published over four hundred years ago, described extreme fussiness as noise and "peine" (pain) in the gut.

It is not hard to understand the origin of this idea. Often in the course of fussing and crying spells, infants draw their legs up to their abdomen and pass gas. Spells of extreme fussiness/colic also often occur after meals, suggesting an issue involving the digestive system. Furthermore, the crying of extreme fussiness/colic has been described as waxing and waning, as if waves of colonic spasms hit the infant (as in some versions of adult stomach flu). Because the smooth muscle in the colon does, in fact, contract in regular waves, pushing food and fecal matter through, observers over the centuries have drawn the connection that extreme fussiness originates in the abdomen. As I will demonstrate in the next chapter, however, research once tried to substantiate this theory. Specifically, Illingworth and others used X rays in association with barium enemas, but were unable to detect any unusual gastrointestinal activity whatsoever during spells of extreme fussiness/colic.

As countless observers have noted, the behavior that gave rise to this theory—drawing up of legs, turning red, clenching fists—also occurs momentarily when an infant receives a shot. In the case of a shot, the behavior does not indicate pain in the abdomen at all—it is simply the way the infant expresses discomfort. As for the gas, as an infant cries, she swallows air that must be expelled. The gas is a *result*, not a *cause*, of prolonged crying. The waxing and waning feature is probably the way any baby would cry who has been at it intensely for hours.

Most convincing, however, is the following explanation: Extremely fussy babies do not have any symptoms of intestinal disorder, that is, no poor weight gain, no excessive spitting or vomiting, no constipation or diarrhea, and no need for extra feedings. Surely, after all these years, some scientific support for this idea of gastrointestinal pain should have shown up. Because it has not, there is presently no reason to believe that extreme fussiness/colic reflects reaction to a gastrointestinal problem. Newer research by my wife, Linda Weissbluth, may suggest that a normally occurring chemical imbalance that develops in many babies causes contractions of the smooth muscle lining the gut. But I will tell you more about this later.

Fallacy No. 4: Something the Baby Has Eaten Disagrees with Her

If you have a food allergy, you might assume that your extremely fussy/colicky baby does too. It is true that some children are allergic to the cow's milk protein in some formulas, but this is much less common than extreme fussiness/colic. Allergy to cow's milk protein usually causes bloody diarrhea. Nevertheless, a common treatment for extreme fussiness is switching formulas from those containing cow's milk protein to those derived from goat's milk or soybeans, or some hypoallergenic formulas.

One published report claimed to prove that cow's milk protein in infant formulas caused extreme fussiness/colic. However, serious errors in that study weakened the authors' conclusions. There was, for example, no randomization in the placement of infants into different study groups. The study was not blind—that is, parents were not unaware of the changes in the type of formula given their infants. Also, investigators never defined what was meant by a "cure." And although they claimed that these extremely fussy/colicky infants were allergic to cow's milk, about 50 percent of these so-called allergic babies failed to show symptoms when given cow's milk at three or six months of age. The authors claimed they had "outgrown" the allergy, when, in fact, they had outgrown the extreme fussiness.

In fact, a careful, objective study by Dr. William Liebman at the University of California School of Medicine concluded that the cow's milk protein allergy has no significant role in infant extreme fussiness. Other modern studies have also demonstrated that food allergies in general play no role in extreme fussiness/colic.

Authors of another study claimed that when a nursing mother has cow's milk in her diet, the cow's milk protein gets into her breast milk, causing extreme fussiness in her baby. This study also suffered serious methodological flaws; for example, the results were based on a sample of only ten infants. To my knowledge there is no reliable research that demonstrates conclusively a connection between the diet of nursing mothers and extreme fussiness/colic.

A related fallacy is that "allergy" in general causes extreme fussiness. This dates from a period in the 1950s and '60s when scientific study of the phenomenon of allergic reactions had just emerged. In this period clinicians of many specialties were inclined to attribute to allergy a wide variety of otherwise inexplicable medical problems. The vague concept of allergy has no demonstrable basis, although it persists as a smokescreen behind which we hide our ignorance.

Another food-related theory about extreme fussiness/colic is lactose intolerance. Lactose, commonly known as milk sugar, is present in all commercial formulas that contain cow's milk. About 10 percent of white Americans, and a much higher percentage of Africans and Asians suffer from an intolerance to lactose. It is known to cause abdominal pain, gassiness, and diarrhea, but does it cause extreme fussiness? Liebman's study evaluated extremely fussy infants for lactose intolerance. He concluded that, in fact, it does not have a significant role in causing extreme fussiness. Prescribing lactose-free formulas or having nursing mothers stop drinking milk, at least according to Liebman, simply does not make sense.

Furthermore, researchers who believe that cow's milk protein allergy or lactose intolerance causes extreme fussiness have never explained exactly how these offending foods, ingested throughout the day, trigger attacks of fussiness only at particular times. As noted, the vast majority of infants with extreme fussiness suffer their worst spells in the evening hours.

As you can see, there is no basis for the strategy of switching to formulas free of cow's milk protein and lactose to treat extreme fussiness/colic. There are, however, enough different brands of formulas so that a pediatrician might suggest a formula switch each week, effectively buying time until the infant simply outgrows the phase. This is a deplorable strategy, especially when doctors know full well that it will not work. A doctor may argue that mothers feel better with something to try; I, on the contrary, suspect this strategy only increases a mother's frustration. Each successive failure (until the infant is about three months old and the difficulty goes away by itself) intensifies a mother's fear that something is dreadfully wrong with her child or herself.

If your physician suggests switching formulas in an attempt to cure your baby's extreme fussiness/colic, do not lose patience. Ask your pediatrician to discuss frankly whether he or she thinks the treatment will really work or whether it is designed to make you feel better.

Fallacy No. 5: The Nursing Mother's Diet

Foods that cause stomach upset or gas in the nursing mother go on to cause extreme fussiness/colic in her baby, right? Wrong! This fanciful notion is contrary to everything we know about how digestion occurs. This makes about as much sense as the argument that when a nursing mother eats chocolate, she produces chocolate milk. Rarely, cows' milk may cause bloody diarrhea in a baby.

There is no evidence that caffeine causes extreme fussiness/colic. Mothers have to drink more than five cups of regular coffee a day before caffeine shows up in their breast milk and in their baby's urine. So if your baby has extreme fussiness/

colic, don't feel that you have to give up your morning cup of coffee!

Here are the facts: Foods eaten by the mother get broken down into elemental nutrients and absorbed by her digestive system. Breast milk is actively made in the breasts from these absorbed nutrients. By contrast, gas in the mother's intestine is formed by the action of bacteria naturally occurring on the food the mother has eaten. It is biochemically impossible that gas in the mother's colon, derived from eating something like beans or cabbage, could pass into her breast milk. Yet some nursing mothers report that eliminating certain foods from their own diets improved their children's behavior. You may have heard some of your friends swear this is true, but it is not. It is only coincidence or wishful thinking.

Mothers who believe their breast milk is causing their children's misery must be reassured that it is not, since it may cause certain mothers to stop nursing prematurely when there is no reason to do so. Since nursing is one of the few things that can sometimes soothe a fussy baby, a mother can be tormented over whether nursing helps or hurts.

In particular, a professional woman torn between staying home to nurse or returning to work sometimes uses her baby's fussiness to resolve the conflict. She may say to herself, "Since I decided to stay home to nurse my baby, but my breast milk disagrees with him, I might as well go back to work and let someone else give him formula." A mother should not use the belief that "bad" or insufficient breast milk causes fussiness as a reason to return to work. "Bad" or an otherwise insufficient quality of breast milk is unrelated to the problem of infant extreme fussiness.

Fallacy No. 6: Breast-fed Babies Have Less Extreme Fussiness/Colic

To go with the prevailing notion that breast-fed infants are healthier in general, many also assume breast-fed infants are protected against extreme fussiness/colic. However, several

studies have shown that extreme fussiness/colic occurs as often
for breast-fed infants as for bottle-fed infants. A study by Dr. T. C.
Boulton of the University of Adelaide noted that extreme fussiness was common in Australia (40 percent of all babies), but
that it was as common among breast-fed babies as those who
were formula-fed. Many subsequent studies have corroborated
Boulton's finding that breast-feeding does not prevent extreme fussiness/colic.

Fussiness has also been studied among non-Western peoples
such as the !Kung San where the mothers practice continuous
care and contact: the baby is always in contact with the mother,
the baby is always carried or held upright by the mother, the
baby sleeps with the mother, the mother responds to every
fussy sound immediately, and the baby is breast-fed several
times an hour. As noted above, though, just like American babies, most fussiness occurs among !Kung San babies during the
first few months, and observers have seen a similar pattern of
increasing fussiness that peaks during the second month of life.
This observation strongly suggests that this pattern of increasing
and decreasing fussiness has a biological basis independent of
any culturally determined parenting style.

Fallacy No. 7: Firstborn Children Have Extreme Fussiness/Colic More Often

Many mothers swear this is so, but why? Probably out of uncer-
tainty and inexperience, parents regard the first child as more difficult in a number of ways, even though ratings of temperament
that strive for scientific objectivity show that firstborn infants are
no different from subsequent ones. There is no biological reason
why a firstborn child should be more prone to extreme fussiness/
colic. As for psychological reasons, this argument is merely a
variation of the maternal anxiety argument. Many studies have
demonstrated that extreme fussiness/colic occurs as commonly
among subsequent infants as among firstborns.

Of course, there may be what we call a reporting bias at
work here. A mother may simply deny or refuse to believe that

a second, third, or fourth child has extreme fussiness. If her first child did not have extreme fussiness, she is perplexed: "It's not supposed to happen this way. I wonder what went wrong." Alternatively, if her first child did have extreme fussiness, she may have even stronger emotional reasons for denying that it has happened again. Perhaps she still feels guilty about "causing" it in her firstborn. Or perhaps she feels that two extremely fussy babies are a sure sign she is doing something terribly wrong. Careful examination of mothers' reports of crying and fussy behavior in non-firstborns corroborates our opinion that their extreme fussiness/colic is not significantly different from that of firstborns.

I had a mother tell me, with a tone in her voice as though she were being punished, "I survived not sleeping for three months with the first two; I guess I can do it again. Anyway, those children are fine now, so we'll just wait it out." Try to tell this mother that extreme fussiness occurs only in firstborn children! Extreme fussiness/colic is, however, not inherited.

Fallacy No. 8: Fresh Air Causes Extreme Fussiness/Colic

Also, several mothers, primarily from rural backgrounds, have described to me what they refer to as "wind colic." The idea here is that taking a baby out in the night air or on a windy day causes cramps and great fussiness the next day. Some of these mothers even warn against leaving the window in a baby's room open at night. There is a long tradition of believing that "night air" causes all sorts of illnesses, but it is no truer in the case of extreme fussiness/colic than anything else.

Fallacy No. 9: Boys Get It More than Girls

The only explanation for this fallacy is that some mothers might perceive problems in their sons more often than in their daughters because boys are stereotypically considered more mischievous, active, and stubborn than girls. At any rate, it is not true. Studies by the Canadian pediatrician Dr. W. C. Taylor and others agree that infant boys and girls share an equal risk in developing extreme fussiness.

Fallacy No. 10: Better-Educated Mothers Have More Extremely Fussy/Colicky Babies

It sounds fanciful, but many people believe that the higher the mother's education level and social class, the more her baby is prone to extreme fussiness/colic. You will also hear it stated in the contrary way: Extreme fussiness/colic is less common among families of lower social status.

These fallacies may arise from the patient selection bias of most pediatric training programs. Pediatric residents often learn from and practice their skills on poorer families without their own private pediatricians. These families tend to visit emergency rooms and clinics sporadically, and often delay seeking medical care. Complaints of extreme fussiness/colic may be less frequent among these families when compared to middle-class families leisurely discussing infant behavior in the privacy of their own pediatrician's office. Then again, perhaps better-educated mothers read more child care books, making them quicker to conclude that normal crying is extreme fussiness/colic. Perhaps they are less tolerant of fussing and crying.

Whatever the stereotype, careful studies show that social class or maternal education level is not connected in any way to extreme fussiness/colic. I myself have examined detailed, narrative descriptions of infant behavior during fussy periods. In these investigations I have observed no correlation whatsoever of extreme fussiness in infants along lines of social class.

Fallacy No. 11: Extremely Fussy/Colicky Babies Are More Intelligent

You may hear it said that children with extreme fussiness/colic are more intelligent than others, or grow up to be more driven, persistent, or ambitious. No study has ever supported or refuted this fallacy. It is generally recognized by pediatricians as a "white lie" intended to help parents endure this difficult period in the life of their child.

Why So Many Myths?

None of these eleven common myths about extreme fussiness is true. None can help you or your baby in any reliable way. All, though, have the potential to distract, upset, and exhaust you.

Why is there so much misinformation about extreme fussiness/colic? Partly, as I have said, it is because of a lack of real factual information—mythology loves a vacuum. Also, because the definition of extreme fussiness/colic has been so vague, people are at liberty to maintain theories they like and dismiss those they do not. Ultimately these theories are derived from the human desire to make sense of our world—to see cause-and-effect relationships wherever possible. Consider these examples: A mother might take her baby out in the cool air one night, and the next day he might have an especially bad fussy/colicky spell; she decides that the night air caused the extreme fussiness/colic. A breast-feeding mother might stop eating gas-producing vegetables for a while, and the baby may then have a couple of relatively quiet days; she decides that vegetables caused the extreme fussiness/colic. Perhaps one baby's extreme fussiness/colic runs its course at the same time his mother switches to a new formula; she may tell all her friends that Formula X causes extreme fussiness/colic. A person may know three baby boys with extreme fussiness/colic and no baby girls with it; he may well conclude that boys have more extreme fussiness.

Their conclusions are, however, all mistaken. But you can see how the myths in this chapter got started, and how they seemed to be "proved" just often enough to keep them alive. While some of the "causes" may seem to explain a small number of cases, and while the "cures" may seem to work for a couple of days, under the weight of real scientific scrutiny, none holds up.

What We Actually Know About Extreme Fussiness/Colic

What modern research tells us about extreme fussiness/colic is nowhere near as colorful as what magazines or mothers-in-law tell us, but it is actually a lot closer to the truth. Some of these bland facts about extreme fussiness/colic must be better publicized if parents are to face it calmly.

What follows is a summary of what I consider to be the key findings of several of the best-conducted extreme fussiness/ colic studies during the past forty years, although not every point in every one of these papers is equally valid. I have cited here those findings that have stood the test of time and which I believe are not only correct but ultimately also useful to parents. Each of these studies has facilitated the exploding of myths and has contributed to real knowledge of the facts. They represent milestones in our current understanding of what extreme fussiness/colic is and is not.

What Kind of Research?

You may be surprised that so little work has been done on the causes of extreme fussiness/colic. Most people think that research always involves looking inside the body, trying to understand what chain of physiological events—involving hormones, chemical changes, electrical impulses, glands, nerves, or organs—leads to a certain condition. Physiological research into something as elusive and transient as extreme fussiness/ colic is almost prohibitively difficult. Most of the usual research tools, such as simple blood tests, show normal results for these babies, and complex or invasive testing is inappropriate for children—infants in particular—who are not sick. Extreme fussiness is not serious enough to justify anything more intrusive than an occasional simple blood or urine test or X ray to rule out specific illnesses.

So you can see that until more subtle experimental procedures are developed and more sensitive experiments conducted, we cannot easily learn about the actual biological causes of extreme fussiness/colic. And, until we understand at least some of the biology behind extreme fussiness/colic, we will probably not be able to understand it very well. The irony of the condition of extreme fussiness/colic should not be missed: If it were a graver condition, we would undoubtedly know more about it.

With what I might call "internal work" on extreme fussiness/colic so difficult, most studies approach it from the outside instead. That is to say, researchers observe a large number of babies with extreme fussiness/colic to observe what they have in common. This allows for generalizations about how often it occurs and how long it lasts. Medical researchers can explore links between extreme fussiness/colic and other physical, environmental, or temperamental variables. They compare extremely fussy/colicky babies with common fussy babies to see if there are any significant differences between the groups that might explain why one group fusses and cries more than the other. This kind of research work poses questions such as: Does extreme fussiness/colic present with a history of allergy in the family? Do more boys have extreme fussiness/colic than girls? Do babies with extreme fussiness/colic have, on average, more frequent bowel movements than babies without extreme fussiness/colic? Questions like these can be answered without any added aggravation to the baby. As we saw in the last chapter, however, if a study is not well designed, it simply serves to generate more fallacies.

Research like this will not give us all of the answers to our questions tomorrow, but it is very valuable. First, it can define the usual course of extreme fussiness/colic to reassure parents that their baby is neither unusual nor ill and that there is an end in sight. Second, it can help us eliminate dead-end recommendations and "cures." For example, it is worthwhile to know that it is useless to have a nursing mother alter her diet continually.

All of the studies below fall into the category of quantitative research. Most began as attempts to prove or disprove some commonly held beliefs about extreme fussiness/colic. They provide the scientific background that falsifies the eleven myths presented earlier in this chapter. Everything we can rule out as not being related to extreme fussiness/colic brings us closer to understanding what extreme fussiness/colic is and what we can do about it.

Dr. Illingworth: It's Not Allergy, Gas, or Spoiling

Our understanding of extreme fussiness study dates from 1954, when Dr. R. S. Illingworth published a paper titled "Three Months' Colic." Dr. Illingworth wrote several popular and influential books on child care and is a British equivalent of the late American Dr. Spock. Dr. Illingworth's landmark paper includes an exhaustive (and frequently humorous) review of the medical literature on extreme fussiness up until that date. He summarizes the assertions of some forty papers in many languages, detailing their contradictory and far-fetched theories on the causes and treatment of extreme fussiness. He found that the most persistent theories involved underfeeding, overfeeding, allergy, flatulence (gas), and spoiling, among others.

In order to get a base of factual information to prove or disprove these theories, Dr. Illingworth performed a careful study of his own. At the Jessop Hospital for Women in Sheffield, England, he studied fifty extremely fussy/colicky babies, all under three months of age, whose behavior is best be summed up by the following definition: "said by their mothers to have violent, rhythmical screaming attacks, which did not stop when they were picked up, and for which no cause, such as underfeeding, could be found."

About 20 percent of the babies the doctor saw in the clinic behaved this way. Every time he found a baby with extreme fussiness/colic, he enlisted the next baby he saw at the clinic that day (provided the second baby had no colicky symptoms) as part of a control group. In this way, he collected two randomly selected groups of fifty babies each for a comparative study.

Dr. Illingworth saw all one hundred babies personally and followed up on them for six months. He collected a great deal of data about them and their families. The majority of his information came from reports by the mothers and not from his direct observation.

Dr. Illingworth was able to report the following data: Forty-four of the fifty had developed extreme fussiness during the first two weeks of life. In all fifty, spells of extreme fussiness/colic occurred in the evening; in eight, the spells also occurred at other times but worsened dramatically in the evening. Typically, symptoms of extreme fussiness began between 6:00 P.M. and 9:00 P.M. and lasted from one to six hours. (This reminds me of a father who referred to his extremely fussy son as "Dr. Jekyll and Mr. Hyde"—when the sun went down, the child was transformed into a monster!) In many of the babies, feeding eased the symptoms for a brief time. Extreme fussiness/colic disappeared, on average, at nine and a half weeks. By twelve weeks, 85 percent of the babies were over it. By four months, all of them were over it. Comparing the extremely fussy/colicky group to the normally fussy group, Dr. Illingworth concluded that extreme fussiness/colic did not appear related in any way to the suggested factors.

Underfeeding? The fifty extremely fussy/colicky babies gained more weight, on average, than the fifty commonly fussy babies did. Some of the commonly fussy babies who gained weight poorly did no unusual crying, while many of the extremely fussy/colicky babies had very good weight gains.

Overfeeding? In Illingworth's words, "I firmly believe that for practical purposes, overfeeding in a young baby is a myth. It is so rare that one can truthfully say that it practically never occurs."

Allergy? There was as much family history of allergy among the babies in the control groups as among the extreme fussiness/colic group. Only seven of the fifty mothers in the extreme fussiness/colic group said that their eating certain foods had any bearing on the child's extreme fussiness/colic, and they all named different foods.

Stomach or intestinal problems? To address this crucial old question, Dr. Illingworth performed X-ray studies on seven of the extremely fussy babies at the height of their spells to see if there was excessive gas in their intestines. No excessive gas was found. To eliminate bias, Dr. Illingworth had these X rays mixed in with a number of X rays of commonly fussy babies and challenged a disinterested radiologist to pick out the seven that were different. The radiologist could not identify a single one. Barium enemas were also performed during the spells of extreme fussiness/colic. No malformation, obstruction, or spasms in the intestines were found.

A previous study in 1952 by Dr. S. Jorup at the Samaritan Children's Hospital in Stockholm also used X-ray studies obtained during the spells of extreme fussiness/colic. He also found no increased intestinal gas connected to extreme fussiness/colic. As further evidence that digestive problems are not to blame, Dr. Illingworth found that the incidence of vomiting and the frequency of stools were the same for both the extremely fussy and commonly fussy groups.

As for spoiling as a cause of extreme fussiness, Dr. Illingworth had this to say:

> It is difficult to understand why rhythmical attacks of screaming, which do not stop when the baby is picked up and such as only occur with pain, should be ascribed to over-permissiveness on the part of the mother. . . . Any parent who has possessed a child with extreme fussiness knows that it is the most worrying and disturbing complaint, and that a baby with obvious pain has to be picked up and cuddled.

In addition, factors that might bear on spoiling, such as the age of the mother, whether the baby is her firstborn, and whether other children in the family had extreme fussiness, appeared identical for both the extremely fussy group and the commonly fussy group. In addition to deflating these five key claims about extreme fussiness, Dr. Illingworth was also able to rule out these other factors:

TABLE 2
**FACTORS RELATING TO INFANTS THAT DO NOT
INFLUENCE EXTREME FUSSINESS / COLIC**
(according to the research of Dr. Illingworth)

Age of the mother
How many children the mother has had before
Maternal illness during pregnancy
Number of fetal hiccups
Family history of allergy
Allergy in infant during the first six months
Sex of baby
Birth weight of baby
Weight gain of infant
Number of feedings per day
Method of feeding (breast versus formula)
Amount of spitting or vomiting
Number of stools per day
Increased muscle tone

To summarize, the group of babies with extreme fussiness/ colic showed no differences—in terms of allergy, frequency of feeding, younger or older mothers, or any other factor—than the group of babies with common fussiness.

Dr. Wessel: It's Not Allergy and It's Not the Family

Also in 1954, Dr. Morris A. Wessel and four associates at the Yale University School of Medicine published results of their extensive project on extreme fussiness/colic. They began their work with the strong suspicion that allergy was responsible for much of what they referred to as "paroxysmal fussing" (extreme fussiness). They hoped, by their research, to test this and other hypotheses.

Over the course of several years, a significant quantity of data had been collected on approximately two hundred mother-infant pairs who passed through Yale's maternity and early infancy project. Data included prenatal interviews, detailed records of the infant's first week, and follow-up reports by pediatricians, in addition to reports from social workers and psychologists. Dr. Wessel and his associates sent a questionnaire about family history of allergy to every mother involved. Ninety-eight of the women filled out and returned the questionnaire. It formed the basis for the Wessel study.

Fifty of the ninety-eight were judged to be "contented" and forty-eight to be "fussy." Of the forty-eight fussy infants, twenty-five were rated "seriously fussy," or "colicky," according to the following definition: "one who, otherwise healthy and well-fed, has paroxysms of irritability, fussing or crying lasting for a total of more than three hours a day, and occurring on more than three days in any one week . . . Their paroxysms continued to recur for more than three weeks or became so severe that the pediatrician felt that medication was indicated."

Irritability, fussing, or crying for more than a total of three hours per day, for more than three days per week, and continuing for more than three weeks has become a standard definition of colic or extreme fussiness. The word *or* in the definition is important because many of these babies cry very little or not at all due to the heroic efforts of their mothers and fathers to soothe them. If these parents were to suspend their soothing efforts, then their baby would cry. The fact is that interminable hours of soothing will often, but not always, prevent crying. It is important to note that Wessel himself focused on fussiness and not crying as the major problem; in fact, he titled his paper "Paroxysmal Fussing in Infancy, Sometimes Called 'Colic.' "

The ninety-eight mothers kept detailed diaries of their children's crying patterns, eating habits, bowel movements, weight gain, and general behavior. By these records, Dr. Wessel and associates were able to make many comparisons among the contented babies, the fussy babies, and the extremely fussy babies.

A problem is built into Wessel's definition, however. It expands the definition of extreme fussiness to include the pediatrician's reaction to the infant's extreme behavior: "so severe that the pediatrician felt that medication was indicated." Whether or not the doctor feels medication is needed probably has less to do with the baby's condition than with the doctor's own training, tolerance, experiences with extreme fussiness, and pressure from the parents.

This theory about allergy, however, was quickly invalidated. There was as much family history of allergy among the contented infants as among the extremely fussy ones. Likewise, there were no significant differences in type of feeding, weight gain, sex, birth order, family history of extreme fussiness, and mother's education level. Dr. Wessel's study confirmed many of Dr. Illingworth's findings as listed in Table 2, adding several more.

TABLE 3
FACTORS THAT DO NOT RELATE TO EXTREME FUSSINESS
(according to the research of Dr. Wessel)

Emotional status of mother
Family history of extreme fussiness/colic
Family tension

My own research has confirmed that many parents have babies who fuss more than three hours a day, for more than three days a week, and for more than three weeks but in fact rarely cry. Parents may invest many hours in soothing their child and would never identify him or her as colicky. They may wonder why their child needs to be held so much or why she sleeps only in their arms. The point is worth restating: Some extremely fussy/colicky babies do not cry very much or at all. Based on the studies performed by Ian St. James-Roberts (cited above), it is clear that fussiness represents a much more common problem than crying.

Dr. Paradise: *It's Not the Mother's Personality*

Directly confronting the question of whether a mother's emotional state contributes to extreme fussiness, Dr. Jack L. Paradise published an extremely useful study. It was a prospective study, meaning that information was gathered as the babies developed, rather than relying on the parents' recollections. Furthermore, it attempted to use a standardized scale to rate maternal personality traits, rather than relying on an interviewer's subjective impressions.

Dr. Paradise, who worked at Rochester (Minnesota) Child Health Services, studied 153 full-term infants who were born at one hospital during a single five-month period. This provided him with a reliable random sample because his study included every baby during this five-month time span without any selection bias. A few of the mothers declined to participate, and a few babies became sick and had to be dropped from the study. Dr. Paradise, therefore, ended up with a group of 146 infants out of the initial 153. He interviewed each mother at least once each month for three months. He gathered information about the baby's crying, eating, and bowel habits and the mother's own attitude. He examined the babies frequently.

Twenty-three percent of the infants turned out to have extreme fussiness/colic, defined as "unexplained episodes of sustained crying of moderate severity occurring often enough to be considered troublesome or distressing; holding or rocking resulted only in partial or inconsistent relief " or "prolonged and intense periods of crying or screaming throughout the first three months or longer, not lessened by any attempted method of control, and of overriding concern to the mother."

As these definitions make apparent, Dr. Paradise admitted the reaction of the mother into the equation along with the infant's behavior. He has also used terms such as "sustained crying," "moderate severity," and "intense crying" without explanation or further definition. Any observer of infant behavior knows how hard it is to determine whether crying is "moderate" or "severe," and, of course, a cause for "overriding concern" to one mother may not disturb another. Despite these limitations, the Paradise study is important because of the way in which he evaluated the mothers' personalities. He had each of the 146 women complete the Minnesota Multiphasic Personality Inventory (MMPI), a widely accepted measure of personality characteristics. The MMPI included five hundred questions and a number of scales designed to correct for distortions that might be caused by illiteracy, defensiveness, or lying. It is an extremely subtle and reliable test used on such a large number of people that the database with which these mothers could be compared was large. With MMPI results (computer-scored) in hand, Dr. Paradise looked for signs of the emotional disorders that previous studies had connected to extreme fussiness: overall psychological disorder, anxiety, "rejection of the female or maternal role," and lack of energy or enthusiasm. For each category, he compared the mothers who scored the highest (for example, the most anxious) and those who scored lowest (least anxious), concluding that extreme fussiness/colic was equally common among the children of both groups. He thus eliminated all of these personality disorders as connected in any way with extreme fussiness/colic.

The occurrence of extreme fussiness showed no relationship to maternal emotional factors, whether estimated clinically or measured by a standardized psychological test. Most mothers of infants with extreme fussiness/colic were stable, cheerful, and feminine. He concludes that his evidence "does not support the frequently stated view that colic [extreme fussiness] results from an unfavorable emotional climate created by an inexperienced, anxious, hostile, or un-motherly mother. By so advising parents, physicians may relieve them of unwarranted self-blame and anxiety."

Dr. Paradise's study also confirmed some of the research done by Illingworth and Wessel, confirming their findings. To the list of factors unrelated to extreme fussiness, he added several.

TABLE 4
**FACTORS THAT DO NOT RELATE TO
EXTREME FUSSINESS**
(*according to the research of Dr. Paradise*)

Amount of constipation, diarrhea, or flatulence
Type of formula
Duration of each feeding

Father's occupation
Maternal intelligence
Family history of gastrointestinal problems
Birth order of infant

Dr. Stewart: It's Tension

In an attempt to explain fussiness/colic from yet another scientific perspective, Dr. A. H. Stewart's behaviorally oriented textbook expresses the notion that unexplained fussiness/colic results from tension. That is, it is caused by external overstimulation of babies. The paper even refers to the phenomenon with technical jargon: "stimulus-overload extreme fussiness." Stewart argues, based on his own observations, that a child who cannot be consoled is signaling that he needs to be left alone to discharge tension by "crying it out." He claims that letting an inconsolably fussy baby cry himself to sleep several times will end, or permanently reduce, the child's crying.

The not-so-hidden message here is that parental attempts to comfort an extremely fussy baby can be counterproductive, returning to the worn-out idea that parents cause or at least aggravate extreme fussiness, either by overstimulating the baby physically or by transmitting their tension to him. Proponents of this theory like to talk about a vicious cycle of mounting tension between baby and parents. Dr. Brazelton speculated that overreactive parents can drive hypersensitive babies to greater and greater agitation, so that "what starts out as a 2 hour period of crying rapidly grows to 4, 8, and 12 hours." An earlier study by Dr. A. H. Stewart similarly proposes that extreme fussiness occurs when unusually sensitive children are matched with unusually stimulating or unusually anxious parents. This paper is so full of muddled reasoning and near slander against mothers and fathers of extremely fussy babies that I am surprised when its message—trickling down in popular wisdom—is still taken seriously. It well demonstrates what mischief a few unfounded conclusions can cause.

Stewart studied a small group of infant-parent pairs to see if "excessively fussy" babies received different treatment than did "quiet" babies. They did. The mothers of the fussy babies re-portedly jiggled, rocked, and carried their babies more. They changed the babies' position more frequently and talked to them more often and more loudly. Stewart—offering no evidence beyond his own observations—implied that all this activity caused the fussiness, as if the babies were being pestered and jiggled to the point of breakdown.

Does this conclusion necessarily follow from the data? I don't think so. If it is possible that a lot of handling can cause fussiness, it is equally possible that the fussiness can lead to a lot of handling. Every mother tries first one thing and then another when her baby cries. Mothers of babies who cry a great deal develop a whole range of consoling motions and sounds. These responses might not appear effective to a researcher during a brief observation, but over the long run this patting and bouncing and talking could well help. Concluding that a mother's comforting gestures are the cause of her baby's distress is totally unfounded.

Stewart made a related error in claiming that inconsistent parenting also caused fussiness. She reported that the mothers of the seriously fussy babies in her study alternated between holding for long stretches and not holding at all, between overfeeding and underfeeding, between overattentiveness and neglect. I doubt that any but the most distraught mothers behave as negligently and erratically as Stewart portrays those mothers of her study, although mothers of extremely fussy infants do behave inconsistently toward their babies. This is, of course, a necessary and practical reaction to the erratic behavior of their infants. Extreme fussiness changes from day to day. What seemed to comfort a fussy baby in the morning might not work that same night. A mother who tries to remain consistent in her responses to a wildly fluctuating condition will be left behind. An extremely fussy baby needs flexible, adaptive, improvisational approaches to management. The inconsistent behavior Stewart suspects of inflaming, if not causing, extreme fussiness is more likely a reaction to it, and a perfectly appropriate one.

What of the theory that an infant can pick up tension from his parents? This is one of those oft-repeated ideas with no basis in fact. Brazelton says that tension in the people around a crying infant can cause the infant's intestinal tract to act up, causing the pain, gas, and drawn-up knees of extreme fussiness, as though extreme fussiness were some sort of infant ulcer. Stewart says that when a tense, anxious, or ambivalent parent holds a baby, the tension is communicated through all the baby's senses, including smell. This observation is yet another version of blaming the mother—her behavior, personality, or her natural anxiety for her newborn.

I continue to believe that attempting to console your extremely fussy/colicky baby through whatever means occur to you is the best approach. Your baby is in some form of distress. Although we have not yet determined the nature of the distress, it is, for all intents and purposes, distress. Your soothing motions, murmuring sounds, and close holding can help. Of course, it is important that you do not let yourself become exhausted, depressed, or overwhelmed. The calmer you are, the more help you will be to your baby and the better you and the rest of your family will come through this brief but trying period of extreme fussiness/colic.

Dr. Schnall and Dr. Shaver: It Is Not Maternal Anxiety

Two subsequent studies have used objective psychological ratings to analyze whether there is a connection between a mother's emotional state and her child's extreme fussiness/colic.

Dr. R. Schnall and his associates examined thirteen extremely fussy/colicky infants brought to the Royal Children's Hospital Clinic in Parkville, Australia. Their mothers were asked to complete a standardized test called the Eysenk Personality Inventory. As a control group, thirteen commonly fussy infants and their mothers were selected, and the same test was used. Dr. Schnall found no more neurosis or anxiety among the mothers of the extreme fussiness children than among the mothers of the nonfussy children.

In a separate study of the same subject, Dr. Benjamin Shaver prefaced his report by reviewing earlier studies that had claimed that extreme fussiness/colic stemmed from a baby's perception of her mother's anxiety. Dr. Shaver wrote:

> We agree with these authors that babies are exceptionally sensitive to their mother's mood. However, colic rarely begins before the second or third week of life. If colic were due primarily to the mother's mood and level of anxiety, we would expect the symptoms to begin in the first few days of life when the mother is the most anxious and unsure of herself. . . . Also, we would expect the first-born of several children to be the most colicky prone. This is not the case, however, for the ordinal position within the family does not appear to be correlated with development of colic.

With these points in mind, Shaver analyzed a sample of fifty-seven mothers from the second trimester of pregnancy through the first six postpartum months. The babies of twelve of these mothers turned out to have extreme fussiness/colic.

To evaluate the mothers' moods, anxiety levels, and adaptation to motherhood, Dr. Shaver chose several characteristics to measure. They included "amount of physical contact," "sensitivity to infant's cues," "sense of humor," and "sense of success as a wife." On all of these items he compared the twelve mothers of extremely fussy/colicky babies to the other forty-five. On none of these measures did the mothers of the extremely fussy/colicky infants show any differences from the other mothers in terms of personality or success at adapting to motherhood. Dr. Shaver did find, however, that extreme fussiness/colic could temporarily disturb the mother-child relationship. The mothers of the extremely fussy babies were less confident and less accepting of their infants when interviewed when their child was three months old. This finding should not surprise anyone who has experienced three months of screaming and crying. When Dr. Shaver repeated these measurements at six months—after the extreme fussiness/colic had passed—the mothers of the formerly extremely fussy/colicky babies were indistinguishable from the control group; full confidence in the relationship and acceptance of their children was restored. Both mothers and babies demonstrate strong resilience through this period of suffering.

Urinary Tract Infection?

The suspicion that extreme fussiness/colic might be caused by an unrecognized urinary tract infection has also generated a lot of speculation. Physicians and parents have spent office time waiting to collect urine specimens. Infants have endured painful bladder punctures and catheterizations and been given unnecessary antibiotics. The study that led to this unfortunate state of affairs is entitled "Colic as the Sole Symptom of Urinary Tract Infection in Infants." This title is misleading. In it, again, no substantial definition of extreme fussiness is given. The authors refer to "the appearance of paroxysmal abdominal pain." Only four infants are reported about, all of whom were sick enough to require hospitalization. Moreover, two of the four babies were six months old at the time of the diagnosis of extreme fussiness. Most reports describe extreme fussiness, as we know, ending between twelve and sixteen weeks of age. The serious methodological flaws of this study require that its conclusions be dismissed. Any future hypotheses that urinary tract infection causes extreme fussiness must be proven. Naturally, infants at any age with poor weight gain, fever, and chronic irritability should be evaluated for disease, including urinary tract infections.

Drugs During Labor?

A study entitled "Drugs During Labor May Disturb Normal Behavioral Development," by the Australian physician Dr. David Thomas, focused on epidural anesthesia during labor as a cause of extreme fussiness/colic. Epidural anesthesia does appear to affect both infant behavior and maternal perceptions for a short period after delivery. However, Thomas's conclusions went much further. He suggested that drugs administered to the laboring mother pass through the placenta such that babies of these mothers are born with high drug levels in their blood. The drug concentration falls after delivery, however, and, of course, no subsequent drug is administered to the infant. So what causes the extreme fussiness/colic in the infant? Thomas speculates that extreme fussiness is caused by drug withdrawal, although no specific definition of extreme fussiness/colic is used. Further disqualifying this study, however, is that the investigator categorizing the selected babies with extreme fussiness/colic knew ahead of time which mothers had received epidural anesthesia. Preconceived bias may have prejudiced his diagnoses. The findings in this study would be more convincing if the assessment of which infant had extreme fussiness had been done blindly. Up to the present, no study demonstrates a direct biochemical connection between epidural anesthesia during labor and extreme fussiness/colic. Also, epidurals are relatively recent and extreme fussiness/colic is not.

Gastroesophageal Reflux

Babies commonly do "wet burps"—spit up—during infancy. This reflux appears to be effortless; she can smile at you and spit up on you at the same time! These babies are usually called "happy spitters," and parents simply learn to protect their clothing and furniture. Though it may be unwanted and undesirable, in the vast majority of babies spitting up is not a medical problem. To reduce or prevent this behavior, however, some pediatricians may prescribe anti-reflux drugs. In either case, no strong data link gastroesophageal reflux to fussiness or crying in most infants even if some children are medicated under the fanciful notion that the baby suffers the pain of "heartburn" or indigestion.

Naturally Occurring Substances
May Cause Extreme Fussiness/Colic

Prostaglandins are powerful muscle contractors. For example, it is probably prostaglandins that cause contraction of the uterus and the painful cramps of menstrual periods. Prostaglandins can similarly contract the muscles lining the intestine. These chemicals have been therapeutically administered to infants with birth defects involving the heart. In one study, the authors observed irritability in two infants who had received therapeutic prostaglandins for heart disease. Unfortunately, their observation has not been confirmed on a larger number of infants.

Progesterone is a hormone made by the placenta. Generally speaking, an infant is exposed to very high levels of progesterone at birth. A provocative old study suggested that progesterone deficiency might be a cause of extreme fussiness/colic. The authors of that study observed that uterine smooth muscle contractions during labor are accompanied by a fall in the mother's progesterone level. Those authors wondered if extreme fussiness/colic might be derived from similar painful smooth muscle contractions (perhaps of the smooth muscle in the gut) caused by low progesterone levels. Perhaps extremely fussy/colicky infants make an abnormally low amount of progesterone. High levels of progesterone from the placenta would protect these infants during the first few days of life, explaining why extreme fussiness/colic has a delayed onset after birth.

Progesterone deficiency as a cause of extreme fussiness is an attractive hypothesis because progesterone and its related chemical products are able to induce anesthesia or sleep. It would make sense that infants with low progesterone levels—and thus less central nervous system depression—might be more intense, fretful, difficult to soothe, and easily startled, and might have more difficulty staying asleep for long stretches.

Unfortunately, the authors of the first progesterone study also did not use an explicit definition of extreme fussiness/colic. Further, there was no blind or double-blind evaluation of their claim that a progesterone-like drug successfully treated extreme fussiness. Additionally, they used a crude urinary analysis technique to determine progesterone deficiency.

To improve upon this study, I directed a group at Children's Memorial Hospital (Chicago) to measure plasma progesterone levels in twenty-five infants at a few weeks of age, when progesterone from their mothers would no longer be present. Infants were divided into two groups: those with extreme fussiness/colic (according to Wessel's exact criteria) and difficult temperaments or low sensory threshold, and those without any of these features. One researcher measured plasma progesterone levels, while a different researcher, working independently, made the diagnosis of extreme fussiness or common fussiness. The study found that among the infants with extreme fussiness who at four months of age had difficult temperament or low sensory threshold, plasma progesterone levels were unusually low. These infants also slept for shorter periods of time and awoke more frequently at night. In a larger study, however, that compared only infants with and without extreme fussiness, regardless of subsequent temperament diagnosis or sleep pattern, the group differences in concentrations of progesterone were less impressive, although extremely fussy babies still had lower concentrations. Reflecting on this study, Linda Weissbluth raised the important question that led to another chemical candidate for extreme fussiness/colic. That candidate is melatonin.

Melatonin is a hormone produced by the pineal gland, located deep within the brain. Linda Weissbluth, who gave up her language studies to raise four sons, developed an interest in child development and asked the perceptive question whether progesterone concentrations were lower at night, thus causing more fussy behavior and crying at night. I told her that I did not know and suggested that she look it up. She walked across the street to the Northwestern University Medical School library, but the textbooks were too old to be useful. So she then went to the medical school's bookstore and sat down on the floor to read a brand-new textbook on pediatric endocrinology. The section on the progesterone was long, complex, and not very helpful, so she decided to browse through other sections of the textbook. That is when she made her discovery. She rushed to my office and exclaimed, "I've found the answer; it's melatonin!" I told her that I knew nothing about melatonin except that it came from the pineal gland, which I had been taught was not supposed to be good for anything, like the appendix. I was wrong; she was right. She published her paper in 1992 detailing how melatonin and another hormone, the neurotransmitter *serotonin,* might cause extreme fussiness/colic. In her study, she describes how the mother's pineal gland produces melatonin that crosses the placenta. The concentration of melatonin is high around the time of delivery and remains high only for several days after the baby is born. After this time, the levels become extremely low in the newborn until between three to four months of age. At three to four months, babies begin to produce their own melatonin. Moreover, at three to four months of age, the secretion rhythm of melatonin begins to show a day/night pattern, with lower levels occurring during the day and higher levels occurring at night. We also know that melatonin is capable of causing drowsiness or sleep and can cause relaxation of the smooth muscle of the intestine. During the first several days of life, high levels of maternally derived melatonin cause the baby to be very sleepy, drowsy, and calm. During the next few months, the absence of this inhibiting hormone allows the baby to become more alert.

In addition, at birth the gut is bathed in naturally occurring serotonin, which has high concentrations in the evening and at night. Serotonin causes contractions of the gut's smooth muscles. This effect of serotonin is unopposed by melatonin, causing intestinal smooth muscle contractions that last three to four months. So according to Linda Weissbluth's theory, the imbalance between serotonin and melatonin causes cramping, abdominal pain, and extreme wakefulness. In 1997, a report was published demonstrating that extremely fussy/colicky infants indeed had higher concentrations of serotonin than commonly fussy infants.

Exterogestation

In 1998, I published a book in which I discuss the concept of exterogestation. The word *exterogestation* means that during the first few months of life, babies continue a developmental process begun in the womb. They behave in many ways like a fetus even though they are outside their mother. How can this be? Consider the following observations. First, the rapid growth of babies during the first several months after they are born mimics the rapid growth of all primates before they are born. Second, in other primates, the rate of brain growth slows soon after birth, but in human babies, the brain continues to grow rapidly after birth. Third, when you compare gestational duration, onset of puberty, and total life span for all primates, the data suggest that human babies have too short a gestational period. Why? The answer is simple. In order to walk upright, as humans have for millennia, the bones of the pelvis and hip region narrowed, making the birth canal smaller. But as humans evolved larger brains, it was more difficult for the larger skull enclosing that bigger brain to fit through the birth canal. So it became necessary for all human babies to be born "prematurely," at least with respect to other primates.

The biological consequences of this relative "immaturity" is that some systems of the body, such as the ability to produce melatonin in response to light/dark cues, the ability to have regular day and night sleep periods, and the time for other systems to mature requires an additional three to four months of development. Also after three to four months, occurrences of sudden infant death syndrome (SIDS) halt. This phenomenon, too, tapers off at the age when extreme fussiness/colic subsides and ends.

The social consequences of this relative immaturity might be that during the first few months, babies feel more comfortable, as if they were in the womb, when they are swaddled and being rocked. Swaddling and rhythmic rocking movements are two of the three most effective methods used to calm babies (the third is to encourage sucking). Some researchers believe that this immaturity of human infants at birth creates a feeling of such severe helplessness in a newborn in order to compel mothers to be extremely attentive, and that this nurturing attention evolves into the maternal attachment or love for a baby necessary for the child to thrive.

Another social consequence is derived from studies of animals: ducklings pipe, lambs bleat, and monkeys make distress vocalizations only when they are away from their mothers. These cries have been described as "proximity-promoting behaviors" because they draw a mother to her baby for feeding and protection. Similarly, the cry of a human infant is a powerful signal drawing parents away from other tasks to the child. The cry demands parental attachment.

Extreme fussiness/colic itself seems not to occur in any other animal. This too, however, offers corroboration of the conclusion that human babies are born "too soon." The fuss/cry signal, a key component of the baby-mother attachment system, represents an imperfect recognition of the world outside the womb. It is as if to say that the baby in his or her immaturity is actually unaware that the mother is, in fact, present. The baby fusses or cries even when the mother is present and soothing her baby.

Babies present a range of immaturity manifested in a range of fussy behaviors, so some babies have more fuss/cry behavior and some babies have less. Furthermore, the ability for a baby to even begin to make a fuss/cry signal requires about 40 weeks' gestation, so babies born before that time do not have more fuss/cry behaviors compared to full-term babies.

Several Physiological Disturbances

Moreover, extreme fussiness/colic may be the outward expression of more than one disturbance. A one- or two-month-old bundle of organs and nerve endings can express discomfort or some kind of physical disharmony in only a limited number of ways. Long periods of crying and inability to sleep well are two of the most unforgettable, at least from a parent's point of view. It is surely incorrect to conclude that every baby diagnosed with "extreme fussiness/colic" suffers the same underlying problems.

There are probably several physiological disturbances, related or unrelated, that are capable of causing extreme fussiness/colic. In some instances, the main problem might be the fussing spells; in other instances the fussing might be less of a problem than the inability to sleep well. The problems may not be entirely biological. It is possible that different biological disturbances in infants trigger irregular, inappropriate, or deliberately inattentive parenting, which in turn aggravates (not causes) excessive crying, sleep disturbances, and/or difficult temperaments.

The State of the Art of Extreme Fussiness/Colic

As you can see, we know much more about what extreme fussiness is not than what it is. It is a poorly understood behavior and quite distressing. Studying extreme fussiness/colic is complicated, and in fact most research has been done around the edges of extreme fussiness/colic rather than on its core cause.

All studies agree on some things. Extreme fussiness occurs in about 20 percent of all babies. These babies may experience periods of explosive, inconsolable crying with the appearance of abdominal pain and gassiness. The outbursts of unmanageable and disagreeable behavior usually start during the first two weeks, occur mainly in the evening, and typically disappear by three or four months of age. The cause of extreme fussiness is unknown, but factors such as birth order, sex, parental social class, allergy, maternal intelligence, maternal anxiety, and maternal personality have not been proven to be involved.

It seems to me that any researcher who seriously maintains that the mother causes extreme fussiness will have to explain three interesting facts. First, why does extreme fussiness nearly always begin within two to three weeks of birth in full-term babies, and within two to three weeks of expected birth dates in premature babies? Even if you believe that the child has to be with the mother a few weeks to feel the full burden of her anxiety, why would a premature baby not fuss until she has been living with her mother six, seven, or eight weeks? Second, why isn't extreme fussiness/colic confined to, or at least much more common among, firstborn babies? Mothers are demonstrably more anxious around their first infant, but all studies agree that extreme fussiness/colic occurs as often among second-born children as among firstborn. Third, why is extreme fussiness almost universally worse in the late afternoon and evening? A mother's anxiety follows no daily pattern; why should a child's response follow one? Brazelton suggested that a mother is more fatigued as the day goes on or becomes anxious over the father's return home from work. Frankly, mothers of extremely fussy/colicky infants are fatigued and anxious all the time. Even when an infant's "day" runs from one in the afternoon to midnight, even when the mother works outside the home and does not see the baby until evening, even when the father works the night shift, extreme fussiness stubbornly worsens at 6:00 or 7:00 in the evening, no matter what.

I believe that these three facts point to a biological rather than environmental cause for extreme fussiness. I believe that a maternal anxiety explanation leaves too many questions unanswered. I want parents to know that tension in the family is simply not the answer to what causes extreme fussiness/colic.

Review all the factors listed in Tables 2, 3, 4, and 5. These are things we can say with confidence do not have any direct connection with extreme fussiness/colic. So if you fear that your own anxiety, your husband's allergies, your smoking, your breast milk, your level of education, or your fondness for lima beans is causing your child's misery—reassure yourself. We do not understand the causes of extreme fussiness, but I am absolutely certain that it is not the parents' fault.

CHAPTER 3

Birth to Four Months of Age: How to Soothe and Help Your Baby to Sleep

Introduction and Advice

Even though you now may understand more about the phe-nomenon of infant extreme fussiness—even given that you know it will, in all likelihood, last until three to four months of age—you still must soothe your infant! Though probably none of the suggestions here is new to you, many warrant back-ground explanations, more thorough presentation, and clari-fication of terms in order to effectively help parents both customize an approach to their fussy baby and to manage ex-pectations of results.

What exactly is soothing? Soothing helps restore your child to a normally peaceful state. To soothe your newborn is to ren-der her calm or quiet, to bring her to a composed condition. You are attempting to establish a peaceful state of tranquility by reducing the force or intensity of fussiness. Your goal is to soften, tune down, or render less harsh her fussiness or crying. Soothing is pacifying or calming. You want to bring comfort to your baby and to bring a cessation of the agitation. Snuggling her close to your body, she feels the warmth of your body and senses your affection and protection. Cuddling with your baby

63

is like a close embrace with someone you love. Sometimes you just want to nestle with her as you take a cozy position and hold her close to you or you lie down close to her. At best, when she is tired, you hope to lull her into a relaxed, sleepy state.

Bodily contact, sucking, and gentle rhythmic motions over long periods of time seem to work best. For some babies, loud mechanical sounds like the garbage disposal, vacuum, or blow dryer seem to help. Be careful, however, not to bombard your baby with stimuli. Initially, try to appeal to one sense at a time: tactile (massaging, rubbing, kissing, rocking, patting, changing from hip to shoulder), auditory (singing, humming, playing music, running the vacuum cleaner), visual (bright lights, mobiles, television). When your baby is drowsy, dim light or darkness or a rhythmic motion (swings, cradles, car rides, going for a walk) may also help. Sometimes doing too many of these things simultaneously or with too much force has a stimulating rather than relaxing effect. If your baby remains fussy, try combinations of these different modalities.

Try to synchronize your actions with your baby's rhythms. If he is tense and taut, with deep, exhausted-sounding, heaving sobs and little physical movement, try rubbing his back gently or moving your cheek over his in a slow rhythm that coincides with his breathing pattern. If he is boxing with his fists, jerking his legs, and arching his back, maybe a ride on your shoulders will grab his attention and arrest the spell. You will find that after a while you become attuned to the nuances of your baby's rhythms and respond accordingly.

Your Relationship with Your Extremely Fussy/Colicky Baby

Extreme fussiness/colic strikes during the early months, when the parent-child relationship is just forming. Daily bouts of screaming, with the attendant guilt and worry, can interfere with this relationship. You must remind yourself continually that although your baby is in distress, he is not rejecting you, disputing your authority or anyone else's, or commenting on your parenting ability.

Parents should be especially aware of their behavior toward their baby during the first few months, particularly when the baby is calm and alert and social interaction is possible. These times will become more frequent as your baby approaches the age of three to four months and should be taken advantage of. Although your behavior may not have a dramatic effect on extreme fussiness/colic, it will have a cumulative effect because you are learning a way of responding to your child. If you tend to respond in a tense, anxious manner even when your baby is not crying, this only robs you of enjoying those "good" times. When your baby is fussy, drowsy, or both, he is almost out of reach. If your baby cries when awake and/or does not rest well when asleep, he is probably not going to be very sociable, attentive, or receptive to the messages you send him. It is crucial that you shower your baby with attention during those times when he is awake and not crying, and be prepared for a burst of interaction as soon as the spell of extreme fussiness/colic goes away.

Do not let the extreme fussiness/colic throw you off balance. Love your baby all the time. If you are able to respond calmly, you will be able to enjoy your baby more during the nonfussy periods, and your baby will enjoy you more. Remember to treat your infant in the same loving way whether he is crying or content. How your child's temperament and sleeping patterns will ultimately turn out are probably related more to your behavior during this time than to the original biological disturbance(s) that caused the extreme fussiness.

Take Care of Yourself

An extremely fussy/colicky baby needs a great deal of attention. You may find your life filled with rocking, walking, feeding, and soothing. But the truth is that most of what you will be doing about the extreme fussiness/colic is waiting it out. Try to keep up your health, good cheer, and loving relationships during this difficult time. Do not forget about yourself and the rest of your family. Then you will all be ready to give the baby your best love and care.

It is normal for parents to feel angry, bewildered, and frustrated sometimes when their baby fusses and cries. All parents are this way. You have had an unlucky break, and you are entitled to feel resentful sometimes. Maintaining a sense of humor is hard, but most mothers with extremely fussy/colicky infants feel better getting their feelings out into the open.

Mothers of fussy infants can easily become worn down or exhausted. When this occurs, a mother should have her husband, partner, friend, or baby-sitter take over care of the baby so she can get away. (Serious consideration, however, must be given to who will care for these high-maintenance babies, especially if it's someone from outside the family. Shaking a newborn will not halt crying or induce sleep and may cause permanent physical damage or even death.) If you feel reluctant, remember that your baby's crying will not be as bothersome to someone else as it is to you. This is not self-indulgence—you must have frequent breaks from your extremely fussy/colicky baby. Call it tag-team parenting or one-on-one defense if you have only one child. If you have more than one child, call it zone coverage!

Spend as much time as you can with your baby, but do not feel compelled to spend six or eight hours consoling him without a break. Many fathers have experienced the pleasure of automobile rides at three in the morning with their baby to give their wives a break. Fathers quickly learn how hard it is to be a loving parent and husband while always on the verge of falling asleep. Mothers should be careful not to behave like a "gatekeeper" and prevent fathers from helping out because they believe that they are better soothers.

As we have seen from studies on crying, responding promptly and consistently when a baby is younger than three months is better than waiting to see if she settles down. If she has extreme fussiness/colic, she probably will not settle down, and the time you spend waiting and listening is unpleasant for you. On the other hand, if none of your efforts seem to calm the baby, it is important not to exhaust yourself totally. If you are alone and you have completely run out of energy, you feel as though you're at your wits' end, and find he is as unhappy in your arms as he is in his crib, then put him down and let him cry just long enough for you to regroup. As noted above, a baby in the midst of an inconsolable spell of extreme fussiness/colic may not know whether he is being held or not. *Taking a break from the continuous fussiness before you break down is prudent, not selfish.* It is far better to let your child cry a little than it is to get angry with a harmless and innocent child. Remember that you must rest at times in order to recharge your battery so that you can continue to comfort your baby.

A popular recommendation is to try for fifteen or twenty minutes to soothe the child; if you see no results, put him down for about 30 minutes and then try again. In my experience, most mothers are able to, and want to, spend more than 20 minutes soothing their babies but are not willing to endure even half an hour of crying. Do whatever suits you, but letting your baby cry should be the action of last resort: an attempt to help a desperate mother, if not the child.

> *Can a mother sit and hear*
> *An infant groan, an infant fear?*
> *No, no! Never can it be!*
> *Never, never can it be!*
>
> WILLIAM BLAKE

Creative Parenting

I believe that over the long run, creative parenting behavior will override whatever temporary disturbances are causing extreme fussiness/colic. The problem is that some parents—especially mothers—become so distraught or fatigued that it prevents calm, well-thought-out parenting. Conflict can erupt among family members over how to handle the problem. Husband and wife may expend energy blaming each other. Everyone's self-esteem can suffer, and no one will have the resourcefulness to try strategies that might end up helping. So try to get enough rest, keep your wits about you, and get away for occasional quiet evenings. Whatever works, do it: wear your baby in a sling, sleep with your baby, use gentle rhythmic motions to help your newborn sleep, try different ways to hold or cuddle with your newborn.

Hospitalization

In the past, extremely fussy/colicky babies were sometimes hospitalized. Frankly, this was done because some doctors believed that colic resulted from a family situation that more or less drove the baby crazy. Today, of course, we know that this is not true. Still, a doctor will occasionally propose to remove a baby from the family for a while, for "tests and observation." You should know that as long as the baby is gaining weight and exhibits no abnormalities apart from the symptoms of extreme fussiness/colic symptoms discussed in this book, hospitalization would not accomplish anything. The real motive is to give the parents some relief.

If a doctor suggests hospitalizing your extremely fussy/colicky infant, talk with her very frankly. Does she have a real reason to believe the problem is something more than extreme fussiness/colic? Exactly what tests will be performed, and what can she learn from them? Why does she feel your baby should be separated from you? What can be learned from observing the baby in the hospital rather than at home? You should probably get a second opinion before even considering this drastic move.

I believe that hospitalization for extreme fussiness/colic is never justified. It is very expensive, and infants can easily catch serious infections in hospitals. Having a baby in the hospital is stressful on parents and can be upsetting to the baby. Even if your baby's extreme fussiness/colic is so bad that the idea of respite looks good to you, there are many cheaper, safer alternatives: hire a full-time sitter or even a private-duty nurse; go to a hotel for the weekend; alternate with your husband spending nights away from home; leave the baby with relatives for a day or two.

Remember that many, many parents have lived through extreme fussiness/colic. It is a trying experience but does not really last all that long. Your extremely fussy/colicky baby—even if her crying is very persistent and very severe—is not sick and does not belong in a hospital. She belongs at home with people who love her.

Caring for a Family with an Extremely Fussy/Colicky Newborn

Caring for a family is different from treating or "managing" extreme fussiness/colic in a newborn. "Treatment" implies the presence of a medical problem that if treated or managed correctly will be solved, restoring health. There is no good evidence that extremely fussy/colicky newborns are unhealthy or are suffering from a medical problem. Fussiness appears to be a pre-cry state. That is, if the parents do not respond to the fussiness effectively, crying usually follows. The more skillful you become, the more effort you are able to put forth, and the earlier you start to soothe your baby, the less likely it is that fussiness will escalate into crying. In other words, skillful soothing of fussiness may prevent much crying.

Prevention of extreme fussiness/colic will be possible when the cause or causes are known. Based on my experience, we should start with prevention of unnecessary guilt, worry, and confusion on the part of the parents. The better you understand the nature of extreme fussiness/colic, the better off you will be. At both prenatal visits with the obstetrician and at the first visit to the pediatrician after delivery, the family should be informed that extreme fussiness/colic might occur and given tools to cope with it if it does. I would recommend that parents ask about extreme fussiness/colic even if the pediatrician does not bring up the subject. This is not borrowing trouble; it is being prepared.

All of the tips for living with extreme fussiness/colic given in this chapter have helped large numbers of parents. The periods of extreme fussiness/colic can be made bearable. Future behavioral and sleeping problems can be minimized. Nothing is more important to parents than a good dose of optimism, because extreme fussiness/colic *does* disappear. Parents will sleep again. In later chapters, you will learn through the experiences of several mothers of extremely fussy/colicky infants which coping strategies are successful and which are less so.

REMEMBER

Fussiness and crying will not continue forever.
You cannot spoil your newborn.
Different soothing tips work better for different babies.

Father Care: Our Secret Weapon for Soothing

Before the baby is born, fathers should make the decision to become involved in caring for the baby right away.

Some fathers hold back initially out of fear that they might make mistakes when holding, burping, bathing, changing, or feeding the baby. For this reason, mothers should deliberately leave the house for a few hours on a weekend to visit a friend, hang out with the older kids, work out, get their hair done, or go shopping at a time when you expect your baby to go through a cycle of feeding, changing, bathing, and going to sleep. Often a father will feel more comfortable in doing those things when the "expert" is not present looking over his shoulder.

Second, fathers should plan ahead for the six-week peak of fussing/crying that occurs in all babies. Plan to come home early or take a few days off from work if you are able. Make adjustments if your baby is born before or after the expected date of delivery because the six-week peak is counted from the due date. Try to give your wife a well-deserved break at this time by taking your baby out for long walks or car rides in the evening or at night. There are many fathers in my practice out at night in Lincoln Park, Chicago, driving around slowly with their baby in the car seat in the back. They meet one another at stop signs or red lights, smile or wave, and continue their circular journey. Music in the car and the gentle rocking motions often calm even the fussiest of babies. Still, even if your baby does not sleep well during these outings, at least you know that Mother is getting a break.

The third point is that fathers can learn how to help their baby fall asleep. For example, after nursing the baby, a mother might pass the child to the father, who rocks the baby gently for a while and then puts the baby down to sleep or lies down with his baby next to him in their bed so they both can snooze. However you choose to do it, putting your baby to sleep will help you gain confidence in becoming a father. If you are giving expressed breast milk in a bottle, sometimes it's easier when the mother actually leaves the house, because the baby can smell the mother's presence and might resist taking the bottle if he knows that Mom is home. So, maybe on weekends when it's time for the baby's nap, Mom can leave the house and have fun while Dad gives the bottle and puts the baby down to sleep.

Fourth, fathers can learn how to soothe fussiness and crying. For example, learn infant massage. Classes are offered everywhere; call your local maternity hospital or go online. Expand your repertoire of lullabies; your baby will not care how well you sing. A bath might be especially soothing; spend time with your baby, letting the warm water calm him. A father can learn to do everything a mother does to soothe a baby, except for breast-feeding. So men, wear your baby in a sling or carry your baby in a backpack or frontback. Walk, rock, and gently swing your baby.

Number five is that a father can request to help feed or soothe the baby in the middle of the night when the mother needs some extra sleep. This is a little bit tricky because many mothers believe that nobody can do the soothing as well as they can and anyway, the father needs his rest so he can go out to work well rested in the morning. With this belief, the mother rejects or resists the idea that baby care in the middle of the night should be a shared experience. For some families, this might be the right course of action. But if the mother is distressed, exhausted, sleep-deprived, or going through the baby blues, then extra help at night from the father is absolutely needed to give the mother a little more sleep. After all, no matter how stressful his job might be, the father always gets some breaks at work. During the day, a mother with a baby might get no breaks.

Last, a father should not encourage the mother to keep their child up past his time of tiredness so the father and baby can play together. Adjust your schedule so that you can spend time with your baby in the morning or whenever he's awake. Tell your wife that as much as you love your baby, he should sleep when he is tired, just as he should be fed when he is hungry. You do not want him to be starved for food or sleep.

Sucking Is Soothing

Anything you can do to encourage your baby to suck will help soothe her. Offering the breast, a bottle, a pacifier, a finger, or a wrist usually helps calm your baby. If you are breast-feeding, one way to help distinguish between sucking for soothing and sucking for hunger is that the sucking for soothing is often rapid repeated sucks with very little swallowing. In addition, the fussy baby does not suck in a rhythmic, steady fashion; instead, she starts and stops, twists and turns. If she is hungry, the pattern is usually a rhythmic suck-swallow, suck-swallow, and so forth. If you are bottle-feeding, do not assume that eagerly taking several ounces means that your baby is hungry. Many babies with extreme fussiness/colic suck more than they need and spit up a lot.

Because sucking is such a powerful way to calm a baby and babies often fall asleep with sucking, I think it is unnatural and unhealthy for parents to deliberately do things that interfere with sucking. For example, in a popular book that promotes "no-cry sleep solutions," the author tells mothers to remove the child from the breast before she falls asleep; if the baby continues to want to suck, the author tells parents to hold the baby's mouth closed to prevent sucking. Another popular book describes sucking as the major way that babies can calm themselves but then goes on to recommend that you wake your baby up during sucking if she falls asleep at the breast—even as early as one month of age! Both books make the assumption that if the baby falls asleep while sucking, you will be creating a sleep problem. There is no good evidence to support this assumption. Both books also incorrectly assume that feeding and sleeping are tightly linked, so they encourage you to force-feed your baby in order to help her sleep longer. Phrases such as "cluster feed" or "top off the tank" or "awake when hungry and asleep when full" reveal a profound ignorance about how the developing brain, not the stomach, controls sleep-wake rhythms. I believe it is much more natural to follow your baby's needs. If your baby is hungry, feed her. If your baby is fussy, soothe her. If your baby is tired, help her sleep. If you're not sure what she needs, encourage sucking at the breast or bottle until she seems satisfied or calm or until she falls asleep.

Here are some common questions about pacifiers.

Q: *My baby is extremely fussy but won't take a pacifier. What can I do?*
A: Some babies reject a pacifier early on but may accept one later, after they are six weeks old. So if she does not want one now, try other methods of soothing but offer the pacifier again when she is older.

Q: *Will using a pacifier create "nipple confusion" and interfere with breast-feeding?*
A: In my pediatric practice the vast majority of mothers breast-feed their babies successfully, and I encourage them to do whatever works to soothe their babies, including pacifiers. I think that "nipple confusion" does not occur with

pacifiers. But if you gave too many bottles of formula or expressed breast milk per day, your baby might learn to reject the breast and wait for the bottle because it takes less effort to suck from the bottle compared to the breast. Sometimes this is referred to as "nipple confusion" and has led to the recommendation of giving no bottles to ensure successful breast-feeding. I recommend that a *single* bottle of expressed milk or formula, mother's choice, be given only *once* each day beginning at two to three weeks of age. This allows fathers, brothers, sisters, and grandparents to enjoy the pleasure of feeding the baby and to give the mother a mini-break. One bottle per day accustoms the baby to taking a bottle but does not cause "nipple confusion" or otherwise interfere with breast-feeding.

Q: *What kind of pacifier is best?*
A: Over the past thirty years I have seen many different pacifiers marketed, and each one is promoted as having some kind of distinct advantage. The truth is that all unit-construction pacifiers (made in one piece so the nipple cannot separate from the flange) are safe. Those that allow air to get on the skin around the mouth are best because this helps prevent irritation of the skin.

Q: *When do I stop the pacifier?*
A: Some babies love to suck the pacifier as they fall asleep. I have had parents come to me for sleep consults who reported that their child had been a good sleeper until they threw away the pacifier. Now the child was having difficulty falling asleep and staying asleep. When I asked why they threw away the pacifier, they told me that they thought that this was something that they were supposed to do at some particular age. This is because there is a common but false notion that if parents do not get rid of the pacifier by a certain age, they will create a dependency or "infantalize" their baby, that is, prevent their baby from developing properly. Other parents get rid of the pacifier because they do not

want their one- or two-year-old walking around with a pacifier in her mouth.

I advise that parents restrict the pacifier to only sleep times beginning at nine months of age. Then they will never have a toddler walking around with a pacifier in his mouth. Exceptions to restricting the pacifier to only sleep times might be a long trip or an illness where the child needs extra soothing. In general, the pacifier becomes associated with the crib and the child does not expect to have it at other times. I tell families that when he goes off to college, he will take your plastic credit card and not his pacifier.

Rhythmic Rocking Motions

Rhythmic motions are usually an effective method of soothing your infant. Use a cradle, rocking chair, baby swing, sling, or front carrier; dance with your baby, simply walk with him, or take your baby for automobile rides. Rocking motions may be gentle movements or vigorous swinging, depending on what your child responds to. Sometimes simply gently rocking the bassinet or crib will be just right. Gentle jiggling on your lap or bouncing may calm your baby. Your baby may be on his back or stomach. Some parents claim that raising and lowering the baby like an elevator ride is effective. Perhaps these gentle rhythmic movements are comforting because they are similar to what a baby feels before he is born.

Swings are popular for soothing babies and are usually safe and effective. Please make sure the head is well supported by having the baby more reclining than upright. If your baby falls asleep while swinging, try to turn off the swing so he will have motionless sleep. This might not work and he might cry. Even if your baby does stay asleep after the swing is turned off, you might not be able to transfer him to a bassinet without him waking. Do whatever works to help him sleep; even if he sleeps in the swing, even if the swing is moving, it is better than no sleep. Similarly, he may fall asleep in a car seat when driving and you will not be able to transfer him into a bassinet. Again, let him sleep in the car seat.

A teenage baby-sitter taught me a trick that she learned from her mother. She showed me how to hold my extremely fussy/colicky son on my shoulder so high on the shoulder that my collar bone was in his stomach and his face was looking down at the floor. It looks funny, but it really was comfortable for him. Before I learned to do this, I held him lower on my shoulder so he was looking backwards but my collar bone was pressing into his chest, and this was not very comfortable. But with this more comfortable position, my walking around (sometimes in circles in my living room) was a more soothing, relaxing experience for both of us.

Swaddling

Gentle pressure, such as when we're embraced or hugged, makes us feel good. Swaddling (gentle wrapping), sleeping in a car seat, or being held in a soft baby carrier or sling are other ways to exert gentle pressure. Take a blanket from the dryer when it is still warm and see if swaddling your baby with it helps your baby calm down. Here too, perhaps the sensation of gentle pressure resembles a state of comfort the baby experienced before he was born. Both rhythmic motions and gentle pressure may be effective because they partially re-create the sensations that the baby felt in the womb.

Here is a simple way to swaddle your baby.

Square Receiving or Baby Blanket
1. **Fold down one corner (the top corner).**
2. **Place your baby down on his back so that the nape of his neck is on the fold.**
3. **Gently hold his arms straight down at his sides.**
4. **Take the right corner and fold it diagonally across your baby so that it crosses in front of your baby, just below the chin. Tug it gently so the material is taut.**
5. **Take the left corner and fold it diagonally across your baby so that it crosses in front of your baby, just below the chin. Tug it gently so the material is taut.**

6. **Trick No. 1: Tickle or tap the baby's toes so that he draws up his legs a little into a slightly flexed position.**
7. **Take the bottom corner and fold it up toward the face. If there is too much material and the face would be covered, fold down just enough of the excess to keep the face clear.**
8. **Trick No. 2: Pick up your baby with one hand on the back and your fingers supporting the head. This will allow you to tightly wrap the material behind the baby.**
9. **Place your baby down on his back. His weight will keep him from being able to kick free.**

Rectangular Receiving or Baby Blanket
1. **Fold down the short side of the blanket.**
2. **Place your baby down on his back so that the nape of your baby's neck is on the fold.**
3. **Follow steps 3–9 above.**

Music

Music may soothe your baby. There is no one type of music that has been shown to be superior to other types. So try different varieties of music or recordings to see what works best for your baby. If the music has many quiet and loud portions, it is probably best to turn it off after your baby has fallen asleep, because the wide changes in volume might awaken him.

Voices

Your voice may be particularly soothing to your baby, so try quietly talking to her or make calming sounds such as shushing sounds. Read or tell a short story, or say good night to things in the room. Tape recordings of other family members' voices such as grandparents saying good night might be useful. Humming or singing lullabies might have a calming effect.

Sound Machines

Your baby may respond well to sound machines—devices that produce white noise or nature sounds such as rain, birds singing, water in a brook, or ocean surf. Like music, the sounds may lull your child to sleep or partially drown out the intermittent street noises that might interrupt sleep. An alternative to a white noise machine is a desktop fan, humidifier, or vaporizer. The humming or whirring sound of these machines is often effective.

Lullabies

What is the power of a lullaby? Babies calm down and slip into slumber; parents relax and feel more at peace with themselves and their baby. Lullabies are the universal musical language of parents loving babies. Gently stroke or massage your baby when singing or listening to a lullaby; feel the waves of calmness sweep over you. The CD of lullabies that I helped produce is called *Sweet Baby Lullabies to Soothe Your Newborn*. Toria Burrell, who did the musical arrangements and also performed both the vocal and instrumental music, described lullabies as follows:

> Rhythm in music can help to calm and soothe by being regular and steady and therefore almost hypnotic. Rhythm conjures up images of motion, like waves breaking, horses running, rain falling, trains chuffing, or our own gentle motions inside us, like our hearts beating or our breath rising and falling. My lullabies have regular, gentle, rocking rhythms like the rocking of a baby's cradle. Regular rhythms can help us to focus our minds away from pain or discomfort, which is unpredictable, irregular, and frightening, and on something predictable, steady, and peaceful. We can trust the rhythm of a lullaby; we can let go and follow it; we need no energy to listen to it, so we can let it lull and relax us.
>
> Melodies in music can help to calm and soothe by being singable, intimate, full of repetitive patterns, and therefore pleasing. Melodies can remind us of bird song, wind whistling, distant train horns, and particularly our own voices (or the voices of our mothers), whether speaking, whispering, or singing. The more repetitive and smooth the melody pattern is, the more memorable it is, and therefore the more singable it is.

My lullabies have choruses that are repeated many times, allowing the listener to become familiar with the melody and therefore able to sing along with it. Melody originated from the speaking voice, which is often melodic and tuneful in itself. Melodies mimic the spoken sentence with a rise in pitch and volume toward the middle of a phrase or verse and drop in pitch and volume toward the end of a phrase or verse. We can bond with the melody of a lullaby; we can let go and forget our burdens and responsibilities and let the melody caress us and relax us.

Harmony in music can be described as the weaving together of several melodies, making them synchronize in a pleasing blend. This synchronization creates a physical vibration of sound waves, which has an effect on your ear and, in turn, your mind, body, and emotions. Harmony requires careful crafting to make various melodic lines build smoothly toward the peak of each verse and fall away smoothly together towards the end. Harmony can therefore enrich and enhance a single melody line and can emphasize a rhythm pattern, giving music more depth, structure, and texture. Feel the harmony of my lullabies, follow it, bond with it, and let it deeply fulfill and relax.

One of her original lullabies was based on the *Aeneid*, an epic poem written by Virgil between 30 and 19 B.C. It illustrates how ancient cultures appreciated the magical power of sleep to heal.

> *As night falls, the weary creatures*
> *of earth. And the woods and the*
> *frothing seas. Grow calm like the stars*
> *as they circle their course. And sleep*
> *with quiet ease.*
>
> *And so all creatures far and wide.*
> *From the craggy fields to the glassy lakes.*
> *Stretch and lie 'neath the silent night. And*
> *Sleep takes away their worries and aches.*
>
> Translated by JED WEISSBLUTH

Massage

Baby massage has been observed in many different cultures and has a long history. Just as prenatal massage benefits a mother because the relaxation allows her to sleep better and be better rested in preparation for childbirth and breastfeeding, massaging your newborn promotes a more calm state, improved sleeping, less fussing or crying, less gas, better nursing, and increased weight gain. Parents, too, benefit directly from massaging their child. While lovingly stroking your baby, you smile at your baby, talk softly, or you might sing or hum. These efforts, while focused on your baby, also relax you! Both mothers and fathers feel closer to their child. They learn how to read their infant's cues and respond more sensitively. For mothers, the soothing effect of massage may mean that the child does less non-nutritive nursing, which might produce less nipple soreness and fatigue. Fathers who spend time massaging their child are also giving their wives free time to rest and relax. Grandparents, too, can massage the newborn or fussy baby, calming the child and giving the parents a little free time. (Don't forget that parents can massage each other, too. Both will be more relaxed and sleep better. A relaxed mother will be more successful at nursing. A relaxed father can be more supportive of his wife and more involved in caring for their baby.)

Baby massage is not a gimmick or a cure for extreme fussiness. However, it does soothe babies. Equally important, it provides you with a singular opportunity to be completely focused on your baby, so turn off your phone and pager. You are doing something quite different from feeding, changing, and bathing. Comforting your baby this way will give you an inner calmness that will help you get through possible rough times when your baby is extremely fussy and not very soothable.

To massage your baby, use a natural cold-pressed fruit or vegetable oil. Gently stroke the skin and gently knead your baby's muscles. All the movements are gently performed. Books with pictures and videos are available to assist you. One popular book is *Infant Massage: A Handbook for Loving Parents* by Vimala McClure, and another is *Massage for Healthier Children* by Marybetts Sinclair. Here are some practical tips and instructions:

1. Plan to provide fifteen to twenty minutes of quiet time, especially before sleep times.
2. Provide warmth, especially after a bath. Consider massaging your older child in a bathtub with soap instead of oil.
3. Provide soft lighting.
4. You can use either massage oil, such as safflower or almond oil, or lotion. At sleep times, lotion is better because it will add moisture to the skin, and unlike oil, it will not soak through the child's pajamas.
5. The massage surface should be firm and flat, such as the child's bassinet.
6. Cover the bedding with a sheet if you are using oil to prevent the oil from soaking the bedding.
7. Wash your hands and remove all rings, watches, and bracelets.
8. Vary the pressure to find one that soothes your child the best.

Instructors who are certified by the International Association of Infant Massage teach infant massage. More information on infant massage is available at the association's Web site (www.iaim-us.com) and at the Website of the International Institute of Infant Massage (www.infantmassageinstitute.com).

Sleep Associations

When you are soothing your baby to sleep, you might play a lullaby that is used only at that time. Then your baby will learn to associate the lullaby with falling asleep. In the same vein, you might turn on a music box, hum a tune, softly repeat a phrase of endearment, or repeat a sound that seems to calm your baby. As an alternative, or in addition to the sounds, you might always give your baby something safe to clutch, such as a small stuffed animal, only when falling asleep. Some parents like to spray the bed with a scent that is used only for sleeping. These pleasant auditory, tactile, and olfactory sensations help communicate to your baby that it is time for slumber.

Respect Your Baby's Need to Sleep: The One- to Two-Hour Window of Wakefulness

Immediately after your baby is born, you will see what people mean when they say, "sleeping like a baby." For a few days, babies sleep almost all the time. They barely suck and normally lose weight during this time. If your baby was born early, this very drowsy time might last longer, and if your baby was born past the expected date of delivery, the drowsy period might be brief or nonexistent. A few days later, babies begin to wake up more. This increased wakefulness reflects the normal maturation of your baby's nervous system. I tell families that the brain wakes up after three or four days just in time to catch the breast milk, which is now available in ample amounts. The baby looks around more, with wider eyes, and is able to suck with more strength and for longer periods. Within days, the weight loss stops and a period of dramatic growth in weight, height, and head circumference begins. Also, longer periods of wakefulness begin to appear after a few days. Although your baby is intently interested in you and is quickly able to recognize your face and voice, she is not curious about objects such as toys or mobiles. She does not appear to care about the general buzz of noises, colors, or other activities surrounding her, and therefore she falls asleep almost anywhere. The extremely fussy/colicky baby often is not this way and appears to have more difficulty falling asleep and staying asleep even at only several days of age. All babies gradually seem to become more aware of action, motion, voices, noise, vibrations, lights, wind, and so forth as they become more curious. Now, they often do not "sleep like a baby."

During the day, you will notice that within one to two hours of being wakeful and alert, your baby will become drowsy and want to go to sleep. If you soothe your baby during the beginning of drowsiness, most babies will easily fall asleep. The extremely fussy/colicky baby will need this kind of help more often. At times, though, in the evening and especially around six weeks of age, all babies are a little fussy and may need a longer period of soothing or different techniques to help them fall asleep.

Drowsy Cues

Here are some ways to recognize when your baby is becoming drowsy. Watch for a decrease in activity, less movement of the arms and legs, eyes that are not as sparkling, eyelids that droop a little, less intense staring at you, fewer or quieter sounds, and weaker or slower sucking. If your baby is over six weeks old, you may notice less socially responsive smiling or that your baby is less engaging. This is the time to begin soothing to sleep. All babies become this way within one to two hours of wakefulness.

What happens if you miss this one- to two-hour window of wakefulness? If your baby cannot fall asleep because of too much stimulation around her, she will become overtired. When you

---

DROWSY SIGNS, SLEEPY CUES, SLEEP SIGNALS

Moving into the sleep zone
Becoming Drowsy
Decreased activity
Slower motions
Less vocal
Sucking is weaker or slower
Quieter
Calmer
Appears uninterested in surroundings
Eyes are less focused
Eyelids drooping
Yawning

FATIGUE SIGNS

Entering overtired zone
Becoming Overtired
Fussing
Rubbing eyes
Irritable
Cranky

or your baby become overtired, the body is stressed. There are chemical changes that then occur to fight the fatigue and this chemical stress response interferes with the ability to easily fall asleep and stay asleep. Babies vary in their ability to self-soothe and deal with this stress, and parents vary in their ability to soothe their babies, so not all babies go bonkers if they are kept up a little too long. But you will have a more peaceful and better-sleeping baby if you respect his need to sleep within one to two hours of wakefulness. I consider this to be the beginning of sleep-training babies.

Sleep training begins with developing a sense of timing so that you are trying to soothe your baby at the time when your baby is naturally getting drowsy. Some young babies will need dark and quiet environments to sleep well, while others will appear to be less sensitive to what is going on around them. Respect your baby's individuality and do not try to force your baby to meet your lifestyle. I like the analogy with feeding: We do not withhold food when our baby is hungry. Instead, we try to anticipate when he will be hungry so that we can be somewhere calm where we can feed him. Nor do we feed him on the run. The same goes for sleeping.

REMEMBER

If your young baby does not sleep, continue to try soothing your baby. Do not let him cry or ignore him. You cannot spoil a baby. You cannot teach a baby a crying habit.

Other Soothing Methods

Be skeptical about the supposed miracles accomplished with crib vibrators, hot water bottles, herbal teas, or recordings of heartbeats or womb sounds. There has been a great deal of nonsense written about burping techniques, nipple sizes and nipple shapes, baby bottle straws, feeding and sleeping positions, lambswool pads, diets for nursing mothers, special for-

mulas, pacifiers, and solid food—even chiropractic spinal ma-
nipulation. But there is no evidence that these things affect
extreme fussiness, crying, temperament, or sleeping habits.

Many useless remedies can be purchased without a prescription. Anti-gas drops, such as simethicone, have never been
shown to be more effective than a placebo in well-conducted
studies. One popular pellet contains chamomile, calcium phos-
phate, coffee, and a very small amount of active belladonna
chemicals (0.0000095 percent). Another remedy contains
natural blackberry flavor, Jamaica ginger, oil of anise, oil of
nutmeg, and 2 percent alcohol. Please read labels carefully—
any natural substance, flavoring agent, or herb might have
pharmacological effects. Call a school of pharmacy or a medical school to find experts in pharmagnosy, the study of natural herbs and plants, to find out if a particular plant or
herb is dangerous. Also be cautious in using home remedies.
One mother almost killed her baby by giving a mixture of
Morton's Salt Substitute with *Lactobacillus acidophilus*, as prescribed in the popular book, *Let's Have Healthy Children,* by
Adelle Davis.

Newborns have drowned in rocking waterbeds, been stran-
gulated by having their necks overhang a trampoline-like crib
platform, been suffocated by having their heads accidentally
buried in a pillow.

Everything Works . . . for a While

When you believe that something is going to calm your baby—
herbal tea, recordings of womb sounds, lambswool blankets,
you name it—it often appears to work for a while. Your fatigue
may breed inflated hopes for a cure, and the day-by-day variability in infant crying creates the illusion that a particular
remedy works, but only for a while. What really is happening is a placebo effect; this is the emotional equivalent of
an optical illusion. If the alleged remedy is tried again later,
no improvement is seen. Still, if a baby coincidentally outgrows extreme fussiness/colic just when a useless remedy is in-
troduced, the mother, the family, and even the doctor might

become convinced that the alleged remedy actually cured the extreme fussiness/colic!

Night-lights

If your baby cries at night, darken his room. Infants are not afraid of the dark. Extreme fussiness is not the expression of bad dreams. A light burning in a closet or even a conventional 7-watt night-light can keep a sensitive baby from sleeping well. If you are absolutely convinced that your baby will not sleep in a totally dark room, I would suggest using a guide light (¼ watt), which produces a faint yellow glow.

What Is Best for You and Your Family?

Because each family and each situation is unique, what worked well for your friends or your sister might not work well for you. So when you are listening to advice or reading a parenting book, always keep in mind that there is no single "right" way to handle a difficult issue like extreme fussiness. Only you can decide what is best for you and your family. Here are some variables to consider as you make decisions for your baby and when you hear advice from other parents.

Breast-feeding Versus Formula Feeding

Breast-feeding is best for baby and mother. Breast-feeding the fussy baby is discussed in detail at the end of the chapter. The decision to breast-feed or not may be influenced by the mother's strong feelings and by the support or lack of support from her husband, her mother, or other family members. However, many healthy babies are bottle-fed because of adoption, prematurity, or medical problems with the baby or mother. Bottles can contain either expressed breast milk or formula, so the phrase "bottle feeding" may include feeding breast milk. Formula-fed babies may grow up to be just as healthy as breast-fed babies. Many research studies have shown that breast-feeding does not prevent extreme fussiness/colic, does not prevent sudden infant death syndrome (SIDS), and does not prevent or cause sleeping problems. At night, breast-fed babies are often fed more often than formula-fed babies, but it is not known whether this is caused by the breast-feeding mother responding more promptly and frequently to her baby's quiet sounds or whether rapid breast milk digestion in the baby causes the baby to wake up more often. In general, research has shown that sleep/wake rhythms evolve at the same pace whether the baby is breast-fed or formula-fed, demand-fed or schedule-fed, and whether cereal is given in the bottle or by spoon. Some babies with birth defects of the digestive system are fed continuously intravenously or by a tube in their stomach, so they are never hungry; these babies have the same development of sleep/wake/rhythms as all other babies. This is why I tell parents that "sleep comes from the brain, not the stomach." Although there are rare medical exceptions, changing formulas in general will not reduce fussiness or promote better sleeping.

Of course, if the baby is not being fed enough, the child might be so hungry that she fusses, cries, or does not sleep well. In this situation, the child is not gaining weight well, and some help is needed to establish a better breast milk supply or evaluate the baby for medical problems that can cause poor weight gain. In my practice, I encourage first-time mothers to begin to give a bottle of expressed breast milk or formula once per 24 hours when their baby is two to three weeks old. This allows fathers and other family members to have the pleasure of feeding the baby, the mother to take a mini-break once a day to rest or allow healing of cracked or painful nipples, husband and wife to have a date to recharge their energy, and the father can be more helpful during fussing/crying periods or middle-of-the-night feedings to give the mother a little more sleep. Some experienced mothers who have previously breast-fed successfully give the once-daily bottle sooner. They have confidence in their ability to breast-feed and either give formula in the hospital or start pumping sooner. They know that giving a single bottle per day does not confuse the child or interfere with breast-feeding. The reason the bottle is given once every 24 hours is to keep the baby adapted to taking the bottle. Some babies do well with less frequent bottles, but others will reject all bottles if days go by without having had a bottle.

Family Bed Versus Crib

Since our goal is a well-rested family, a family bed may be right for your situation. Sometimes this is described as co-sleeping or bed sharing. The decision to sleep with your baby might be made before you have your baby because this is what you want for your family. You might decide that unrestricted breast-feeding day and night, always carrying your baby, and sleeping with your baby at night or day and night will promote a tighter or more sensitive bond between you and your baby. Parents then begin the practice of co-sleeping as soon as the baby is born. Researchers use the term "early co-sleepers" to describe these children. Alternatively, you might not have thought about or not really wanted to have a family bed, but you discovered that your baby was so fussy/colicky or was sleeping so poorly that the only way anyone got any rest was to sleep with your baby in your bed. Researchers use the term "reactive co-sleepers" to describe these children. Scientific studies have shown that co-sleeping in infancy is often associated with the later development of sleep problems. I suspect that the majority of these problems occur among the reactive co-sleepers. In other words, some parents find that the family bed is a short-term and partial solution to sleeping problems, and the sleeping problems continue after the child has been moved to his own crib or bed.

Sleeping with your baby might include day and night or just at night, all night or part of the night, in your bed or using a small crib attached to your bed, with other children in your bed or with other children in your bedroom but not in your bed. All of these variations are collectively called "family bed." In many cultures, families usually sleep together because of tradition or a limited number of bedrooms. It is rare in Japan or traditional or tribal societies for children to sleep apart from their parents. There is a great appeal in sleeping together; after all, one powerful word to describe soothing is "nestling," and this easily brings forth the image of creating a nest for your baby in your bed.

Both the United States Consumer Product Safety Commission and the American Academy of Pediatrics actively discourage the family bed because of the risk of trapping the child between the mattress and the structure of the bed (headboard, footboard, side rails, and frame), the wall, or adjacent furniture. There is the hazard of suffocation by overlying by an adult who is in an unusually deep sleep caused by alcohol or mind-altering drugs. Also, soft surfaces or loose covers can cause suffocation. They point out that there is no evidence that bed sharing protects against sudden infant death syndrome. Also, from other research, there is no evidence that bed sharing prevents extreme fussiness/colic

So if you want to use a family bed, try to make it a safe environment by not drinking alcohol at night, and make sure your baby is always sleeping on his back. Also, fill in the spaces between the bed and any walls or furniture and eliminate loose bedding.

Back Sleeping Versus Side Sleeping

"Back to sleep" is the motto of the campaign to reduce Sudden Infant Death Syndrome. Putting children to sleep on their back is safe and will reduce the risk of SIDS. There is no reason to put a child on her side, and side sleeping might not reduce the risk of SIDS. Some parents worry about creating a flattened head from back sleeping, but this is rarely a persistent problem.

New Mothers Versus Experienced Mothers

A first-time mother may be bewildered about all the advice she has heard about child rearing and may not know whom to believe or what to try. This state of confusion is made much worse if she is sleep-deprived and struggling with an extremely fussy/colicky infant. In response, she might rigidly try to raise her child "by the book." Experienced mothers have the advantage of confidence compared to new mothers when it comes to breast-feeding their baby, balancing baby care with other demands on their time, knowing that baby fussiness does not last forever, and knowing the time will come when she will again get some sleep. Also, the experienced mother might be more sensitive to her baby's cues of drowsiness, and thus her baby may be less likely to become overtired. This mother might come across as sounding too scheduled or inflexible. On the other hand, with more than one child, the experienced mother might be exhausted or distracted by caring for several children and so may miss her baby's drowsy cues. This is especially likely if the older child has many scheduled activities. Do not assume that your second child will be like your first child, and be prepared to modify your child-rearing style.

The bottom line is for you to reflect on your own experiences, resources, and your baby's personality. Advice from an experienced mother may or may not be right for you and your baby. Do not blindly follow advice from a book, a friend, or a relative.

Older Mothers Versus Younger Mothers

Older mothers might be able to afford to hire more help for child care and housework, and may not feel very distressed during fussy times. An older mother might not have to return to work soon or even at all, as a younger mother might. So her experience with fussiness or a wakeful baby might be dramatically different from those of a younger mother. Thus, when sharing experiences with other mothers and hearing what works for them, be mindful that their resources may be dramatically different from yours. On the other hand, an older first-time mother might not have the energy to actively play with her older baby or feel comfortable hanging around the park chatting with much younger mothers. This child, when older, might not get enough outdoor sandbox time and may not be able to burn off enough energy to nap well.

Singletons Versus Multiples

If you have twins or more, it will be a challenge to get them on a synchronized sleep schedule. "A baby is inestimable joy, and bother," said Mark Twain. Two babies can create double the pleasure and double the bother. Because nighttime sleep rhythms develop at about six weeks of age, I do not think you should even try to put the babies on a schedule until after six weeks. To the best of your ability, try to maximize sleep, especially during the day, and minimize crying. Forget the formation of habits; just try to do whatever it takes to keep them well rested. The reason for this is because the better rested they are, the more adaptable they are. After six weeks, counting from their expected date of delivery, you will be better able to put them on the same or similar sleep schedule for night sleep. Day sleep patterns or naps will not change until twelve to sixteen weeks of age, so we have to wait a little longer to co-ordinate naps.

Return to Work

Returning to work when your child is around six weeks of age is hard. Commonly fussy babies are just beginning to sleep longer at night and are giving you more social smiles. Extremely fussy/colicky babies are usually at their worst, which means you are still in a major zombie-like, sleep-deprived zone. Rarely, a mother is so desperate for some sleep before going to work, she wants to do something dramatic to try to help her baby sleep better. Real life forces some tough choices on people, and it is not fair to be judgmental, because all of our circumstances are different.

When your baby is extremely fussy/colicky, how can you cope with the complexities, tensions, and anxieties of modern life? How can you deal with the conflicts between what is needed to take care of your family, yourself, your work, and your marriage? Under these circumstances, sometimes a mother will give her baby less attention at night to see whether the baby will sleep longer. This will cause crying, and because this is a controversial subject, it will be discussed later in more detail.

"No Cry" Versus "Let Cry"

"No cry" versus "let cry" is debated among parents and some professionals. Parents are divided into two camps: those who think helping their children learn to sleep involves "crying it out" and those who think that the family bed, unrestricted night nursing, and never letting your baby cry, or "gently to sleep," is the right way. The debate over the merits of "crying it out" versus "gently to sleep" is confusing because the way children learn to sleep depends on the age of the child and whether or not the child has extreme fussiness/colic. Certainly with a newborn who is just a few days or weeks old, helping your baby learn to sleep does not involve letting him cry.

If sleep training is done correctly, most children will sleep well without crying. Sleep training is a process to *prevent* sleep problems and should not involve crying. However, crying might be needed to treat sleeping problems in older infants.

Sleep Training Does Not Mean "Let Cry"

When you bring your newborn baby home from the hospital, you can help your baby learn to sleep. At this time, with your newborn who is just a few days old, this process does not involve letting your baby "cry it out." Some parents like to sleep with their baby in their bed and breastfeed throughout the night; they call this choice "gently to sleep." Other parents mistakenly do not want to think about their child's sleeping until some age in the future when they plan to do sleep training, which they incorrectly think means letting their child cry at night. When the baby is older, these parents think that they have to let the child "cry it out" in order to sleep well and advocates of "gently to sleep" think that this is harmful to the child and selfish of the parents. The proponents of "gently to sleep" believe that they are more child-centered because they always respond to every cry, thus developing a stronger attachment between the parent and child.

Sleep Training: My Idea

Sleep training involves several general principles to allow the natural development of biological sleep/wake rhythms to assist your child to learn to sleep. This is similar to the natural development of coordination, strength, and balance that allow your child to learn to walk. So we might call it "sleep learning." However, "sleep training" is the phrase I coined to suggest that parents could assist their child to learn the habit of how to sleep in the same way that parents can assist their child to learn the habit of how to use the toilet, that is, toilet training.

The concept of sleep training does not mean letting your child "cry it out." For 80 percent of babies, sleep training will **_prevent_** sleep problems.

The patterns I describe below are mostly for commonly fussy babies. As I note, these stages may occur later in extremely fussy babies.

Newborns

Sleep training means avoiding the overtired state by soothing your child to sleep as the moment of drowsiness develops, before the child becomes overtired. However, in the beginning, there are no clear circadian rhythms of drowsiness. So for the newborn, sleep training means trying to soothe your baby to sleep after one to two hours of wakefulness. *Brief intervals of wakefulness* are a major part of sleep training. The goal is to maximize sleep and minimize crying. Learn to recognize *drowsy cues*. Soothing may include anything and everything, including the family bed, breast-feeding, car rides, swings, sleeping with your baby in your bed, quiet walks in the park. *Stationary sleep* is probably better than sleep in motion, but do what works. Twenty percent of babies have extreme fussiness/colic and require enormous soothing effort and they still do not sleep well; do what works for these extremely fussy/colicky babies. This is an important point and needs to be repeated: If you work hard to soothe these extremely fussy/colicky babies, they will not cry very much, if at all, but they still will not sleep well. Never ignore crying.

Babies a Few Weeks Old

After a few weeks, babies become more alert and curious. Now, be more careful to not allow noises, vibrations, bright lights, and other forms of stimulation to interfere with sleep; sleep now occurs best in the crib or your bed at home. *Not letting outside stimulation mess up sleep* is part of "sleep training." Again, keep the intervals of wakefulness to no more than two hours. Again, do not ignore crying; if your baby cries, pick him up and soothe him and try again later. Do whatever you can to soothe your baby to maximize sleep and minimize crying. Realize that extremely fussy/colicky babies do not sleep well at all, despite being constantly held, rocked, or nursed.

If you do not have an extremely fussy/colicky baby and this is not your first baby, then consistently use *Method A* for daytime sleep. This means that after several minutes of soothing, you always put your baby down to sleep in the crib or with you in your bed, whether your child is or is not yet asleep. Soothing may include breast-feeding. Start this when you come home from the hospital. *Starting early* with consistent soothing styles and brief intervals of wakefulness is also part of "sleep training."

Method B for daytime sleep means that you always soothe your baby until she is in a deep sleep state; you never put your baby down until she is really asleep. This may take a long time, but this method often is needed for extremely fussy/colicky babies.

Method A and method B are only for daytime sleep.
At night, do whatever you can to help your baby sleep.

If you do have an extremely fussy/colicky baby, or if you simply prefer this style, especially if this is your first child, you might find sleeping with your baby in your bed is the best way to maximize sleep and minimize crying. You may not see *drowsy cues* if your baby is extremely fussy/colicky. Try it if you want to.

Six-Week-Old and Older Babies

At six weeks of age (or six weeks after the due date), infant fussing, irritability, and crying peak and tend to occur mainly in the evening hours. Do whatever works to prevent crying. You can't spoil your baby at this age. Try to put forth as much effort as you can to soothe your baby and prevent crying. You don't always have to use the same technique; in the daytime you might put your baby down drowsy but still awake, and at night soothe your baby until she falls into a deep sleep. You might use a crib during the day and a family bed at night.

After six weeks of age, babies start to have longer (four to six hours) sleep periods occurring mainly at night, and they begin to get drowsy earlier in the evening. Watching for earlier signs of drowsiness and *putting your baby to sleep earlier at night* is part of sleep training at this age. Use the crib or a co-sleeper attached to your bed. Extremely fussy/colicky babies do not usually show this tendency for earlier bedtimes until they are older, so do not force an earlier bedtime on your baby. Look for drowsy cues starting earlier in the evening. If your baby has extreme fussiness/colic, you may not see drowsy cues, so experiment with slightly earlier bedtimes and slowly, gradually try to move bedtime earlier.

Remember, if you fail to keep the intervals of wakefulness brief, if you allow too much external stimulation, or if you fail to respect the need to fall asleep earlier, then you will have an overtired baby on your hands. Consistently doing this can lead to sleep problems. On the other hand, if you have an extremely fussy/colicky infant, then accept the fact that he was born with a temporary difficulty regarding sleep no matter what you do.

If you have an extremely fussy/colicky infant, consistently use Method B for naps. That is, always try to spend as much time as needed to soothe your baby into a deep sleep. *Consistency* in *soothing style for naps* is part of sleep training.

At about four months of age, major naps begin to occur more regularly. First, the morning nap develops (9–10 A.M.). Later, a second nap develops in the early afternoon (12 noon–2 P.M.). A third, minor nap may occur in the late afternoon, but it is irregular and brief. Begin your soothing-to-sleep routine with the onset of these daytime drowsy periods. This *synchronization of the beginning of your soothing and baby's drowsiness* is part of sleep training. Be aware that extremely fussy babies tend to show nap rhythms later than commonly fussy babies.

Also, at four months of age, formula-fed infants seem to need to be fed only once or twice at night. The social stimulation associated with lifting them from the crib, giving the bottle, and returning them to the crib might be too much stimulation if it occurs too often. *Not stimulating your baby at night when she is not hungry* is part of sleep training.

What if your bottle-fed four-month-old baby wakes up more than two times a night and you are not sure that she is hungry? Try first having the father give a bottle for a few nights, measuring how much she eats at the feedings to determine whether she is really hungry.

If you are breast-feeding and if your baby is in bed with you at night, go ahead and feed your baby as often as you want because both of you are probably more asleep than awake and no real social stimulation is occurring. If you are breast-feeding but the child does not sleep in your bed, pay attention to her sucking rhythm at the breast. If she's hungry, the rhythm is usually suck-swallow, suck-swallow, and this continues until the baby is sated. If she is fussy, there is much less swallowing.

To sum up, if your baby is four months old and does not seem especially hungry at night, then consider going to her not more than twice at night, even though she may cry a little for a few nights. (Remember that this stage may occur later for extremely fussy babies, perhaps at six months.)

This is the first time that some parents might deliberately attempt to help their baby sleep by letting their baby cry. Up to now, it's all been gently to sleep. However, if sleep training went smoothly, and your baby was not colicky, then there should not be any "crying it out."

Problems in Older Babies

After four months of age (or maybe six months in an extremely fussy child) there may be problems because sleep training did not go smoothly or the baby was extremely fussy. Either way, the baby may now have gotten into a pattern of being over-tired and/or dependent on parental efforts to soothe to sleep. "Crying it out" may be thought of as a form of damage control to correct problems created by the parents in common fussy or non-colicky babies. "Focusing on the morning nap," which will be described later, and slowly establishing age-appropriate sleep rhythms in the post–extremely fussy/colicky baby might also involve some crying. Sleep training is intended to prevent sleep problems in the first place. "Crying it out" is associated with correcting those sleep problems. Extremely fussy/colicky babies at four to six months might have to be weaned from the expectation of always being held. This process might involve some crying, because some sleep problems are intimately associated with colicky infants. Remember, colicky infants need more attention when they are less than four months old, and during this time they come to expect this extra attention even when older. After four to six months, the major problem with these post-colic infants is receiving too much attention at night. This extra attention causes a night-waking habit to develop.

After four to six months, extremely fussy/colicky babies or babies who've developed the habit of getting overtired may benefit from being allowed to cry at night, assuming they are not hungry and nothing else is wrong. Extremely fussy/colicky babies may also need to be allowed to cry at the time of the first morning nap at this age.

The major potential problem with sleeping with your baby after four to six months of age is that the child might fall asleep too late. Using a co-sleeper—a separate bed that attaches to the side of the parents' bed and allows easy access—you can put your baby down to sleep early, before you yourself go to sleep, and then there are no problems.

Mistaken Ideas About Sleep Training

Some parents believe that sleep training is something that should be started at a specific age—say four months. These parents may incorrectly think that sleep training means letting the child cry it out at this age, and that this in itself will get the child on a schedule.

The fundamental error here is to assume that during the first few months of life, it does not matter how the child is sleeping. In fact, sleep training means instilling good sleep habits right from the time your child is born.

SLEEP TRAINING: NO CRY VERSUS LET CRY

Prevention of sleep problems younger than 4 months: no cry.

Treatment of sleep problems at 4 months: let cry.

Different Decisions for Different Babies

Introduction

Answer these three questions: (1) Do you spend a total of more than three hours per day soothing your baby to prevent crying? That is, when you add up the total amount of minutes spent walking, rocking, driving around in the car, swaddling, singing, humming, running water, offering the breast or bottle even when not hungry, using a pacifier, and so forth, does the total exceed three hours? (2) Do you behave this way more than three days per week? (3) Have you been doing this for more than three weeks? If you answer yes to all three questions, then your baby has extreme fussiness. Because of your soothing effort, there may be no crying, just endless fussing. Or she might sometimes cry anyway despite your soothing efforts. If you answer no to any of the three questions but your baby fusses often, especially in the evening and especially around six weeks of age, then your baby has common fussiness.

My research and that of others has shown that about 80 percent of babies have common fussiness and 20 percent of babies have extreme fussiness/colic. A combination of inborn predispositions and how you react to your baby determines the kind of temperament your baby will have at four months. Some children are super calm, stay on a regular schedule, smile all the time, and are good sleepers. Other babies are the opposite. The good sleepers are described as having an "Easy" temperament and the opposite as having a "Difficult" temperament. Some children are more in between and are described to have an "Intermediate" temperament. How you care for your baby influences the temperament at four months of age.

These temperament terms discussed below are explained in more detail in the next chapter. Please be patient while I lead you through a numerical exercise involving a hypothetical group of 100 babies. The reason that this exercise is useful is because it might: (1) Help you set your expectation on what you will need to do with your individual baby both during the first several weeks (for soothing) and the following several months (to prevent sleep problems). (2) Help you decide whether you will breast-feed or bottle-feed. (3) Help you decide whether you will use a family bed or a crib. Remember, out of a group of 100 babies, 80 percent will have common fussiness and 20 percent will have extreme fussiness/colic. My research has shown that these two groups of babies differ in how their temperaments develop.

Consider the 80 percent of babies who have common fussiness at four months of age. Of these,

- **49 percent or 39 babies are temperamentally Easy.**
- **46 percent or 37 babies are temperamentally Intermediate.**
- **5 percent or 4 babies are temperamentally Difficult.**

The 20 percent who are extremely fussy/colicky babies also can be divided into three groups at four months of age.

- **14 percent or 3 babies are temperamentally Easy.**
- **59 percent or 12 babies are temperamentally Intermediate.**
- **27 percent or 5 babies are temperamentally Difficult.**

Of the original 100 babies, the largest temperament group is Intermediate. Forty-nine babies or 49 percent are in the temperamental category of Intermediate. Temperament measurements form a gradation and the temperament categories represent arbitrary cutoff points. So it is possible that the 37 babies with Intermediate temperament, who had common fussiness, tend toward being temperamentally easier and the 12 babies with Intermediate temperament, who had extreme fussiness/colic, tend toward being more difficult. I suspect that the parents of these 12 babies had to put forth much more soothing effort to get to this Intermediate temperament group than the parents of the 37 babies who had common fussiness.

Of the original 100 babies, the next largest temperament group is Easy. Forty-two babies or 42% are in the temperamental category of Easy. Of these 42 babies, 39 babies had common fussiness and were born mellow, self-soothing, and calm and/or their parents were unusually skillful in soothing or their parents had vast resources to help them soothe their babies. Not so with the three babies who had extreme fussiness/colic at birth. They were not born mellow, self-soothing, or calm. I think these lucky three babies had super-hero parents who put forth enormous efforts to soothe their baby and probably had lots of other resources to help them maintain this effort over four months.

The smallest temperament group is Difficult. Only nine babies, or 9% of the original 100 babies are in this temperament category. Four babies had common fussiness but they may have been almost, but not quite, extremely fussy/colicky. Remember, the measurements used to determine whether a baby has common fussiness versus extreme fussiness/colic are graded and arbitrary cutoff points are used to make the determination.

Alternatively, for these four common fussy babies who developed a Difficult temperament, maybe *something went wrong* with the parents' ability to soothe their baby.

Why might parents be unable to really soothe their baby? Some factors are: maternal depression, an unsupportive husband, too many other children to care for, medical problems, financial problems stressing the family, marital problems, and so forth.

The five babies who had extreme fussiness/colic and developed a Difficult temperament may have overwhelmed all the resources that the parents could bring to bear on soothing their baby. This implies that factors within the baby were so intensely powerful that no matter what parents did, the baby's extreme fussiness/colic led to a Difficult temperament at four months of age. It is also possible that the Difficult temperament evolved because there was a combination of factors within the baby plus problems within the parents or family, as mentioned above, that conspired to create an overtired child. Preexisting problems such as marital discord only get worse when a couple is faced with trying to cope with an extreme fussy/colicky baby. Some problems with the parents' ability to soothe may grow out of or be a response to the fatigue, frustration, and exhaustion of trying, without much success, to soothe an extreme fussy/colicky baby.

There is some research to suggest that parents who made the commitment to use the family bed from day one and stick with it will wind up with better rested babies than those families who initially wanted to use the crib but later brought their baby into their bed because it was the only way the parents, or a parent, could get some sleep. In the former group, sleep problems are less likely to develop, as the children get older. But in the group where the family bed was used only in response to soothing or sleeping difficulties, the family bed often mistakenly appears to be a short-term solution that contributes to or creates a long-term sleep problem. What really is happening is that for parents who are overwhelmed by the fussy/crying behavior and have limited resources for soothing their baby, they reluctantly use the family bed that gives some relief, but the limited resources for soothing persist and may cause sleeping problems in older children. This occurs primarily because the child develops a need for an earlier bedtime, but the parents continue to use a late bedtime plus family bed. This will be discussed more in Chapter 5.

I believe that how babies sleep modulates or influences the development of temperament at four months of age. And how babies sleep during the first few months is a combination of both factors within the child and the parents' ability and skill to soothe their baby. It is also my belief that at four months of age, the Difficult temperament represents an overtired baby and the Easy temperament represents a well-rested baby. The temperament that your baby has at four months of age is **not** permanent. Temperament changes over time as babies develop and parents change how they soothe their children.

> **Sleep habits probably affect how much change or persistence of temperament occurs over time.**

Stability of individual temperament measures does appear to develop during the second year of life or shortly after the second birthday. If you are reading this book before you have your baby, be prepared to invest enormous efforts in soothing your baby and consider yourself unlucky if your child is among the 20 percent of extremely fussy/colicky babies. However, if you have already had your baby and you are in the midst of suffering through four months of extreme fussiness/colic, reevaluate some of your decisions, if necessary, regarding how you soothe your baby and what is best for your baby and family. Be optimistic because everything settles down at about four months. Everyone gets a second chance at about four months to help their child sleep better.

Common Fussiness

Eighty percent of babies have common fussiness. These babies tend to be self-soothing, mild, and calm, and they easily fall asleep and sleep for long periods.

Breast-feeding these common fussy babies is relatively easy because the mothers tend to be better rested and the babies tend to fall into a regular schedule. The duration of a breast-feeding, how long you nurse, may be relatively short and infrequent because nursing is mainly for satisfying thirst and hunger. When these babies are fussy, methods of soothing other than breast-feeding often work. In fact, the popularity of many different techniques or strategies for soothing babies is due to the fact that, for these babies, most everything works well!

Bottle feeding these common fussy babies either formula or expressed breast milk with or without breast feeding is a family decision that is usually easily made. Some considerations are whether to allow the father or other children the pleasure of feeding the baby, the mother's need to get some extra sleep at night, the mother's anticipation to return to work shortly and to continue to pump her breasts at work, or the natural desire for the parents to want to go out on a date.

Before your baby is born, you might decide that you want to sleep with your baby or that you prefer to use a crib or bassinet. If you decide to sleep with your baby, then you might decide to do this at both naps and at night, or only at night. At night you might decide to sleep with your baby when she first falls asleep or perhaps you will want to put your baby down in a crib and then at the first night feeding, bring your baby to you. Or you might decide that you want to have a co-sleeper attached to your bed and use it for part of the night or all of the night. For 80 percent of babies with common fussiness, because they are fairly adaptable and self-soothing, any of these plans usually works well. If you try to put your baby to sleep within one or two hours of wakefulness, watching for drowsy cues that are usually obvious in these babies, then any

soothing-to-sleep method is likely to work. As a result, the baby
and parents usually sleep well. Parents are at a low risk for feeling distressed, and I think maternal depression is not very
likely. However, some of these common fussy babies will behave a little like the extremely fussy/colicky baby and your plans
might have to be altered as described below. Only about 5 percent of these babies seem to develop into overtired four-
month-old babies.

Extreme Fussiness/Colic

Twenty percent of babies have extreme fussiness. These babies
tend to not be self-soothing and require a lot of parent soothing. They often appear intense and agitated, and they have
difficulty falling asleep and staying asleep. As many as 27 percent of extremely fussy babies are at risk for becoming overtired four-month-olds—babies with a Difficult temperament.

Breast-feeding these extremely fussy/colicky babies is often
difficult because the mothers tend to be exhausted or fatigued
from sleep deprivation and the babies tend not to fall easily
into a schedule. Nursing sessions may be long and also frequent because in addition to satisfying thirst and hunger, sucking helps reduce fussiness. When these babies are extremely
fussy, methods of soothing other than breast-feeding and/or
family bed often do not work. Frustration or despair is common because many of the popular techniques or strategies for
soothing babies often fail, even though many other mothers
(80 percent of mothers) swear by them.

Some considerations going through the mind of the mother
are whether something is wrong with her breast milk, whether
her breast milk is sufficient, or whether her diet or the current
formula is causing the extreme fussiness/colic. Because soothing at the breast often seems to work when other soothing
methods fail, the mother does not want to give it up. But
painfully dry or cracked skin around the nipple may make
breast-feeding an ordeal. Discomfort and pain associated
with breast-feeding plus unrelenting exhaustion from sleep deprivation may conspire to cause so much stress that the breast

milk supply becomes insufficient. Mothers who have enormous support such as dedicated husbands who spend a lot of time soothing and helping with baby care and the house can get through this difficult time much more easily than mothers who lack a support system. Mothers who have other children to care for, pressure to return to work soon, medical problems, the baby blues, or postpartum depression may find the additional stresses associated with breast-feeding these extremely fussy babies to be overwhelming.

Because these babies are difficult to soothe, breast-feeding in the family bed may be the best strategy, or the only one that works. Although the mother's sleep may be fragmented by frequent feeding for both nutrition and soothing, this is probably the most powerful soothing method for these babies.

Bottle-feeding these babies either formula or expressed breast milk may be a benefit to some mothers, but it may create more stress in others. The benefit of complete or partial bottle feeding is that the mother might get more rest because others can feed her baby. And because they can see how much the baby is swallowing, the parents are calmer. They know for certain that their baby is not hungry. In other mothers, giving bottles might create the feeling of having failed as a mother. Recognizing that bottles are not as soothing as the breast, she might feel guilty switching from breast to bottle because she thinks she is causing her baby to fuss or cry more. Further, she might worry that something in the formula is causing the fussiness or crying. If you want to breast-feed, a compromise position is to have someone else give a single bottle of expressed breast milk once per 24 hours. This will not cause "nipple confusion" or interfere with lactation. It will give mothers a mini-break, allow them to get a little more sleep, and allow parents to go out on a date.

Keep reminding yourself that extreme fussiness is not indigestion. It is not caused by formula or breast milk. Switching from one formula to the other will not help stop the crying. Some manufacturers of infant formula try to sell their product by claiming that their product will reduce fussiness. The so-called research they cite to support their claims is weak and unconvincing and has not been reproduced.

If you are nursing and fear your baby is crying from hunger—nearly all nursing mothers wonder at times if they have enough milk—arrange to have the baby weighed at a doctor's office several times over the course of a week or two. Chances are you will find her gaining weight nicely.

Do not let extreme fussiness make you give up breast-feeding if you want to continue. Your baby is still getting all the benefits of breast milk, even if she seems at times not to appreciate them. If you stick with it, you can look forward to many calm, pleasant months of nursing once the extreme fussiness has run its course.

Still, nursing an extremely fussy baby is undeniably a challenge. When nursing, infants with extreme fussiness/colic tend to be gulpers, twisters, and forceful suckers. Sometimes they seem to reject the breast entirely. The determined nursing mother is in a bind: It is difficult to nurse a tense, twisting infant, but this is one of the few maneuvers that appear to calm the child (at least temporarily). The mother finds herself nursing very often—either because she interprets the extreme fussiness/colic as a sign of hunger or simply to get some peace. She is often rewarded with painful cracked nipples and/or exhaustion. Non-nutritive nursing—using your breasts as pacifiers—may calm the baby, but it is no picnic for the mother! Here is a description of the nursing predicament by the mother of one of my young patients:

The first three weeks of Michael's life led me to believe that having a baby would be a breeze. His behavior was almost identical from day to day. He was very calm, and so were my husband and I. Michael would breast-feed about eight to ten minutes on each side. He had no problems burping after each meal. Then I'd either hold him for a while, lay him on his back, and talk or play with him. The usual schedule, from the time he got up until he went to sleep, would be one to one and a half hours. He would usually sleep anywhere from two and a half to four hours. Everyone would say to me, "Boy, are you ever lucky to have such a good baby."

As the fourth week approached, Michael's behavior changed dramatically. He no longer wanted to sleep during the day. I felt like all he wanted was my breast. I concluded that he either was continually hungry or had strong sucking needs.

By the middle of each afternoon, I was exhausted. Almost every hour I found myself breast-feeding. Sometimes I could put him off for two hours, but he'd cry a lot. I'd change his diaper, walk him, hold him, rock him, sing to him, change his position, and so on. Nothing would please him except my breast, which was terribly tiring, to say the least. The thing that saved our lives is that he slept long hours through the night—probably because he was exhausted from being up all day. The worst times were midafternoon, and again between 5:00 P.M. and 10:00 P.M. He would fuss and cry and nothing would calm him except when he was nursing. After that he would sleep for around five hours straight.

If you are in a predicament similar to this mother's, give yourself some relief by trying the following suggestions:

1. **Space feedings a few hours apart. If you last nursed your baby well (not a snack or a sip) less than two hours ago, he has no room in his stomach for more milk and your breasts contain little or no milk for him. Nursing too frequently is pointless, and if it causes you pain or exhaustion, it is destructive. See if your baby will accept a pacifier instead.**

2. **Ask your doctor about hydrocortisone ointment. A famous pediatric dermatologist who nursed her own children suggests treating cracked nipples with 1 percent hydrocortisone ointment. It is safe for mother and the baby, and seems to work better than any other treatment. Many of my patients' mothers have reported rapid healing of sore nipples by using this treatment. After nursing, allow your breasts to air-dry.**

Then apply a thin film of the hydrocortisone ointment to the dry or cracked areas. Make sure that you use ointment, not cream, because cream might cause a painful burning sensation. When you are about to nurse again, do not wipe off or wash off any of the ointment. Most of it will have been absorbed into your breast skin, and the small amount that your baby will ingest will cause no harm.

3. Don't exhaust yourself. One mother of an extremely fussy infant stored breast milk so that her husband could feed the baby once during the night and her mother could handle a similar daytime feeding. In this way, she was able to get some extra rest. When the baby was several weeks old, the baby's grandmother went home and the father returned to work. Now, all alone and very busy, the mother saw her previously ample supply of breast milk dwindle to almost nothing. We discussed how she had decreased her fluid intake, how she was worried about her mother's departure, and how she was generally under strain. I reassured her that while it was important to continue having the child suck at her breasts to stimulate milk production, a single bottle of formula for one or two days would not harm the baby or inhibit lactation. She increased her fluid intake, rested more, and after four to five days was again nursing with more than ample milk production. Throughout this period, the child continued to have spells of extreme fussiness/colic spells with periods of inconsolable crying. This mother knew that the crying was not related to nursing.

Another mother of one of my patients felt especially bad when nursing failed to calm her baby:

In the early evening my daughter would be screaming and restless. Nothing seemed to calm her, not even nursing. I didn't think Chelsea was colicky, but she sure was fussy. Although her fussiness wasn't an everyday occurrence, it persisted from her second or third week of life until about two months of age.

At first I thought something I was eating was causing her to have gas. Then I felt her behavior was due to my inexperience as a mother. As these episodes continued, I began to feel inadequate, desperate, sad, and exhausted.

I felt inadequate as a parent. I didn't know what to do to comfort my child, or whether what I was doing was right. I especially felt inadequate when Chelsea rejected my breast. It seemed as if nothing could console and comfort her.

We had visions of a child who could be comforted at the touch of her mom or dad. Soon all the sleepless nights and exaggerated feelings of incompetency led to exhaustion. Would this cycle ever end? Well, it finally did. With the help of our pediatrician, we soon began to realize that this behavior was normal and would not last indefinitely. I also found that her fussiness was neither caused nor enhanced by my behavior. Along with this realization came the light at the end of the tunnel. I then knew her fussiness would not last forever.

I became aware of certain behavioral changes that manifested themselves either before or after each fussy period. She would startle easily, have difficulty falling asleep and then would sleep for shorter periods of time. Also, during her fussy periods, she exhibited different behavioral characteristics. She was restless and would scream with a quivering chin. She would become stiff or have rigid movements. She would not nurse, or when she did she would suck frantically. She would become overtired but would not sleep. Sometimes she would be wide awake one moment and sound asleep a second later.

Chelsea is now three months old. Her fussy periods have ceased and she wakes in the morning with a smile that lasts all day. We really love our "perfect" child.

Sometimes a nursing mother notices that the baby seems calmer in her husband's arms than in her own. She may feel that her husband does a better job of soothing the baby, that perhaps the baby "prefers" him to her. What is really happening is quite simple. The baby recognizes that his mother is the source of milk. When she holds him, he quite naturally squirms and twists, rooting around, looking to suck, even when he is not hungry.

I want to encourage every mother's desire to nurse her extremely fussy/colicky baby. It is an important accomplishment for both of them. One mother called me when her extremely fussy/colicky baby was exactly three months old. She was determined to continue nursing and to start working part time. Her husband was a fireman and found it very difficult to be around his crying baby on days off. She was under enormous stress. All her friends claimed that if she would feed her baby formula, then the crying would disappear. She wanted to—and did— keep on nursing after the extreme fussiness/colic disappeared to show them, and herself, that nursing was not the cause of the crying. Here is a report from the mother of another one of my patients; persevering with nursing helped her maintain her confidence and self-esteem.

Both my husband and I questioned our judgment and our ability to care for Lisa. At one point I questioned my ability to nurse and felt that I was literally poisoning my baby. Her screaming episodes came a predictable ten minutes after every feeding. At times I felt tortured. I consider myself a rational and caring person, yet often found myself crying in the shower or praying that my husband could somehow relieve the tension, anger, and helplessness that I felt.

At six weeks, Lisa seemed to be easing into patterns and appeared to be getting good, deep sleep. Her smiling times were numerous, but she still had hours of screaming. I overcame my fear of nursing and decided to continue weeks after I had planned to stop. Nursing became the one pleasurable experience the baby and I had together. When I finally did wean Lisa, it was a sad time; we were separate after being together for so long.

Six weeks of age (or six weeks after the due date) is truly a magic turning point for many babies.

Breast-feeding the Fussy Baby

Nancy Nelson, RN, IBCLC

One of the most difficult things for many breast-feeding mothers is not knowing how much milk your baby is getting. When you are the mother of an extremely fussy baby it can be even more of a concern. When a baby is crying, most well-meaning observers will comment that the baby must be hungry. As the mother, these comments may cause you to feel frustrated and guilty. After all, you are responsible for feeding the baby! To allay your fears, keep track of the baby's output of urine and stool. After the sixth day of life, your baby should be producing six or more wet diapers and one or more stools in a twenty-four-hour period as a sign of adequate intake of breast milk. Babies usually need to feed eight to twelve times in a twenty-four-hour period in the first few weeks of life. In the beginning they may cluster-feed. This means that they may want to feed very frequently for a few hours and then go into a sleep stretch of four or five hours. As they become more efficient, they decrease the number of feedings. The baby should be back to birth weight by two weeks of age and should gain a minimum of five ounces a week for the next two to three months.

If you are concerned that your baby is fussy because you have a *low milk supply*, it would be helpful to see a lactation consultant, who will do a feeding observation. This includes a study of your baby's ability to transfer milk from your breast by a strong nutritive suck followed by audible swallows. A pre- and post-feeding weight should be included in order to get an idea of how much milk the baby is taking in during the feeding. The baby should be weighed both before and after the feeding (with a diaper on, so as not to lose the weight of urine or stool that may have been produced during the feeding). This can be reassuring if the baby gains between two and four ounces during the feeding. If the baby gains less, it might alert you to a problem with either the baby's method of transferring the milk or your milk supply. If the milk supply is low or the flow is too slow, a supplemental feeding system may help to improve the suck and give the baby the additional calories he needs. Use of a hospital-grade electric breast pump can augment the breast milk supply as well. Some mothers may decide to feed the baby additional pumped breast milk by bottle or feed formula if they are unable to pump enough milk to meet the baby's needs.

Occasionally *breast engorgement* may cause the baby to be fussy at the breast. To deal with engorgement, use warm compresses or take a warm shower prior to feeding the baby. Use breast massage as well. You may be able to express some milk by hand, or use a good-quality breast pump to take out a little milk and make the breast softer and easier for the baby to latch onto. Do not pump too much milk because it could continue an oversupply problem and prolong the engorgement. In between feedings use cold compresses on your breasts in order to decrease the swelling and give pain relief. Engorgement may occur within the first week after your baby is born, or later, when the baby begins to skip feedings as he gets older.

A baby may be fussy at the breast because the mother may have *flat or inverted nipples*. Breast shells may be worn in between the feedings in order to evert the nipples. Using a breast pump for a few minutes prior to putting the baby to the breast will help to pull the nipples out and also start the flow of milk so the baby will get milk right away and be more likely to continue sucking instead of pulling off the breast and crying. Seek the help of a lactation consultant as soon as possible if you are having difficulty with the feedings because of flat or inverted nipples.

A baby may be fussy at the breast because of *poor positioning*. Both mom and baby may be uncomfortable, and that may lead to inadequate let-down and poor milk production as well. With a fussy baby, a football or cross-cradle hold works best because you have more control over the baby's head. You can direct him to the breast and keep him there by using these two positions. The baby's nose and chin should indent the breast. Babies usually nurse better when they are held more firmly by the mother. A firm pillow that supports the baby at the level of the breast is preferable to a soft pillow. A chair that gives good support is better than a soft couch. I cannot emphasize enough that a fussy baby will respond better to being held tightly and close in to the breast. Contact a lactation consultant if you are uncomfortable during breast-feeding. This may be a reason why your baby is fussy.

Almost all babies have some degree of *gastroesophageal reflux*. This is a medical term, which means simply that the sphincter muscle leading to the stomach is immature and may not close completely all the time. This may allow some milk, along with stomach acid, to come back up into the esophagus, leading to a feeling we would call heartburn. As anyone who has experienced this can attest, it is quite uncomfortable. Just as sitting upright can help an adult with heartburn feel better, holding the baby upright usually helps the baby feel better too. Sometimes these episodes can occur during breast-feeding. Holding the baby more upright during the feeding or interrupting the feeding for a short time to comfort the baby by holding him in an upright position should help. Using a swing or a car seat may also help. As the baby matures, so does the muscle, and the episodes become less frequent. Sometimes a baby has a severe problem with reflux and is unable to feed well at all. This may be a case where prescription medication will be needed. Your health care provider should be consulted.

All new babies experience *gassiness*. When the baby begins to feed, it sets off a reflex that produces gas so that the baby will be able to pass more quickly whatever waste products are produced during the feeding. This avoids problems with constipation. Breast milk moves through the baby's system very quickly. You can often hear the sounds while the baby is still feeding. Although all babies are gassy, some babies are not as upset by it as others seem to be. The time of day may be a factor as well. It often seems like this gas problem becomes worse at the end of the day, traditionally the "fussy" time of day. Babies seem to want to stay at the breast constantly, and this may exacerbate the gas problem. The baby may need comforting or some cluster-feeding. It is a good idea to pump a bottle of breast milk in the morning when the baby is calmer and not feeding so often. Have this milk available during this fussy time to allow another family member to feed the baby so you can get a break. As babies mature this problem resolves.

The milk at the beginning of the feeding from the breast is higher in lactose. This is called the foremilk. The milk that comes after about 10 to 15 minutes of nursing from that same breast is called the hindmilk. It is higher in fat and balances out the lactose so as not to produce so much gas. If the baby takes in too much foremilk and too little hindmilk, it may result in *lactose overload* and more gas production. Try to keep the baby on one breast for at least twelve to fifteen minutes in order to get the hindmilk. As the baby gets older and becomes more efficient at nursing, he will be able to get to the hindmilk in a shorter period of time. Hindmilk can have a sedating effect on the baby and help a fussy baby to fall asleep. Most new babies will naturally fall asleep at the end of a feeding because of the sedating effects of the hindmilk. Recently there has been advice given to awaken the baby at the end of the feeding in order to allow him to fall asleep in the crib on his own. I feel that as babies get to be three or four months old, they will remain more awake at the end of the feeding. This is the time for them to learn how to put themselves to sleep. This pattern should be allowed to develop naturally.

When the baby is just learning how to breast-feed, the *let-down reflex may be overwhelming* and lead to gagging and choking. This may cause the baby to pull off the breast and become fussy. Put firm pressure over the breast for a minute to stop the rapid flow and put the baby back to the breast. Try to pump a little milk prior to the feeding to see if you can elicit the let-down before the baby goes to the breast. This may not help too much because usually the baby will elicit a more forceful let-down, but it is worth a try. Football hold or holding the baby in a sitting position on your lap might help. The baby straddles your body with his legs and faces you directly. As the baby gets older, he will be able to handle the let-down reflex without a problem in any feeding position.

Allergic reactions to foods in the mother's diet are rare but may sometimes occur. The most common cause of allergy is cow's milk. Besides extreme fussiness with feeding, there is frequent spitting up, blood in the stool, and poor weight gain. The baby's health care provider should be contacted if these symptoms occur. If you must go on an elimination diet, make sure that you get information about how to supplement your diet so that you remain in good health and can continue to produce enough breast milk for your baby. It usually takes at least 2 weeks in order to see results from an elimination diet.

Rarely *soaps or creams being used on the breast or nipples* may cause the baby to fuss and pull off the breast. If you have started using something new on your skin and the baby fusses, clean it off and start over.

Yeast infections may occur in the baby's mouth or on the mother's nipples. You might see white patches in the baby's mouth. The baby may also develop a diaper rash. Your nipples could be very red or itchy. There is a burning sensation on the nipples following the feeding. Your baby may be fussier during his feedings. See your health care provider. If a yeast infection is diagnosed, both you and the baby should be treated. If the baby is using bottle nipples or pacifiers, these should be replaced with new ones. They should be washed daily with hot soapy water and allowed to air-dry. Change your diet by eating more yogurt or drinking milk with added acidophilus daily.

Some babies may become fussy if they are *overstimulated*. They may have better breast-feeding sessions if the lights are dim and they are allowed to feed with only ambient sounds.

These are some other reasons why a breast-fed baby may be fussy while feeding. It may be that the baby is not hungry but is drawn to the breast for comfort. Remember that a baby under twelve weeks of age does not have much ability to self-soothe. As parents, we need to meet these needs just as much as we need to provide them with the other necessities of life. Many of the things that seem to help soothe them are measures that imitate the environment in the uterus. Make sure that the baby is comfortable—not too warm or too cold. A clean diaper should be provided. The baby may be comforted by being held tightly and cuddled or rocked. Besides cuddling and rocking, swaddling and sounds like music, dryers, or fans may help. Perhaps a pacifier will give your baby some additional soothing. The use of a sling or front carrier will give you the chance to get other things done at the same time you are providing comfort for your baby. Another person such as the father or a grandparent may be able to calm the baby without the baby being stimulated by the smell of the breast milk when she is being held by her mother. This also gives you a chance to get a little time for yourself. Try to take a nap or get some exercise. These are activities that help you feel refreshed. Later, after the baby has been calmed by other methods, she may be ready to breast-feed more calmly.

It takes time and trial of different techniques to find out what your baby needs and how best to meet these needs. Feel free to experiment. The baby may respond to certain things at one time and to other things at another time. Remember that it is a learning period, and don't expect yourself or your baby to be perfect.

Take good care of yourself during this time. Eat well. Take your prenatal vitamins. Stay well hydrated and get outdoors to get some exercise at least 5 days per week, if not daily. Try to use relaxation techniques such as yoga, meditation, massage, or a warm bath to help you get through the difficult times. Share your feelings with the baby's father or other family members and let them take turns walking, rocking, and cuddling the baby. Set small goals for yourself, like reading one chapter in a book or taking a fifteen-minute walk.

New-mother support groups help a lot because you will find out that many other mothers and babies are going through the same learning and adjustment period that you are. Most reasons for infant fussiness will be worked out within the first six weeks of life. A few may take a little longer, but by three months of age it is usually resolved. Remember that overall this is a very short time in the life of you and your baby. Try to hug and cuddle your baby as much as you can in order to help her get through this rough time. Together you can do it.

As discussed by Nancy Nelson, lactation consultants can be very helpful, and I would encourage you to seek one who has been certified by the International Board of Lactation Consultant Examiners (IBLCE) and is entitled to use the title International Board Certified Lactation Consultant (IBCLC). In general, successful breast-feeding will require that the family adjusts to fit the needs of the baby; breast-feeding may not work well if the parents attempt to force the baby to fit into predetermined patterns, especially if the baby has extreme fussiness/colic.

CHAPTER 4

Temperament at Four Months of Age

Some parents can be philosophical about extreme fussiness. They can say, "Well, he's just that kind of baby." They may be right. There turns out to be a significant association between extreme fussiness and a certain kind of infant personality. One mother asked me if we could cure her fussy baby by performing a personality transplant!

That newborns have personalities is not news. Every mother of twins or triplets knows that this is true. Your baby has an individual style of behavior at a very early age. Some mothers know before delivery that their baby will be unusually active. Behavioral differences present at birth might reflect inherited or genetic traits. They might also be acquired traits, possibly reflecting environmental influences during pregnancy. Many child development specialists believe that both genetic and environmental factors combine to affect the behavior of newborn infants. It is important to understand that although our genetic makeup contributes to temperament, our genes do not determine temperament. Biology is not destiny. Parenting helps shape or modulate how our children develop.

Extreme Fussiness and Temperament

Chapter 1 described extremely fussy/colicky infants as vigorous, intense, and energetic. As you read in the last chapter, Dr.

Brazelton has called extremely fussy/colicky infants active and sensitive. Dr. Jorup in his classic study mentions that extremely fussy/colicky babies are excessively sensitive to sound and light, sleep for unusually short periods, and seem restless in general. What is the truth about extreme fussiness/colic and a certain kind of temperament? Since temperament is such a subjective factor, could an extreme fussiness/colic temperament even be measured?

A Standardized Temperament Rating

The term *temperament* means behavioral style or the manner in which the child interacts with the environment. It does not describe the motivation of an action. All parents naturally make their own assessment of their babies' temperaments. You may be surprised to know that there is a standardized system for evaluating infant temperament. It is not absolutely objective, and it has a number of limitations that I will point out later, but it has proved over the years to be very useful.

The researchers who developed this system, Drs. W. B. Carey and S. C. McDevitt, did not have extreme fussiness/colic anywhere in their minds. There is not even a crying dimension in their system. No one connected temperament, as rated on this scale, with extreme fussiness until much later. However, as you will see, the connection proved to be striking.

Infant Temperament Characteristics

Carey and McDevitt refined their method of measuring infant temperament in 1977. Starting with nine characteristics that had been described earlier by Alexander Thomas and Stella Chess of New York University, Carey and McDevitt developed a parent-response questionnaire that has been widely used around the world. It measures the following nine temperament traits: activity, rhythmicity, approach/withdrawal, adaptability, intensity, distractibility, and threshold.

Activity (General Motion, Energy)

Does your baby squirm, bounce, or kick while lying awake in a crib? Does she move around when asleep? Does she kick or grab during diapering? Some infants always appear to be active, others only in specific circumstances, such as bathing. Activity levels in infants have nothing to do with hyperactivity in older children. I have examined a few babies who previously had been referred to a pediatric gastroenterologist because of extreme fussiness/colic. When he recognized that there were no gastrointestinal problems, he decided that the problem was "hyperactivity." This diagnosis was made on the false notion that wakeful, reactive, or difficult infants are hyperactive. There is no proven association between high activity levels in infancy and hyperactivity when older.

Rhythmicity (Regularity of Bodily Functions)

Rhythmicity is a measure of how regular or predictable the infant appears. Is there a pattern in the times he is hungry, how much he eats at each feeding, how often bowel movements occur, when he gets sleepy, when he awakens, when he appears most active, and when he gets fussy? As infants grow older, they tend to become more regular in their habits. Still, some babies are very predictable at two months, while other babies seem to be irregular throughout the first year.

Approach/Withdrawal (First Reaction)

Approach/withdrawal is a temperament characteristic that defines the infant's initial reaction to something new. What does he do when meeting another child or a baby-sitter? Does he object to new procedures? Some infants reach out in new circumstances; accept, appear curious, approach; others object, reject, turn away, appear shy, or withdraw.

Adaptability (Flexibility)

Adaptability is measured by observing such activities as whether the infant accepts nail cutting without protest, accepts bathing without resistance, accepts changes in feeding schedule, accepts strangers within fifteen minutes, and accepts new foods. It is an attempt to measure the ease or difficulty with which a child can adjust to new circumstances or a change in routine.

In my research, this was the only temperament trait that showed individual stability between four months and three years of age. That is, extremely adaptable infants turned into adaptable children. The longer the child sleeps, the more adaptable he is. At age three years, adaptability is the only temperament trait associated with naps. In other words, three-year-olds who are more adaptable sleep longer during the day. Also, adaptability is the temperament trait that is most highly associated with night sleep; children who are more adaptable sleep longer at night. I think that this tendency to be adaptable or not, like other temperament traits, is partly biologically based and partly molded by the environment. However, adaptability seems more connected to sleeping behavior than the other traits.

The following story describes an unusual family that luckily had adaptable infants and how they were able to maintain schedules but also enjoy the occasional spontaneous disruption of those schedules, and how their children were able to stay up later than usual sometimes but also sleep in later than usual and so still be well rested. Although the mother attributes her children's sleeping patterns to parenting, in my discussion with her she acknowledged that all of her children were very adaptable from the beginning. This family may represent one extreme of high adaptability in their children; most families, especially if your baby is extremely fussy/colicky, are not so lucky and have to be more mindful of early bedtimes and schedules. On the other hand, the more careful you are to keep your baby well rested, the more likely he will become more adaptable and then your family will be more able to enjoy the flexibility described in this story.

We have two sets of twins who are 13 months apart. They were 38 and 37 weeks' gestation and are now two and a half and three and a half years old, respectively. We have been fortunate that we have not had the challenges of medical disorders, which strongly influence sleep behavior. All four children have the same sleep habits—they sleep straight through the night from 8:00–9:00 P.M. to 7:30–8:00 A.M. With the exception of illnesses and occasional off nights, our children fall asleep and stay asleep easily. If they awaken during the night or early morning, they are generally able to soothe themselves back to sleep.

The fact that all four of our fraternal twins have the same sleep schedule suggests the possibility that the sleep pattern in our home was more influenced by parental sleep strategies than by individual genetic predispositions or personality of each child. We also wonder if the "twin thing"—for example, the twins sleeping in the same room—positively influenced their sleep habits and may have helped them conquer certain challenges such as separation anxiety.

So what are our strategies? In general, our outlook on sleep mirrors our general parenting style in that we have consistent schedules and rules, but we are happy to break them in order to enjoy the fun moments in life, which often cannot be predicted or planned. Although it is very important to establish a consistent schedule, we feel it is equally important not to be neurotic about deviations from the norm. This is a critical point. If we are relaxed, our kids remain relaxed, and they adjust to changes easily.

As Dr. Weissbluth advises, we started very early to train our children with good sleep habits because we couldn't afford to have four young infants and toddlers control the sleep pattern in our home. We did not give our children the opportunity to develop unhealthy sleep habits. When we perceived a potential threat to our sleep routine, such as toilet training or removing the crib rail, we immediately sought the advice of Dr. Weissbluth, our family pediatrician, rather than wait for serious problems to develop. The bottom line is that as a working pediatrician-mom and working dad, we needed our sleep so that we could function at home, in our workplace and socially. Everyone needs their sleep and sanity regardless of their own personal situation and lifestyle.

For our twin babies, our strategy included putting the children to bed in a tranquil but awake state. We held them for a few minutes without rocking them and we put them to bed with their eyes open. However, there were times after breast-feeding that the babies went to bed with their eyes closed. Our infants slept in the same bed side by side until they grew bigger and needed their own space at about three or four months of age. In addition, we allowed thumb sucking and transitional objects (stuffed animals, blankets) and avoided pacifiers. (My sister, who has one-year-old twins of her own, thought that pacifiers were helpful and avoided transitional objects!) Whether you breast-feed or supplement breast-feeding with formula, as I had to do, having twins is exhausting. We kept to demand feeding and sleeping initially, so all our kids had their own schedule until about three months of age, when we synchronized their routine. We stopped nighttime feedings at approximately six months of age. Although the beginning months are tiring for everyone, regardless of whether you are caring for one, two, three, or more babies, instilling healthy sleep habits early on allows you to catch up on sleep sooner!

We actually discovered advantages to having twins with regard to sleep. We took full advantage of the fact that they had a twin roommate. Even while they were still infants, we discovered that they would sometimes awaken earlier than our 8:00 A.M. wake-up time but would babble with each other for quite some time before crying. Now we often hear them talking in bed. A few times the three-year-olds have awakened early, gotten out of bed, and started their own reading session around a small table. This is great for us as it protects our sleep time in the mornings.

One of the most important strategies that we implemented at six months of age, when they no longer had nighttime feeds, was letting the kids cry themselves to sleep rather than going into their rooms. We sometimes let them cry for as long as an hour and a half (sneaking peeks to make sure there was nothing seriously wrong). They learned early on that we were not going to help them fall asleep or stay asleep! We tried to get to know the different cries of our babies to be better able to decipher the instigating event. If the crying became extensive, we would give them a quick pat without picking them up out of bed. We never brought the kids to our bed, even though the cuddling and pacifying were tempting. In our case, we learned that they do not awaken their twin with their screeching. Interestingly, however, sometimes they have awakened the other pair of twins, who sleep in the adjacent room. (My sister's twins, however, sometimes wake each other up with their cries, but she mostly allows them to fall back to sleep by themselves without intervention.) Listening to them cry was extremely hard for some of the grandparents, and we were very strict with the grandparents and sitters about respecting our sleep practices. This was not always easy, but it was important that everyone be consistent.

We kept scheduled naps, according to Dr. Weissbluth's time and age guidelines. We have always had scheduled naps and bedtimes, but we don't hesitate to break them to enjoy ice-cream outings, visits with friends and family, or just a nighttime stroll. One of our best moments was taking the kids out of bed at midnight to see fireworks! But when the fireworks were over at 12:30 A.M., we were able to put them peacefully to bed. At this point we think that our kids know that we have confidence in their ability to sleep, which may help perpetuate our healthy sleep pattern. As Dr. Weissbluth suggests, if we do detect that they are looking a bit weary-eyed after too many breaks in their schedule, then we make an effort to catch up on their sleep by resuming our traditional scheduled naps and bedtimes, or even lengthening the naptime or giving them an earlier bedtime.

In order to have a life, we decided that our children had to be capable of sleeping in different settings, including napping in strollers and car seats. We didn't go out of our way to ensure complete darkness during naptimes, and we never whispered while they were sleeping. These strategies kept the kids from becoming dependent on a specific sleep environment. Both sets of twins have traveled frequently, sleeping in different beds and cribs and even on blow-up mattresses. They adjusted extremely well to new time zones, even on a trip abroad. Just recently, while on vacation, my two-and-a-half-year-old daughter started to cry every night at 2:00 A.M. This was so unusual that it was the only hint that maybe she was ill. It turned out that she had an ear infection and after two days on antibiotics, her regular sleep habits resumed.

As our kids have gotten older, we added some additional rituals at bedtime, including fifteen to thirty minutes of winding down with music, massage, books, and singing. We expect that we will amend our sleep rituals to make them more relevant as the children get older. Our most recent change with our older twins was the removal of their transitional objects, their little bunnies, for sleeping. Without their bunnies, they have decreased the frequency of their thumb sucking, which was their main technique of soothing themselves to sleep since birth. So far they are requiring some extra attention before bedtime, requesting extra songs and conversation. For the moment we are going along with their demands to help them through the adjustment, but we will pull in the reins soon.

As a former resident in pediatrics and a part-time hospitalist doing twenty-four-hour shifts, I know what it is like to be sleep-deprived. In my own life, I experienced the negative consequences of disorganized sleep, or what Dr. Weissbluth describes as the "internal desynchronization of circadian rhythms." It's not fun for anyone. So it was extremely important for me and my family to be well rested in order to enjoy our lives.

Structured sleep habits are extremely important, but we try to balance the rigidity with flexibility so that we won't miss out on life's fun moments. This system has worked well with our two sets of twins, and we have not experienced any sleep problems from our perspective. My own sister has the same philosophy with her twins but has some different sleep strategies, which suit the specific needs of her family. This illustrates that each family has its own culture, which may dictate different needs of children, even between twins, just as there are different sleep habits among adults. The age of a child, the specific sleep problem or disorder, and/or possible medical issues are additional factors that may warrant tailored approaches to sleep with the help of professionals.

We have learned in our household, with four children having very different personalities and temperaments, that the caregivers have a tremendous influence on the sleep environment of the home. We hope that our story illustrates that it is possible to sleep well in a home with multiples who have a structured sleep program without sacrificing some of the precious, spontaneous, and happy moments in life.

Intensity

Intensity is the degree or amount of an infant's response, either pleasant or unpleasant. Think of it as the amount of emotional energy with which they express their likes and dislikes. Intense infants react loudly with much expression of likes or dislikes. During feeding they are vigorous in accepting or resisting food. They react strongly to abrupt exposure to bright lights; they greet a new toy with enthusiastic positive or negative expressions; they display much feeling during bathing, diapering, or dressing; and they react strongly to strangers or familiar people. One mother described her extremely fussy/colicky baby's intense all-or-nothing reactions: "Her mood changes quickly. She gives no warning—she can go from loud and happy to screaming." Intensity is measured separately from mood. Infants who are not intense are described as "mild."

Mood

If intensity is the degree of response, mood is the direction. It is measured in the same situations described above. Negative mood is the presence of fussy/crying behavior or the absence of smiles, laughs, or coos. Positive mood is the absence of fussy/crying behavior or the presence of smiles, laughs, or coos. Most intense infants also tend to be more negative in mood, less adaptable, and more withdrawn. Most mild infants also tend to be more positive in mood, more adaptable, and approaching.

Persistence

Persistence level, or attention span, is a measure of how long the infant engages in activity. Parents may value this trait under some circumstances but not under others. For instance, persistence is desirable when the child is trying to learn something new, like reaching for a rattle, but it is undesirable when the infant persists in throwing food on the floor. Unfortunately, some babies persist in their prolonged crying spells and their prolonged wakeful periods. One father described his persistently crying baby as follows: "We have an alkaline-battery-powered baby and we're powered by regular carbon batteries. He outlasts us every time."

Distractibility

Distractibility describes how easily the baby may be distracted by external events. A distractible baby who is hungry or tired can be easily consoled by being picked up; soothing can stop fussing during a diaper change. New toys or unusual noises easily distract the infant. Distractibility and persistence are not related to each other, and neither trait is related to activity or threshold levels.

Threshold (Sensitivity)

Threshold levels measure how much stimulus is required to produce a response in the infant in specific circumstances, such as loud noises, bright lights, and other situations previously discussed. While some infants are very reactive or responsive to external or environmental changes, other infants barely react.

To determine a temperament profile, you would rate your baby on a six-point scale for each of ninety-five questions about his behavior. For example:

	Almost Never	Rarely	Variable, Usually Does Not	Variable, Usually Does	Frequently	Almost Always
The infant reacts strongly to foods, whether positively (smacks lips, laughs, squeaks) or negatively (cries).	1	2	3	4	5	6
The infant cries when left to play alone.	1	2	3	4	5	6

The first question is about *intensity* and the second question is about *mood*.

Difficult Temperament

While observing many children and analyzing many question-naires, Drs. Thomas and Chess noticed that four, and only four, of these temperament traits tended to cluster together. In particular, infants who were extreme or "intense" in their reac-tions also tended to be slowly adaptable, negative in mood, and withdrawn. This appeared to be a personality type.

According to their parents' descriptions and direct observa-tion by the researchers, these infants seemed more difficult to manage than other infants. Consequently, a child whose tem-perament scores fall into this pattern is said to have a "difficult" temperament. Infants with the opposite temperamental traits are said to have "easy" temperaments. One father described his easy infant as a "low-maintenance baby."

The difficult temperament and the easy temperament are only descriptions of a behavioral style. Temperament research usually does not ask why a child behaves in a particular way. There is no scientific basis for labeling a child with a "difficult" temperament as a "high-needs" child. In fact, there is no scientific support for labeling a child "high-needs" under any circumstances. Later, I will explain why so many so-called high-needs children are really very overtired children.

Of the original group of infants Thomas and Chess studied, about 10 percent fell into the difficult-temperament category. These infants also tended to be irregular in terms of sleep schedules and night awakenings. There were more likely to have behavioral problems—particularly sleep disturbances—when they grew older. One of the most interesting differences between difficult and easy babies is the way they cry when they are past the extreme fussiness period, that is, when they are three or four months old. Published research found that moth-ers listening to the taped cries of infants rated difficult (not their own babies) described the crying as more irritable, grat-ing, and arousing than the crying of easy infants. They said that the first group sounded spoiled and were crying out of frus-tration rather than hunger or wet diapers. An audio analysis of cries helped explain why this should be. The crying of the difficult infants was found to have more silent pauses between crying noises than that of the easy babies. These silent pauses caused the listener to repeatedly think that the crying spell had ended. Also at its most intense, the crying of difficult infants had a higher pitch. These two differences can make the crying seem much more piercing and annoying.

Why do babies with difficult temperaments cry this way? Do they learn to do it? Is it genetically prewired? Is it connected with other factors that make up a difficult temperament? These are questions that should be explored.

Some professionals contend that the diagnosis of difficult temperament paves the way for future behavioral problems; in general, using infant temperament ratings to predict future development is controversial at best. Many pediatricians have a natural dislike of labeling any behavior just because it is at one end or the other of an arbitrary scale. They also do not like to attach labels that have negative implications. They point out that unusual behavior in adults is often accepted as an "idiosyncrasy" or "eccentricity" and can, in fact, indicate intelligence, creativity, or a drive to achieve. Some professionals believe that "undesirable" infant temperament traits mature into adult virtues. For example, the trait of persistence drives you crazy when your child persists in doing something that you do not want him to do, but the same trait might be likened to ambition later on, which fosters success. Certainly children with so-called difficult temperaments are every bit as lovable and promising as easy children. They are just a bit more of a handful for their parents. A diagnosis of difficult temperament is useful only if it can help parents be prepared and understanding.

Limitations of Temperament Measures

I want to make it clear what the Temperament Profile is and is not. It is a statistical tool used to describe groups of babies. It is not a very good way to evaluate one specific baby; your own observations are much better. What the Temperament Profile does is put into fairly simple, numerical terms that infinitely complex structure called personality. When done on large numbers of infants, it provides a reliable standard for studies that seek to relate certain factors (in our case, extreme fussiness/colic) to temperament. But using the results obtained for one infant to make predictions about his or her future is an unsound business. If your child should be given one of these tests, and if you are told the results, remember that it is just a snapshot, and a blurred one at that.

There is a certain built-in limitation to the Temperament Profile. Ratings can be obtained during the first few months of life, but your baby does not really show stable behavior patterns yet. This is demonstrated when different rating instruments—the Carey Infant Temperament Questionnaire, the Brazelton Neonatal Assessment Scale, the Bayley Scales of Infant Development—used on the same infant do not yield internally consistent results. Temperament measures obtained later, at age four to eight months, are moderately stable but can only weakly predict temperament measures taken for the next three to seven years. Temperament measures obtained during the second year of life are more strongly predictive of future temperament measures.

Make sure you understand the time frame. When we talk about most temperament measures and extreme fussiness/colic, we are talking about a baby with extreme fussiness/colic (before three or four months of age) developing into a baby with a certain kind of difficult temperament (not measured until about four months of age). We are measuring two different things at two different times.

Another limitation to the Temperament Profile is that the infant does not fill out the questionnaire himself. So the ratings might reflect the preconceptions and temperament of the mother who does the rating. Here we see one of the many built-in quandaries of studying very young children. Unless ingenious tests are devised, an adult must interpret everything. Perhaps it is fitting that this Temperament Profile measures both infant behaviors and parental perceptions. After all, how a mother views her infant is probably as important for the mother-child relationship as is how the infant is actually behaving. There is a chance of problems developing when a mother merely perceives her infant to be "difficult" when he is objectively not a difficult child. A dramatic example of the difficult child's behavior and parental response spiraling out of control would be child abuse or infant homicide.

A third limitation is that this Temperament Profile, just like our definition of extreme fussiness/colic, uses arbitrary criteria in order to put labels on things. But infant behavior is a continuum, a gradation of measures. It has no natural cutoff points. There are some children who are almost but not quite difficult enough in their behavior to earn the label "difficult," just as there are children who cry almost but not quite enough to be diagnosed with extreme fussiness/colic. In addition, if an infant does not rate a difficult temperament, the parents and pediatrician should not assume that all will be rosy.

In spite of these limitations, there is value in using statistical analyses and numerical ratings to identify difficult temperament, and to find relationships between temperament and other dimensions of child development.

Difficult Temperament and Extreme Fussiness/Colic

It is important to note that an infant's temperament does not appear to be associated with the infant's sex, birth order, or social class. It does not seem to be related to the method of feeding (breast or formula) or to birth weight. Curiously, it might be related to ethnic group; one study shows that Chinese infants are more difficult than are non-Chinese infants.

Most significantly for our purposes, Carey found that difficult temperament is associated with extreme fussiness/colic. He studied a group of infants with extreme fussiness/colic. Later, when they were old enough to be given the Temperament

Profile, four were rated as difficult, four as almost difficult, four as almost easy, and only one was easy. There was, as Carey noted, "a significant concentration in the first two groups." The association between difficult temperament and extreme fussiness/colic might have appeared stronger if Carey had included those difficult children who had almost but not quite enough crying behavior to be diagnosed with extreme fussiness/colic. Please remember that infant behavior is a continuum, while definitions, by their nature, impose arbitrary cutoff points.

Carey's findings do suggest that extreme fussiness/colic is a combination of excessive but still normal crying and tendencies toward intense reactions, slow adaptability, negative mood, withdrawal, and irregularity. These behavioral tendencies, which make up difficult temperament and the crying of extreme fussiness, may be two facets of the same problem. For example, an overtired baby under four months of age who cannot sleep well may fuss and cry a lot and then may develop later, at four months, into an overtired child who shows a difficult temperament. They may have a common cause.

If your baby seems difficult whether or not she had extreme fussiness/colic, hug her, love her, and look forward to the time when she is older. Many parents find that their sour babies really do turn sweet after three or four months. My research has shown that when infants with extreme fussiness/colic learn how to sleep well, before or after four months of age, they are not likely to develop a difficult temperament. You'll read more about this in later chapters. There is hope that soon you will all sleep through the night and enjoy your days together as well.

CHAPTER 5

After Four Months of Age: How to Prevent Sleep Problems

Introduction: Sleep Before and After Four Months

Is Extreme Fussiness/Colic a Sleep Disorder?

At the Children's Memorial Hospital in Chicago, my colleagues and I did a study of extreme fussiness/colic. We looked at many of the factors listed in Tables 2, 3, and 4, but concentrated on possible relationships between extreme fussiness/colic and sleep patterns. We asked the parents of children between four and eight months to complete our written questionnaire about their children's sleep patterns. The questions covered the time the child usually fell asleep, when he woke up in the morning, how often he awoke at night, and whether or not the child had extreme fussiness/colic. We received 202 completed questionnaires and, after excluding children with medical problems that might have affected their sleep patterns, we ended up with a sample of 141. Twenty percent of them had suffered from extreme fussiness/colic (exactly as defined by Wessel). We found that the following can be added to the list of factors that are *not* connected to extreme fussiness/colic:

TABLE 5
FACTORS THAT ARE NOT
CONNECTED TO EXTREME FUSSINESS/COLIC

Hour asleep and hour awake
Duration of night awakenings
Parents' attempt to maintain regular sleep schedules
Parents' willingness to allow infant to cry himself to sleep
Consistency and promptness of parents' reaction
when infant awakened at night and cried
Maternal prenatal smoking or caffeine consumption

However, we did find one significant difference between the babies who had been extremely fussy/colicky and those with common fussiness. Infants who had extreme fussiness/colic when younger than four months awoke at night far more frequently than the others when they were four months old. They also tended to have less total sleep (day sleep plus night sleep) and to require more time to fall asleep. Remember this is well after extreme fussiness/colicky symptoms had disappeared. You will read more about the relationship between extreme fussiness/colic and sleeping problems later.

Some extremely fussy babies have difficulty falling asleep and staying asleep during the day and fuss or cry in the evening, but at night they fall asleep easily and sleep well. Others sleep better during the day, fuss/cry in the evening, and at night fall asleep with difficulty and sleep only for a few hours. Some researchers have claimed that difficulty falling asleep and frequent night awakenings are a basic part of extreme fussiness/colic, but it has been my experience that sleeping problems at night may not be apparent during the first few months—some extremely fussy/colicky babies exhaust themselves crying all evening and sleep soundly through the night—but often show up later. Before we look more carefully at the connection between extreme fussiness/colic and infant sleep, let us review what we know about how our babies sleep.

Newborn Sleep Patterns

At about six weeks of age (or six weeks after the due date for babies born early) *night sleep organization* develops. What does this mean? Before six weeks, the longest single sleep period is not very long and does not occur at the same time each day. In other words, there are many short sleep periods that occur totally unpredictably. There is no predictable pattern. But at about six weeks of age, there will start to be a four-to-six-hour sleep period occurring in the evening or at night. This is night sleep organization—the end of "day-night confusion."

During the day, at three to four months of age, a midmorning nap emerges first, and an early afternoon nap emerges second. Note that *day sleep organization* develops after night sleep organization, and it may occur later in extremely fussy babies.

Over those first sixteen weeks, there are gradual changes in the infant's sleeping pattern. There is a small decrease in the total hours asleep, a doubling of the longest sleep period, and an increase in the amount of sleep occurring at night. By sixteen weeks, most infants are sleeping a total of about thirteen to seventeen hours, and the longest single sleep period at night is about seven to ten hours. Around this time mothers often start feeding solid foods with the hope of getting the child to sleep, but the introduction of solid foods does not alter the development of these sleep patterns. In general, by three to four months of age most children are sleeping for longer periods of time, and primarily at night.

Your infant sleeps as long as infants in previous generations slept. Age-specific sleep durations have not changed over the past sixty years. A study at Children's Memorial Hospital in 1981 found today's sleep durations consistent with those measured in 1911 and 1927. Social changes during the past sixty years—differences in family size and how people spend their time, the introduction of central heating and air-conditioning, television, and personal computers—have also not had a significant impact on how much children sleep. This would lead me to believe that sleep patterns reflect biologically and

genetically driven behavior as opposed to learned, environ-
mentally driven behavior.

Sleeping Positions

In England and China, it is customary to place infants on their
backs because of the fear that they might bury their heads into
the mattress and suffocate. In the United States, it used to be
customary to keep babies on their stomachs because of the fear
that they might vomit and choke. These are not reasonable
fears; preferred sleeping positions in different countries only
reflect different customs. On an individual level, some babies
sleep well in any position, while others appear to cry less, move
less, and sleep better in one position compared to others. We
still do not know why some babies sleep better in one position
or another. However, we know that the risk of sudden infant
death syndrome (SIDS) is less when babies sleep on their back.
Therefore, please put your baby to sleep on her back.

Understanding Sleep: Sleep States

Studies done in sleep labs have helped us to understand some
of the mysteries of the state we call sleep. Sleep is not one constant state. Brain activity during sleep is not static and unvary-
ing, like a TV test pattern. On the contrary, sleep is an active,
multileveled, frequently changing condition. There are qualitative differences in sleep patterns throughout the night. And
we have learned that the sleep of young infants is different
from the sleep of older children.

Sleep researchers have identified two basic sleep patterns.
In active sleep, also called rapid eye movement (REM) sleep,
the eyes move back and forth rapidly under closed lids. REM
sleep is associated with irregular breathing and heart rhythms
and with many fleeting body movements. Dreaming mostly occurs during REM sleep. The opposite state, called quiet or
non-REM sleep, is associated with decreased body movements
and slow, regular breathing and heart rhythms. The active
(REM) and quiet (non-REM) sleep states alternate in a usually
predictable fashion throughout the night.

Newborns Have a Unique Sleep Pattern for Three to Four Months

Researchers have measured the number of REM periods, the duration of each individual REM period, the total duration of all REM periods per twenty-four hours, and the percentage of total sleep time spent in REM sleep in subjects of all ages. They have found these measurements are basically similar for older infants, children, and adults. A noteworthy exception is that newborns *less than three months old* show a different pattern. This means that during the first few months of life, REM sleep patterns may be undergoing organization.

One way newborns differ is that younger infants spend much more time in REM sleep state than do older children and adults. Another difference is that an infant less than three months old enters a REM state immediately upon falling asleep. After three months, sleep always starts with a non REM period, which is the pattern seen in adults. Why this is and why it changes at that age are not known.

Also, the cycle of alternating between the sleep states is much shorter in the infant than in the older child or adult. That is to say, each state lasts a shorter amount of time and one follows the other more quickly. It takes about four months to establish the adultlike periodic organization of sleep states, which will last throughout a lifetime.

Day Sleep Versus Night Sleep

Research has shown differences between daytime and nighttime sleep in infants.

During the first three to four months of life, REM sleep diminishes significantly during the day, as the number of daytime REM periods decreases, though the length of each stays about the same. In other words, there are fewer bouts of REM sleep but no change in the duration of each bout during the day. Non-REM sleep increases during the night as the duration of each non-REM period increases significantly, though the number of non-REM periods stays the same. In other words, there are longer bouts of non-REM sleep but no change in the number of bouts during the night.

This is an example of how sleep evolves in a complex process. What it highlights is that not all sleep periods are created equal and that we should think of *sleep quality*, not just *sleep quantity*.

Something in the developing baby's nervous system causes a decrease in the number of REM sleep periods during the day and an increase in the duration of non-REM sleep periods during the night (Table 6). This may reflect what people mean when they say a baby has to "learn to tell day from night." Clearly there is a lot of behind-the-scenes activity, sometimes called "day-night confusion." For young babies, each twenty-four-hour period is divided into REM sleep, wakefulness, and something called ambiguous sleep because it looks a little like both REM and non-REM sleep. As you will see, ambiguous sleep may be related to extreme fussiness/colic.

TABLE 6
**CHANGES IN SLEEP PATTERNS
FROM 0—3 MONTHS**

	Day Sleep (Naps) *8:00 A.M.–8:00 P.M.*	*Night Sleep* *8:00 P.M.–8:00 A.M.*	*Overall Effect on Sleep*
REM Sleep	Fewer REM periods (no change in duration)	No change in number or duration	Less REM sleep
Non-REM	No change in number or duration	Longer duration of non-REM periods (no change in numbers)	More non-REM sleep

Possibility No. 1: Extreme Fussiness/Colic Is Connected with Disorganized Sleep

Not all babies get their sleep organized at the same rate. Let us consider some of the possibilities for a two-month-old baby. Sleep organization may have developed normally, with increasingly long phases of non-REM sleep mainly at night. Or sleep organization might be delayed or abnormal, in which case we might see too many REM periods, or REM periods that are too long, or REM periods occurring at the wrong time. Sleep patterns can be disorganized in terms of either the number, duration, or timing of the sleep states.

Many researchers think that REM sleep has a stimulating effect on the baby's developing brain and that this internal stimulation represents a biological form of learning. This is similar to the external stimulation from the environment that triggers the learning of languages and abstract concepts. For adults and older children, it is thought that REM sleep is especially important for emotional or psychological restoration, helping us wake up feeling less stressed or tense, while non-REM sleep seems especially important to physically restore fatigued muscles.

We do not know what it is in the baby's brain that controls the development of sleep patterns, nor do we know the effects of abnormal sleep patterns. Perhaps extreme fussiness results from internally disorganized sleep patterns. Alternatively, sleep patterns might be desynchronized with other vital functions such as breathing control, as discussed in the next section.

Sleep and Breathing Rhythms

The rate of breathing is a relatively stable individual characteristic—some infants tend to be fast breathers and some tend to be slow breathers. However, the rate of breathing during sleep is related to the specific sleep state: people always breathe faster during active sleep states and slower during quiet sleep states. This relationship between sleep state and breathing rate develops during the first few months of life.

It is possible that in some babies, this relationship between sleep state and breathing rate takes longer to develop. These babies might not be able to breathe regularly enough to keep themselves asleep. They may sometimes have to fight for air. What better way for a baby to keep her lungs inflated and get plenty of oxygen into her bloodstream than through several hours of lusty crying?

Charles Darwin, in his book, *Expression of the Emotions of Men and Animals,* was the first to point out the important breath-control component in crying. He described in great detail how during crying the arrangement of the facial muscles, gasping sounds, lingering shudders, and the way the nose clogs and the eyes close, can all be traced to changes in respiration. Crying, we might conclude, is a strange, overwrought kind of breathing. It is not too much of a leap to suggest that when breathing becomes disordered because of lack of coordination with the sleep cycles, the infant might compensate with spells of agitated persistent crying that we call extreme fussiness/colic. Looking at it this way, the paroxysms of extreme fussiness/colic paroxysms might be more like breathless gasping than adult grief- or pain-related crying.

Other studies at the Children's Memorial Hospital showed that babies who are active, intense, and stimulus-sensitive, as determined by the Temperament Questionnaire, have more regular breathing when asleep at night, with fewer respiratory pauses than infants who are inactive, mild, and less responsive to environmental stimulation.

I believe that the sleep-breathing-crying connection might hold an answer not only to the puzzle of extreme fussiness/colic, but also to the tragedy of sudden infant death syndrome. That, too, might be some sort of sleep-related breathing disorder. It is, I believe, significant that when babies are having spells of extreme fussiness/colic, they are almost never SIDS victims.

Sleep, Temperature, and Endocrine Rhythms

If a sleep cycle that is not yet synchronized with breathing rate could cause an infant distress and lead to extreme fussiness, a sleep cycle not synchronized with temperature or hormone rhythms could have the same effect.

Body temperature and levels of certain hormones go through predictable daily ups and downs. These rhythms develop during the first year of life. During the first few months especially, temperature and hormone variations are quite irregular, but we now know that serum cortisol concentrations in the blood begins to show a pattern very early, leading to a distinct twenty-four-hour pattern. Melatonin is another hormone that develops a regular nighttime peak at about three to four months of age.

Also in newborns, human growth hormone is secreted throughout a twenty-four-hour period. By four months of age the pattern of secretion becomes organized into a circadian pattern. That is, during every twenty-four-hour period there are dramatic differences between the highest and lowest hormone levels, and these peaks and valleys occur at about the same time every day. Once the pattern is established, the hormone is released at night after the beginning of sleep, and most of the hormone is released during the deeper, later stages of sleep. We do not understand the biological mechanism that links sleep rhythms to endocrine rhythms, but these rhythms might offer a key to understanding extreme fussiness, especially why extreme fussiness so often occurs in the late afternoon or evening hours.

Many people, including Dr. Brazelton, explain evening fussiness by saying that the child senses the mother's increasing eagerness or anxiety as the time comes for the father to return home. I think this is a clever but unfounded suggestion. It is an example of how male pediatricians or psychiatrists tend to blame everything undesirable about children on the mother! Much more plausible is that the occurrence of most spells in the evening is related or linked to distorted biological rhythms.

Can extreme fussiness be considered an infant form of jet lag syndrome? Biological rhythms that are out of sync with the normal cues of daylight and darkness cause us to feel slightly sick, and jet lag syndrome in adults is an example of this. With jet lag syndrome, we may feel awake, alert, and attentive but have difficulty thinking, focusing, or concentrating. We may ache or feel worn down but still can have difficulty in falling asleep. Another example of not feeling well because biological rhythms are out of sync with daylight cues are the symptoms experienced by shift workers. Sleep loss from jobs that require you to be up at night cause headaches and stomach pains. Extreme fussiness certainly appears to be a painful condition, especially pain in the abdomen.

> **Severe fatigue alone is painful; you ache. The inability to sleep well may cause painful fatigue.**

So here is one possible line of thinking that would link sleep with extreme fussiness: lack of synchronization between sleep-wake rhythms and breathing, temperature, or hormone rhythms may cause distress in an infant. The more disorganized these rhythms are, the more severe the extreme fussy behavior. Then, at three months or so, when the transition to a normal adult-like sleep-cycle pattern is complete, the evening spells of extreme fussiness/colic may disappear.

Possibility No. 2: Extreme Fussiness/Colic Is an "Acted-Out" REM Period

Studies in adults suggest that during rapid eye movement sleep, brain wave patterns superficially resemble the brain wave patterns during alert wakefulness. However, during REM sleep the body is "paralyzed" by an active neurological inhibition of muscle movement. (Now you know why it is so hard to run away from danger in a nightmare!)

In a study done on cats during REM sleep, this muscle inhibition was experimentally blocked and the cats behaved as if they were awake. They appeared to be hunting or pouncing on mice while asleep! One case where we can observe something like this phenomenon in humans is the shaking and jerky movements seen in alcoholics with delirium tremens. This seems to result from an uncoupling between active (REM) sleep and the muscle paralysis that usually goes with it.

Perhaps the increased motor activity during spells of extreme fussiness—twisting, turning, stiffening, and clenching—

represents a breakthrough in this muscle inhibition. That is, the baby might be, in a sense, in a state of REM sleep without having yet fully developed the characteristic accompanying muscle paralysis. Typically, a child ends an extremely fussy spell by suddenly falling asleep. This could, in fact, be the onset of a quiet (non-REM) sleep state.

On the surface, it seems absurd to claim that a crying, writhing baby is more asleep than awake. But in very young babies, the line between sleep and wakefulness is not all that clear. Often the electrical recordings from the brain cannot distinguish between sleep and wakefulness until at least ten weeks of age. To distinguish between REM and non-REM sleep, measurements of eye and chin muscle activity or of breathing and heart rhythms must be taken. It is hard to tell exactly what state an infant is in during an extremely fussy/colicky spell. Behaviorally, during these periods babies appear to be "out of touch," inconsolable, and unreachable. Perhaps they are in a strange sleep state and thus are not really conscious or awake. In this theory, the writhing and screaming of extreme fussiness might be the behavioral reflection of dramatic shifts in breathing and body temperature that we know occur during REM sleep—shifts we usually do not see acted out because the muscle paralysis keeps the body still.

Indirect evidence suggesting an association between extreme fussiness/colic and REM sleep was published by Dr. Robert Emde at the University of Colorado Medical Center. In a well-documented series of detailed observations, Dr. Emde noted that infants may appear to be awake—sucking, fussing, crying, or smiling—at a time when rapid eye movements are observed under closed eyelids. Sometimes this is called "ambiguous" sleep. These "active" behaviors that occur during rapid eye movement sleep tend to disappear by age three months. Over and over again, it appears that the age of three to four months is a crucial turning point. Although it is only speculation, I suspect that unexplained common fussing or extreme fussiness/colicky behavior in some infants is linked with this REM sleep state. Another study showed that intensive eye movements during sleep, called "REM storms," occurred more often in those infants who showed dramatic "neurobehavioral instability"—that is, infants who showed greater behavioral irregularity, or shifts in behavioral states, from week to week than other infants.

Extreme fussiness/colic disappears at about three to four months of age. Sleep state control matures at about three months. Each spell of extreme fussiness almost always terminates with the infant falling asleep. I doubt that all this is coincidence.

With the passage of time, your baby's developing brain becomes better able to inhibit the ever-present background restless, random fidgety behaviors—both when awake and when asleep. Also, circadian rhythms develop and become synchronized with each other and with day/night schedules. If these are neurologically related events, then both possibilities—that extreme fussiness is related to disorganized sleep and that extreme fussiness/colic is an "acted-out" REM period—may be partially correct. The infant with disorganized biological rhythms might have his greatest distress at about the same time every day, and the child who lacks active inhibitory development appears "wired" or "turned on" during the day and always seems to sleep in an active fashion. Extremely fussy/colicky babies usually behave as if they're suffering from not enough sleep. So there may well be support for the idea that extreme fussiness/colic is a neurological development condition.

The Crying-Temperament-Sleep Connection

I have talked about many factors that seem to be related to extreme fussiness, including crying, temperament, and disorganized sleep. I believe that the eventual solution to the extreme fussiness/colic puzzle will draw all of these factors together. For now, I can only suggest where the connections might be made.

Table 7 summarizes a frequently seen relationship between a certain kind of awake behavior and a certain kind of sleep pattern.

TABLE 7
**RELATIONSHIP BETWEEN AWAKE BEHAVIOR
AND SLEEP PATTERNS**

AWAKE BEHAVIOR	SLEEP PATTERNS
Colic	Sleeplessness or "insomnia"
Low Sensory threshold	Easily aroused from sleep
Easily startled	Increased frequency of night
Difficult temperament	awakenings
Increased crying	Increased frequency of sleep/wake
Active, vigorous	transitions per twenty-four hours

Infant temperament assessments taken between four and eight months, using the questionnaire developed by Carey, showed a clear relationship between difficult temperament and brief sleep durations. Infants with a difficult temperament slept significantly less than infants with an easy temperament. Briefer sleep durations were also observed among infants with extreme fussiness/colic. It is possible that insufficient sleep causes a difficult temperament.

> **At four months of age, the difficult temperament might be closely connected with an overtired behavioral style.**

Factors such as parental behavior and neurological immaturity, acting separately or in combination, also may influence both sleep duration and infant temperament.

Several other studies suggest a relationship (as shown in Table 7) between (1) extreme fussiness or excessive crying, (2) low sensory threshold, and (3) difficulty in sleeping—either brief sleep durations or frequent night awakenings.

Low sensory threshold, as discussed earlier, refers to infants who are easily startled or who respond dramatically to small changes in their environment. These infants are described as "sensitive." In the study that connected temperament and extreme fussiness, Carey concluded that extreme fussiness was common among infants who turned out to have difficult temperament and/or low sensory threshold. Sensory threshold is a component of temperament; however, it is not part of the easy/difficult diagnosis. Yet it does prove to have an additional link to extreme fussiness because Carey also found that low sensory threshold was associated with frequent night awakenings.

My impression is that babies with extreme fussiness/colic who learn to sleep well after three or four months of age do not develop a low sensory threshold. However, babies who had been extremely fussy during the first months and who subsequently do not learn to sleep well become more stimulus-sensitive, easily started, and easily upset because they are severely overtired. Just think of how sensitive you are to little things when you are overtired.

A study at Children's Memorial Hospital tied extreme fussiness/colic to a definite increase in the number of night awakenings. Older studies have suggested that night waking in children (with or without extreme fussiness/colic) is associated with brief sleep durations. Night waking also appears to be a problem associated with an abnormal sleep schedule.

We have a set of convincing linkages here. Clearly, the problems of extreme fussiness/colic, difficult temperament, low sensory threshold, frequent night awakenings, and brief sleep durations are interrelated. Perhaps these are different facets of the same problem. None of these characteristics tends to be subject to much parental influence in very young infants. None shows much individual stability during the first months of an infant's life. All develop a sharper focus and more enduring pattern after about three to four months of age. This suggests that either (1) time is required for infants to learn behavioral styles and sleep patterns, (2) some biological maturation takes place, or (3) both learning and maturation occur.

Support for a biological view comes from several studies that show that extreme fussiness/colic occurs in premature infants within a few weeks of the expected birth date, and peaks at six weeks after the expected birth date regardless of the gestational age at birth. In other words, extreme fussiness/colic appears to be time-locked to biological development counting from conception, not from birth. Extreme fussiness/colic most likely has more to do with the biological, rather than the behavioral, maturing of the child.

Extreme Fussiness/Colic May Be Part of a Larger Problem

The evidence seems convincing that infants who suffer from extreme fussiness/colic in their first few months of life have a better-than-average chance of having a difficult temperament at age four months and/or having sleeping problems later in infancy. Researchers who feel strongly that extreme fussiness/colic before three months has no aftermath blame this later difficult temperament on parents. They say that living with a crying baby for three months causes parents to permanently change their behavior toward the child. They might, for example, become inattentive or "emotionally unavailable" to the child, either out of exhaustion and distress, or as a deliberate management tactic to prevent indulging their baby. It is this parental behavior that, according to this theory, causes behavior problems in the child.

My colleagues and I had a chance to test this theory when we conducted a study of the drug dicyclomine as a treatment for extreme fussiness. Several previous studies had indicated that dicyclomine could relieve the symptoms of extreme fussiness/colic. We studied forty-eight extremely fussy/colicky infants, some given dicyclomine and some a placebo (plain cherry syrup), and found dicyclomine to be, in many cases, an effective treatment for extreme fussiness. Dicyclomine could exert its effect on the brain or gut.

We thought that if dicyclomine eliminated the inconsolable crying of extreme fussiness/colic, we would see less of the inattentive or emotionally distant parental behaviors described above. If parental behavior were the problem, we expected to find that infants successfully treated with dicyclomine would emerge from extreme fussiness with easier temperaments and fewer sleep disturbances than those infants who had received the placebo and kept on crying.

To our surprise, this was not the case. The infants in our study, all of whom were diagnosed as having extreme fussiness/colic, did show a higher likelihood of difficult temperament and sleep disturbances as compared to common fussy babies. This was equally true of the infants successfully treated with dicyclomine and those who had received a placebo. In other words, effective treatment for symptoms of extreme fussiness did not alter later temperament ratings or sleep patterns when the infants were four months old.

This led me to originally conclude that difficult temperament and briefer sleep duration in babies over four months of age who had been extremely fussy/colicky under four months of age did not result from the parents' response to extreme fussiness/colic crying. Many of the babies in our study had their crying greatly reduced or almost eliminated by the drug, and they still showed a higher-than-average incidence of difficult to mange temperament and sleep problems.

I originally thought that parents are not the cause of a four-month-old's brief sleep durations, just as they did not cause his crying as an extreme fussiness/colic two-month-old. At that point I believed that extreme fussiness/colic, difficult temperament, and sleep disorders all shared an underlying biological cause—that is, they are all manifestations of the same problem. But after many years of reviewing additional research and discussing these issues with other professionals, I have revised my opinion somewhat. I think that elevated serotonin concentration and other biological factors cause extreme fussiness. But I do also believe that parents' ability to soothe their baby and to help instill good sleep habits has an effect on the child as well. For example, in some families, parents have less ability to soothe their baby for personal or family reasons—the baby blues, postpartum depression, or medical problems in the mother, the father's refusal to help soothe, other children's demands for attention and energy, a mother's conflict between wanting to restart her career and staying at home, or preexisting marital problems.

To sum up, while many of the factors involved in extreme fussiness may be out of your control, your soothing responses to your child have some effect. You can keep a tendency toward difficult temperament from growing into a long-term behavioral problem. You can teach a child with brief sleep durations to sleep longer and more soundly. Your soothing can make extreme fussiness more bearable for both you and your baby.

As Extreme Fussiness Ends

Through draggy afternoons, arsenic evenings, and long nights you probably have sometimes thought that your baby's extreme fussiness/colic would go on forever. But eventually, when your baby is around three or four months old, you should begin to notice a letup in the fussing/crying. The baby may be more able to be soothed, skip days of crying, or may have fewer spells or briefer ones. The change in her behavior may be abrupt and dramatic, or it may be gradual and erratic. After months of disappointment with temporary improvement cruelly followed by even worse relapses, you may not dare believe what is happening. But one day you will say to your husband, or he to you, "You know, she really is a lot better."

This is certainly a time for celebration. You have lived through extreme fussiness, but you may not have reached the promised land yet. Sometimes a miracle does occur, and within days the baby becomes quiet, cheerful, relaxed, and a good sleeper. Other children, however, do indeed cry less, but they remain irritable and hard to soothe, and awaken easily from sleep because they have become very overtired. With careful handling, you may be able to prevent the overtired state before it becomes serious.

Time for a Change

During the period of extreme fussiness/colic, your child has learned to associate falling asleep with specific behaviors such as extended rocking, walking, hugging, and feeding. She has learned to expect extra attention as she drifts off to sleep. The process of falling asleep is learned behavior, and she may never have learned to fall asleep by herself. She may have, in a sense, become dependent on social soothing interaction in order to fall asleep. After three or four months of age, some of these babies become chronically overtired because the parents failed to establish healthy sleep habits. So even after the biological causes of the fussing and crying (whatever they are) have disappeared, the old fussy pattern might remain if your child is overtired.

Parents, too, become conditioned after several months of coping with extreme fussiness/colic. They have grown used to lavishing prompt, continual attention on their crying baby. The variable nature of extreme fussiness/colic has taught them to shift strategies frequently. They have become improvisers— trying what worked last night, trying what worked this morning, or trying something new. It has never been practical for them to have a plan; they just responded. However, around four months old, babies who used to be extremely fussy/colicky need consistent, thought-out management to prevent bad habits.from developing. Parents must make a transition too.

Mothers' Descriptions of Their Babies at Age Four Months

As part of a study on extremely fussy infants, I had the opportunity to study the parents' responses to the Infant Temperament Questionnaire, filled out when the infants were about four months old. Several mothers included a narrative account of the changes they had seen, and I quote from these below. None of these infants was in my practice; I had not given any advice or counseling to these mothers. All the infants had extreme fussiness (as defined by Wessel), and the extreme fussiness had disappeared by the time the parents filled out the questionnaire.

These comments from mothers of different background and

circumstances illustrate the variety of ways extreme fussiness can resolve itself. As you read on, you will see that behavior during the extremely fussy period makes babies appear as alike as peas in a pod. There is not much individuality among crying babies, especially to their exhausted mothers. However, the children outgrow this awful period with vastly different temperaments. I hope you have a sweet baby at four months!

"HE'S COME A LONG WAY"

With the extreme fussiness months behind us, I find Jacob very enjoyable and really no problem at all. Jacob has really come a long way from two months ago. He went from being a crying, crabby baby to a basically happy baby. His routine is, for the most part, regular. He tends to be a bit cranky around the dinner hour but is calmed by being picked up and just being in the middle of the activity. He enjoys being right in the middle of everything and everyone and is up quite a bit. He gets excited watching his brother and sister play. He gets really excited and laughs when he plays with Daddy. If he's crabby and squirming, you know he's either wet or sleepy or it's time to eat. On the whole, I would say he is a fairly content little guy!

"HE BECAME A NEW BABY"

At almost three months to the day, I felt Daniel was over his extreme fussiness. He became a new baby with long times of playing and watching and seemed very happy. He suddenly established a routine of sleeping, eating, and being awake. He followed it faithfully if my husband or me were the ones taking care of him. With everyone else, the routine of sleep was shortened and awake times lengthened, so he'd be fussy at the end, but it is amazing what a happy baby he has become. The only times that are still rather difficult are when he is in a car seat. When I hold him in the back of the van he is perfectly content. However, I drive a small car and then he is in a car seat, which proves to be distressing. Daniel does not take a pacifier on his own and will spit it out unless I help hold it. Rarely does he keep the pacifier in for more than sixty seconds if he's fussy, and he does not suck his thumb or fingers in place of the pacifier. Before with colic, he needed constant attention and there was no solution to his crying. Now he is becoming a happy person. Fussiness now means specific problems: diaper, food, sleep, etc.

Daniel's mother, a thirty-two-year-old teacher, described her baby as not sucking very much. Brazelton reported that crying and sucking behavior were inversely related to each other. That is, babies who cry a lot do not suck very much, and thumb suckers do not cry very much.

"SHE CAN FOCUS HER ENERGY INSTEAD OF CRYING"

Katherine's extreme fussiness varied widely from day to day. On a good day, there might have been only two to three hours of mild fussiness in the evening. She took naps, sleeping perhaps four hours during the day. She always slept from midnight to 7:00 A.M. There were several play periods of twenty to forty minutes, and she certainly was fun! On bad days, the colic lasted from six to eight hours, most of it in the moderate category, maybe an hour or two really severe. On these days, she was unable to sleep during the day. She would fall asleep but awaken a few moments later. Holding, rocking, and the pacifier helped, but she was unusually jumpy. The sound of my breathing startled her, for example. She still had some play periods after eating, but they were much shorter and less frequent. I ended up holding her most of the day. In an average week she had three bad days. One of the fussy days was due to her first DPT shot. I also noticed that on bad days, she looked pale and there was some perspiration on her forehead before she began crying. I could sometimes tell ahead of time that she was going to have problems.

[At about four months], in general, Katie has had less severe extreme fussiness, fewer hours of extreme fussiness, and has slept more. It has been easier to get her to sleep and easier to keep her asleep. Her play periods are longer, and it's been interesting to watch her focus her energy on looking, reaching, batting, and feeling things instead of having it tied up in crying. There has been only one instance of severe colic since, and it was short. She still has some "jittery" times, but on the whole they seem less severe. She still tends to have at least one very active period in the evening during which she energetically leaps, smiles, frowns, coughs, burps, widens her eyes, and so on. However, she is less apt to disintegrate into screaming. More often, she falls into a light sleep and the rapidly changing facial expressions and panting continue for a few moments. Then she either awakens in a quieter mood or goes into a sound sleep.

The comments regarding panting are interesting because many mothers noted that just prior to the onset of extreme fussiness the babies might breathe rapidly and shallowly. Other mothers noted deep or labored breathing, like rapid sighs, just before the extreme fussiness occurred. These changes in breathing patterns were previously reported by Wessel. Perhaps smooth-muscle contractions in the lung are causing increased resistance to breathing, similar to what occurs in asthmatics. The comment regarding perspiration or pallor before the crying started had not been previously reported, but perspiration was noted in the following mother's report.

"SHE FIGHTS SLEEP"

My four-month-old infant, Marjorie, cries and fusses after her bath, almost always for two to five minutes. She fights sleep continuously (one to two hours), rejects the last bottle, stiffens her body and when held pushes away from me by bending her legs, passing gas, and her body perspires. Rocking, being held, played with, walked, etc. does not stop her shrill crying. The difficulty in the evenings has left me feeling either she is spoiled or I'm not following a schedule properly and am promoting this overtired, extremely fussy period myself. Marjorie has been this way for ten weeks, but in the past six weeks she's become even more difficult to get to sleep.

"CRIES HERSELF TO SLEEP"

Tai is strong-willed, yet usually agreeable. She laughs and smiles very easily and is not fearful of strangers. She generally has a very good disposition. She is very inquisitive and very vocal. Tai frequently moves her arms and legs vigorously when playing with toys. She is very affectionate and generally likes to be held. When tired and fighting sleep, Tai becomes much more difficult. Even when she falls asleep while nursing she usually awakens when put into her crib and cries vigorously (i.e., red face, with tears and perspiration) for five to fifteen minutes until she falls asleep. Tai rarely sleeps longer than four hours at a time. During the daytime, naps range from thirty minutes to two and a half hours. She usually awakens from naps more calmly than she did a month or so ago. That is especially true if she has slept for a longer period of time.

During the night, Tai usually sleeps for about four hours and awakens whimpering or crying. She is easily calmed by holding and nursing and falls asleep readily. When returned to her crib, however, she almost always cries for a few minutes before settling down to sleep. She does not cry if she is nursed in our bed and not moved.

"VERY OPINIONATED"

Charles has definitely calmed down but is still very active during the day. When extreme fussiness was bad, it was at its worst during the day, no matter what I did. He is very opinionated as to what he'll eat and has lost interest in his bottle already. He still gets spurts of gas once in a while.

What Mothers Say About First Babies After Extreme Fussiness/Colic Ends

Here are some young mothers describing their first-born babies after they've grown out of a bout of extreme fussiness.

"HE DOESN'T SLEEP LIKE OTHER CHILDREN"

David is a happy boy in general. He loves to take baths and kick in the tub. He also loves to have his hair brushed, his body rubbed with lotion, nails cut, ears cleaned, nose cleaned, etc. David is big on eating—anything he can suck. He still sucks his thumb when sleeping. He loves to be put on the changing table to dress and have his diaper changed. And he loves to be talked to! He is very friendly toward everyone and smiles and coos a lot. David is just great when we take him out—stores, houses—loves all the new things. He is easily stimulated by sights and sounds. David still doesn't sleep like other children, as long that is, but he does sleep seven to eight hours each night, and one hour in the morning and one hour in the afternoon for naps, which sure beats being up every two hours!

"I FEED HER VERY OFTEN"

It is very hard, even impossible, to put Stephanie on a feeding schedule. When I do feed my child, she never eats. I'm talking about nursing her not more than ten minutes total, so I don't think she's very full. I find myself feeding her frequently. She gets very, very angry sometimes and will scream, and sometimes I can't tell if she might be in extreme pain.

"NIGHTS ARE STILL DIFFICULT"

Previously, Matthew's extreme fussiness could be described as moderate in nature with a total duration of about six hours each day—usually three hours in the early morning (3:00 A.M. to 7:00 A.M. or so), 11:00 A.M. to noon, and 4:00 P.M. to 6:00 P.M., and sometimes again between 9:00 P.M. and midnight. He usually had about ten wakings between midnight and 9:00 A.M. One rocking movement that he often responded to when crying intensely was an elevatorlike movement—up and down on his back. However, this is physically demanding and can't be done for long. Now, his general behavior pattern is characterized by pleasantness. Matthew smiles most of the day and maintains the ability to charm, play, and coo. However, night wakings are continually a problem. For the last three weeks he has awakened every hour.

"DEMANDS A LOT OF ATTENTION"

I have noticed marked improvement in Jonathan's behavior during his fourth month. Since his colic pains have subsided, he seems to be enjoying what life has to offer. However, when he gets tired of a certain activity (play, bath, swing, etc.), he is very impatient and screams continuously until I pick him up and move on to something else. I can't coax him to stay with a task if he doesn't want to. He is at a point now where he is showing a lot of emotion. He smiles and giggles out loud for long periods of time, but he can cry two minutes later because he wants a change of activity. Jonathan demands a lot of attention, and I wonder if this is because of when he had colic. Dinner is a difficult time because Jonathan does not like to sit and amuse himself while we eat. This is a problem we are still working on. Maybe this is true with many children. This being my first child, I'm not sure what is typical behavior, but I would consider his temperament to be more difficult than average since he demands so much attention.

"SHE'S USUALLY CALMER"

Annie has a generally sunny disposition and is extremely gregarious. She does have strong negative reactions to things she's not ready for, like dressing or being put to bed. When she was younger, Annie seemed to overreact to stimulation and had many more fussy periods. She still reacts strongly, but not necessarily negatively, and is usually calm.

"DEPENDENCY IS A PROBLEM"

Nelida has a very high level of activity and expresses her emotions through her physical movements. She seems to prefer communication through body language rather than vocal expression. When she vocalizes it's more through a demanding cry rather than cooing and being pleasant. She's a very alert, attentive child with good concentration and attention span, especially when her energy is at its peak in the evening. Being with us makes her feel secure and it is essential for her becoming sociable and outgoing. This has developed into a problem because her attachment and dependency has developed to such a degree that Nelida refused to develop independence, or allow us to have ours.

Second-Born Infants Are Like First-Borns After Extreme Fussiness/Colic Ends

Second-born children who have had extreme fussiness/colic are described in terms similar to those used by mothers of first-born infants.

"REQUIRES A LOT OF SLEEP"

Elizabeth is only getting a formula for feedings—no solids. Four eight-ounce bottles keep her full. Her sleeping patterns and preferences are giving us the most problems. She requires a lot of sleep and is only awake six to seven hours a day. The problem is she will only sleep on her stomach in a crib. Sleeping in cribs other than her own also shortens her naps. She does not particularly enjoy stroller rides or car seats and never falls asleep in them. Her favorite activities involve being with other people. She enjoys being held, walked, talked to, and played with. We are trying to encourage longer play periods alone. It's hard to take her places. She requires a lot of holding and walking.

"NO TWO DAYS ALIKE"

Scott's behavior varies from day to day. It seems there are never two days in a row that are alike. He does follow something of a schedule for eating and sleeping but his behavior during waking hours changes a lot. He can almost always be comforted by holding.

"NO PROBLEM AT ALL"

At first, Nathaniel's crying was a problem because I didn't feel emotionally strong enough to handle it. A three-month span of extreme fussiness seemed like it would be forever to me. We had trouble taking him visiting because right after supper time (about 7:30 P.M.), he would start to cry and wouldn't quit. Once he got wound up, he had a hard time relaxing and calming down. Now his temperament is no problem at all. I enjoy him. I think he's a cute baby. Maybe I'll have a third sometime!

"I Can See More and More How to Help Her"

Although Lauren has greatly improved since the time of her colic, she can't relax in her environment. If she ever must wait for something, especially a nap or feeding she will begin by fussing and then dissolve into tears. If this occurs around naptime, she will take about twenty minutes to settle herself down, during which time there must be no stimulation at all. If she fusses at feeding time, she will generally refuse the breast. The only solution is to place her in the crib and let her cry it out, the end result being a short nap, after which she wakes up cheerful and ready to eat.

However, Lauren more than makes up for these angry outbursts by being a very responsive child. She smiles a lot, freely giving belly laughs. She especially loves playing with her older sister and me. She can maintain cheerful play for up to an hour and sometimes more after a feeding. Her motor development is very good. One thing I've noticed is that she doesn't sleep well anywhere but in her own crib—she's very aware of changes in bed. For example, she won't fall asleep in a restaurant in a car bed, but she can sometimes sleep in a Snugli. It feels good to see the light at the end of the tunnel. I can see more and more how to help Lauren over her sometimes very difficult irritability. I'm feeling much better about our relationship.

Experienced Mothers and Extremely Fussy/Colicky Babies

Experienced mothers with two or three previous children may also experience an extremely fussy/colicky baby.

"A Joy to All of Us"

Before, Michael would scream and cry for hours and nothing we did seemed to help him. We would rock him, walk with him, and he would still scream. He even fought the bottle. This would go on for four or five hours straight; then he'd fall asleep and sleep for approximately an hour, then start all over again. We didn't know what to do to pacify him because nothing seemed to help him. Once Michael started sitting up, it relieved him somewhat and now he is a very happy and content baby boy. He smiles, coos, and is starting to sleep more, and it seems to be a peaceful sleep. When he is awake now, he is content and doesn't have to be held, rocked, or walked constantly. He is a joy to all of us.

"TREMENDOUS DIFFERENCE"

David seems to be very content in whatever we do with him; he also is very content on where we lay him down, observes everything quietly and amuses himself by watching the mobile in his crib. He also accepts changes in his routine very well. It's a tremendous difference from when he had colic.

Perhaps you will recognize in these descriptions of children during and after extreme fussiness/colic ends some of the things that your child is going through. Be comforted. This is all very typical. As these testimonials show, even the fussiest children outgrow extreme fussiness/colic and become sweeter. Some turn into dream babies; others continue to be more assertive, but all become much more responsive, predictable, and easy to live with.

Labeling your child's fussiness or crying as "extreme fussiness/colic" tends to emphasize her worst behavior. Her good behavior is just as much a part of her personality. Closely observe your baby at her best and her worst, when awake and when asleep. Treasure the beautiful, smiling moments. This is your preview of the baby you may be living with soon.

Sleep After Extreme Fussiness/Colic Ends

NATURE CONDITIONS NURTURE

Your newborn's fussiness compels you to put forth more effort to soothe.

NURTURE BECOMES NATURE

Your extra effort to soothe your newborn will create a sweet baby.

There is, as we have seen, a significant connection between extreme fussiness/colic and later sleep problems. Not all extremely fussy/colicky babies become poor sleepers, though, and not all babies with sleep problems went through a period of extreme fussiness/colic. So let's look at infant sleep disorders in a more general way.

What Is a Good Night's Sleep?

We do not know what sleep is for. That is, we do not understand the biological function of sleep. Some say that sleep evolved to prevent our prehistoric ancestors from hurting themselves by bumping around in the dark!

The restorative power of sleep is a medical mystery. Ideally, sleep makes us feel at peace with ourselves and the world. However, some adults who were observed in a sleep laboratory said that they did not feel restored or rested even after appearing to sleep well. When their brain wave activity was analyzed, it sometimes appeared distorted. As I've noted, apparently the *quality* of sleep is as important as the *quantity*. The brain is not simply a chemical battery that is recharged by sleep.

We cannot ask babies if they have had a good night's sleep. We know about the qualitative differences in newborns' sleep patterns compared to those of older children and adults, but we cannot say what exactly are the elements of sleep that constitute "good-quality" sleep. We do know that tired parents, kept awake because their baby is crying, cannot easily function as loving mothers and fathers. A sleeping problem for your baby means a sleeping problem for you. You will be encouraged to know that many infant sleep disorders can be modified.

Does Your Baby Have a Sleep Problem?

Sometimes it is hard to tell if there is a sleep problem. Most mothers do not mind getting up a few times at night to feed their babies during the first few weeks. Typically, these babies awaken once or twice and immediately fall asleep after a ten- or fifteen-minute feeding. By several weeks, many babies awaken only once. Consider yourself fortunate if your baby sleeps this well. Not all infants do.

One mother of an extremely fussy/colicky infant told me that she had fantasies of having just one night of uninterrupted sleep. She could not remember, she said, when she last felt rested. In the playground, when other mothers talked about their babies rolling over or sitting up, she talked only about her baby not sleeping. She felt as though she wanted to attack those mothers whose children slept though the night; what had they done to deserve such luck? Her baby was several months old and still got up frequently every night and seemed never to want to sleep. There was a sharp edge of desperation in the mother's request for help. She was almost out of patience waiting for the baby to outgrow this problem.

What's Enough Sleep for a Newborn?

Sleep patterns in the newborn and during the first few months of life develop in a predictable fashion. During the first few weeks of life, there does not seem to be too much individual stability regarding the duration of sleep time. That is, some babies change from being good sleepers to bad sleepers and back again. However, between six and thirty-three months of age, the total sleep duration and longest sleep period didn't seem to change much in individual children. Individual infants who are brief-duration sleepers tend to remain that way. In this respect, sleep duration is like crying behavior and temperament—it shows little consistency at first, but after a few months it develops into a moderately stable individual characteristic. There are no significant sleep duration differences between boys and girls.

Solid Foods

Contrary to popular belief, sleep duration is not influenced by introducing solid foods. Slipping a little cereal into that night-time bottle will not really help. This fact has been documented in several studies where parents kept careful daily records of feeding and sleeping patterns. In France, there was a study of a group of infants who were never hungry. Because of birth defects involving their intestine or stomach, these infants were fed continuously through their veins. Even when their hunger rhythms were suppressed, the sleep-wake patterns remained unchanged. These babies had partial awakenings, called arousals or light sleep stages, just as often as healthy babies did. It seems that older infants partially or completely wake up because sometimes their brain, not their stomach, turns on an alarm clock. Of course, the infant will drink or nurse if offered the opportunity, but this is probably only to encourage the parent to stay a little longer. Frequent non-nutritive or recreational snacking in the middle of the night is a form of social interaction that soothes the baby back to sleep, but older infants learn quickly that if they do not suck when offered the opportunity, even if not hungry, then their mother or father will more quickly put them down and leave. Of course, sometimes a baby is hungry and does awaken to be fed.

Do breast-fed babies awaken more often than bottle-fed babies? Two studies on this subject, one of which was mine, reached opposite conclusions. However, there is no doubt that switching from breast to bottle or giving a supplemental bottle at night does not help babies consistently sleep through the night.

Night Wakings Are Normal

Awakenings at night are common in healthy infants, perhaps more common than their parents realize. Videotaping of infants at home has shown that they often awaken and return to sleep without calling out or crying. Brief episodes of night waking may reflect the biological sleep rhythms occurring at night. We know that during the non-REM state, sleep alternates between deep sleep and light sleep. In some children, the "light" stage is probably so light that they awaken partially or completely. This is not a problem unless it regularly disturbs the parents or keeps the child from getting enough sleep. As he grows, a child should develop his own resources to return to sleep without his parents' help.

In one study of over a hundred infants, researchers focused on awakenings that were accompanied by crying or fussing between midnight and 5:00 A.M. and that occurred at least once a week. By age three months, 70 percent of the babies had no night awakenings. By age six months, 83 percent of all babies were sleeping through the night, and by one year of age, 90 percent of babies slept through the night. Again, it should be noted that settling, or no night waking, was not related to birth weight or weight at age three months. Nor did the mother's personality appear to influence night waking. Also, the sex of baby was not a factor—in our study, girls awoke as often as boys. Interestingly, though, in our study parents perceived night waking to be a problem in their sons more often than in their daughters. Therefore, the *perception* of night waking as a problem—unlike extreme fussiness or difficult temperament—might be a bit sex-specific.

Parental Response

Infants who cry more and infants who sleep less over a twenty-four-hour period tend to have more night wakings than infants who cry less and sleep longer. In one study, the mothers' behavior toward the night waking was divided into three patterns: always feeding, never feeding, and sometimes feeding. The group of babies who were fed sometimes (described in the study as receiving "inconsistent handling") had significantly more awakenings.

It seems that inconsistent parental responses to night waking in older infants may encourage the habit, leading to more crying at night and more difficulties in the infant returning to sleep. This pattern is referred to as "trained night crying" and may be a common sequel to extreme fussiness/colic.

When Older Babies Wake at Night

Interestingly, about half of all infants who slept through the night before five months of age will begin night waking between six and twelve months. Many mothers have asked me, "What am I doing wrong? Why is he getting me up now after sleeping through the night these past months?" Perhaps the baby is now more curious and attentive to his surroundings. Another explantation is that at about four months of age, the baby's bedtime naturally drifts earlier, to between 6:00 and 8:00 P.M. With an earlier bedtime, it is also natural to feed him earlier. Thus, do not be surprised if between four and nine months of age, your child is now awakening once or twice for a feeding.

Night waking is a very common problem in older babies. Up to 40 percent of mothers describe problems in putting their children to sleep or problems in having them sleep through the night. If your child has a sleep problem, you are not alone.

I advise mothers of older babies to be consistent in their response to night waking. During the first few months, always respond promptly to your baby's crying. After four, five, and certainly six months, it might be time to change your tactics. Begin by trying to analyze whether there is any special reason for your baby waking at night.

Why Older Infants Awaken

The Wrong Sleep Schedule

Frequent night awakening sometimes seems to stem from an inappropriate sleep schedule. As you know, the body has its own internal rhythms, which ideally are in synchronization with deep sleep, light sleep, and wakefulness and collectively in sync with external light-dark cycles.

An imposed sleep schedule that is out of sync with the child's biological rhythms (such as body temperature, hormone secretion, etc.) might distort sleep patterns. Healthy, restorative sleep depends on timing the evening sleep onset and morning awakenings so that they occur when the body's temperature and endocrine levels are right. Sleep **timing** is as important as sleep **duration**.

Do not become fooled by claims that babies simply fall asleep whenever they are tired, regardless of circumstances. Yes, there are infants who can nap in the stroller, at a party, in the car, but most of these are exhausted infants who have collapsed. Most older infants never adapt to this kind of behavior. They do not rest well unless it is dark and quiet. Protect your baby's natural sleeping schedule. Do not try to force the baby to adjust her sleeping patterns to your lifestyle.

Parental Reinforcement

Parents often unintentionally contribute to their child's bad sleep habits. This is particularly true when the baby has been extremely fussy and the parents have gotten used to rocking and walking with him. When the child continues to want this attention at night, the parents do not realize they are reinforcing a bad habit. Often they are on "automatic pilot": it is 3:00 A.M., they are half asleep, and all they know is that they must promptly attend to the baby or the crying will surely get worse.

The same thing might happen during the day. Older infants who awaken frequently at night also take abnormally brief naps. The baby loses sleep, and the mother misses an opportunity to catch up on her own rest. Often these babies would learn to take longer naps if they were not picked up from their cribs at the first whimper or sleep sound.

Your Cranky Baby May Just Be Tired

Some parents, especially parents whose children have been extremely fussy/colicky, seem unable to tell when their babies are simply exhausted. Mothers often tell me that their infants do not need as much sleep as other infants. They report, no doubt accurately, that their babies never rub their eyes, yawn, put their heads down, or appear to be tired. These mothers do not realize that short-tempered, irritable, wigged-out behavior is also a sign of fatigue. Some mothers use the fact that their child occasionally falls asleep in stores, parks, or other noisy places as "proof" that the child has no sleep problem. On the contrary, this could mean that the infant has become so totally exhausted that he simply conks out.

Sleep deprivation affects mood much more than it does activity. We see this in adults who as part of an experiment reduce their nightly sleep duration. They were usually able to function well the next day. As long as they get about five hours of sleep a night, they can complete tasks, show adaptive physical skills, and appear to be quite capable of thinking through problems. But they feel awful. They report feeling slightly or very ill. Their temperament changes radically. So imagine the effect of insufficient sleep on a young child.

A good way to tell whether your child is getting enough sleep is to observe how he behaves when awakening. Babies who are sleeping enough are pleasant and playful; babies who never get enough rest awaken crying and grimacing and appear to be uncomfortable for no apparent reason. Remember that fussy, overactive behavior is as clear an indication of fatigue as is yawning or dozing off. It is not true that infants simply doze off whenever they are tired. Many need help in getting themselves to sleep.

Breast-feeding Versus Bottle-feeding and Family Bed Versus Crib

Introduction

As you read earlier, for 100 babies, about 80 percent will have common fussiness and of these 80 babies, 49 percent (39 babies) will have easy temperaments, 46 percent (37 babies) will have intermediate temperaments, and only 5 percent (4 babies) will have difficult temperaments. However, for those 20 percent of babies who had extreme fussiness/colic, the outcome at four months is quite different. In this group, only

14 percent (3 babies) will have easy temperaments, 59 percent (12 babies) will have intermediate temperaments, and 27 percent (5 babies) will have difficult temperaments. It is important to recognize that the largest group is the intermediate temperament group comprised of 49 babies or 49 percent of the total. Some of these babies with Intermediate temperament will closely resemble the Easy temperament babies or Difficult temperament babies. So for almost half of all babies (49 percent with Intermediate temperament) the advice regarding common fussiness leading to an Easy temperament and extreme fussiness/colic leading to a Difficult temperament only approximately fits. So please read the entire section and take out of it only that which applies to your baby.

The risk of developing sleeping problems after four months of age probably looks something like this:

LOWEST RISK FOR
SLEEP PROBLEMS AFTER 4 MONTHS

39% of common fussy babies who develop Easy temperaments

3% of extremely fussy/colic babies who develop Easy temperaments

37% of common fussy babies who develop Intermediate temperaments

12% of extremely fussy babies who develop Intermediate temperaments

4% of common fussy babies who develop Difficult temperaments

5% of extremely fussy babies who develop Difficult temperaments

HIGHEST RISK FOR
SLEEP PROBLEMS AFTER 4 MONTHS

Different temperaments and perhaps different paths to these temperaments will lead to different sleep strategies for your own child. It appears to me that the difficult temperament at four months mostly represents an extremely overtired baby and the easy temperament represents an extremely well-rested baby. Please keep in mind that biological factors within the baby such as elevated serotonin levels or immature development of sleep-wake rhythms may contribute to your baby's behavior during the first four months. But it is equally important to remember that there is enormous variability regarding the resources parents can draw on to soothe their babies. These are factors within the mother (for example, baby blues or postpartum depression), the husband (forcing a too-late bedtime, not helping to soothe the baby), the marriage (disagreements regarding family bed or breast-feeding), and the family (too many conflicting time pressures regarding other children, career events, not enough bedrooms, ability to hire housekeeping or baby care help, and so forth). So it is important to look at the big picture: your baby and the resources that you have available to help you soothe him. What will work for one family and their baby may not work for you and your baby. The goal is to develop a caring environment for the family.

"No Cry" Versus "Let Cry"

Some parents are strong believers in only one approach to soothing to sleep. They believe that there should never be any crying and that by always holding their baby, frequently nursing their baby, and sleeping with their baby, they can prevent extreme fussiness/colic and sleep problems from developing. They characterize their approach as "gently to sleep" or "attached parenting," a gentle, warm, child-centered style that enhances a sense of security because the baby is taught that the mother is always there. Proponents of this characterize other approaches as "cry it out" or "detached parenting," a cold, rigid, parent-centered style that creates a sense of abandonment because the baby is taught that the mother is unresponsive. They say that when the baby stops crying and sleeps, the baby has "given up" trying to communicate with his mother.

They claim that this stark contrast in parenting styles produces differences in babies and differences in the bonding between the child and her parents. However, there are problems with this outlook.

First, there is no evidence that one style or another produces a specific outcome. Second, babies themselves contribute a lot to what will easily work or not work. Third, fathers, siblings, and real-life family issues help shape how you soothe and comfort your baby and help her sleep. Fourth, there are methods in between always attending to night crying and never attending to night crying, such as "check and console" or "controlled crying," whereby the child is allowed to cry for only short periods of time. Fifth, there is evidence to show that with judiciously ignoring night crying, everyone becomes better rested and more able to deal with the stresses of raising a child.

"Attachment parenting" may or may not be your decision, but it may work well for 39 percent of babies who had common fussiness and developed an easy temperament. For these babies, everything you read in popular books about soothing and sleeping will likely work. This might even be true for the additional 40 percent (3 percent plus 37 percent) of babies in the next two groups of babies at a low risk for developing sleep problems. So, perhaps the majority of families, 76 percent (39 percent plus 37 percent), will have a fairly smooth course from common fussiness to easy soothing and sleeping and an additional 3 percent struggled from extreme fussiness/colic to get to a place where sleeping became easy at four months of age. Perhaps, for the majority of parents, the path did not involve any crying. There is no reason to be judgmental and criticize other parents who were not so fortunate.

However, there is an unfortunate minority (9 percent) of families who I believe become distressed or overwhelmed with the arrival of their baby because they lack sufficient resources to soothe their baby and/or the baby has extreme fussiness/colic, so the baby develops into an overtired four-month-old with a Difficult temperament. These parents may have started out with the crib, decided later to use the family bed for soothing and sleeping, but are still frustrated because after four months the baby still does not sleep well. Flexibility and sensitivity to your own baby and your own family situation are key.

Common Fussiness (80 Percent):
Low Risk for Sleep Problems After Four Months

Breast-feeding becomes much easier around four months of age or sooner for these babies because everyone is better rested and life is more predictable. At three to four months, your baby will start to show drowsy signs earlier in the evening. Instead of becoming sleepy between 8:00 and 10:00 P.M., she will become sleepy between 6:00 and 8:00 P.M. Respect her need to sleep and *begin the soothing process at night at the earlier hour*. If you are using the crib, simply put her to sleep earlier, but if you are using a family bed, you have to make some choices. The first is to go to bed much earlier yourself, but this is not usually practical. The second would be to lie down with her in your bed and create a safe nest or use a co-sleeper where she will sleep and then leave her after she has fallen asleep. The danger if you do not use a co-sleeper is that, unattended, she might roll off the bed and injure herself. The third is to transition her to a crib for the beginning of night sleep, and when she awakens for her first night feeding, then bring her to your bed for the remainder of the night. Because these are well-rested four-month-old babies, they are more adaptable and easy to transition to a crib. One strategy is to breast-feed at night, then pass the baby to the father, who soothes the baby in his arms and then puts the baby down in the crib. This breaks up the previous pattern of "mother, breast-feeding, sleep in parents' bed." If your baby cries, soothe your baby without picking her up. But if this fails, pick up your baby and, after soothing, try again.

If you are bottle-feeding your baby (formula or expressed breast milk) or breast-feeding and using a crib, expect to feed your baby about four to six hours after her last evening bottle and again early in the morning, around 4:00 to 5:00 A.M., until about nine months of age. Some bottle-fed babies are fed only once, around 2:00 or 3:00 A.M. If you are breast-feeding and using a family bed, you might feed your baby many times throughout the night.

If you are using a crib, there is more social stimulation as you pick up the baby, more time required to prepare the bottle, and more handling as you put your baby down to sleep again. Under these circumstances, feeding your baby more often than twice at night is likely to create a *night waking habit*. If you are breast-feeding, the obvious question is whether the awakenings at night, other than the two times mentioned, are due to hunger. If your breast milk supply has not kept pace with your baby's needs or has decreased, then your baby will awaken more at night because of thirst and/or hunger. Here are some ways to help determine whether the breast milk supply is sufficient. Are you thirsty throughout the day? If so, you are not drinking enough fluid. Are there some unusual stresses in your life, such as an important trip that you have to take, worry about balancing child care and working, or worry about returning to work and continuing to breast feed? Is your baby producing less urine? Has the volume of your expressed breast milk decreased? When offered a bottle of expressed breast milk or formula, does your baby now take a much larger feeding? Does he sleep better or longer after taking a bottle? Is he gaining weight at a slower rate? If you think that your child is hungry and you want to continue breast-feeding, then contact a lactation consultant through your pediatrician or maternity hospital.

"Check and Console" or
Graduated Extinction ("Controlled Crying")

If you are using a crib and your child is up frequently at night, consider using the method called "check and console" or "controlled crying" (also called "graduated extinction"). "Check and console" means that you go to your crying child promptly, or at most after five to ten minutes of crying, to soothe your baby either partially or completely back to sleep. You then leave your baby but return again when he next cries and repeat the process. The theory is that you are providing reassurance that you are still there. However, for an overtired or formerly extremely fussy/colicky baby, your repeated consoling efforts might be more socially stimulating than soothing, and therefore the method is likely to fail.

"Controlled crying" or "graduated extinction" means that when you hear your baby crying all night and you do not think your baby is hungry, delay your response for five minutes. Then go to your baby and soothe him back to sleep. Later if you again hear your baby, delay your response for ten minutes, and repeat the soothing procedure. At each time of crying that is not for hunger, delay your response an additional five minutes more. Alternatively, do a five-minute delay at first and increase the delay by five minutes every two days. Eventually, during one of the crying spells, your child will fall asleep before the delay period has ended. This is the beginning of returning to sleep unassisted and the beginning of the development of self-soothing for your baby.

If you are using a family bed, feeding often throughout the night is not likely to create a night waking habit. This is because your baby is partially asleep or barely awake when fed. Therefore, the risk of sleep fragmentation for both mother and baby from too much social stimulation is low. With early bedtimes in place, the family bed does not create any sleep problems, and in fact the family bed may have been part of the soothing solution during the first few months.

After the development of an earlier bedtime, the next sleep change is the evolution of a regular nap, around 9:00–10:00 A.M. This nap may initially be about forty minutes but will lengthen to one or two hours. The rest of the day may be snatches of brief and irregular sleep periods. After the morning nap develops, when the baby is a little older, the next regular nap develops and occurs around noon to 2:00 P.M. This nap will also lengthen to become about one to two hours. There may be a third mini-nap that is irregular and brief in the late afternoon.

These biological sleep rhythms are maturing for night sleep and day sleep. A common mistake is to approach the timing of naps and night sleep by strictly enforcing a by-the-clock routine. A temperamentally very regular baby might appear to be sleeping by the clock, but watching your baby's behavior for sleepy signs is more important than watching the clock.

Consider our original group of 100 babies. At four months, of the 49 babies with an Intermediate temperament, 37 of these babies (about 76 percent) had common fussiness when younger. Also, at four months, of the 42 babies with an Easy temperament, 39 of these babies (about 93 percent) had common fussiness when younger. So, out of the original 80 babies with common fussiness, the vast majority, 76 of these babies (37 plus 39) or **95 percent** of babies with common fussiness, is at a low risk for developing sleep problems because:

Parents are not likely to be stressed during the first four months.
The infant is likely to be well rested.
The infant is likely to be able to self-soothe.
At night, consolidated sleeping (long sleep duration) develops early.
During the day, regular and long naps naturally develop early, without parental scheduling.
If sleep problems exist, "no cry" solutions usually work.

Out of 100 babies, 80 have common fussiness and of these, 76 (95 percent of babies who had common fussiness) are good candidates for "no cry" sleep solutions.

Examples of "no cry" sleep solutions are the family bed, short intervals of wakefulness, watching for drowsy signs, and bedtime routines. All of these are more effective in babies who had common fussiness compared to babies with extreme fussiness/colic, but they are worth trying in all babies. Decrease the amount of stimulation for bedtime routines before sleep times during the day and at night. Reduce the level of noise, light, handling, playing, and activity. Choose from the following list those items that seem to work best for you and your baby, and try to be consistent in doing all of them in the same order.

Bedtime Routines

> **Room should be quiet, dark (use room-darkening shades), and warm, but not too warm**
> **Bathe**
> **Massage after bath, with smooth and gentle movements**
> **Dress for sleep**
> **Gentle rhythmic rocking, swinging in arms**
> **Swaddle if it comforts and relaxes baby, use warm blanket from clothes dryer**
> **Feed**
> **Lullaby, quiet singing or humming**
> **Favorite words, sounds, or phrases**
> **Put down drowsy but awake if possible (does not usually work for extremely fussy/colicky babies and may not work for commonly fussy babies around six weeks old), but do not deliberately awaken a sleeping child before putting her to bed**
> **Do not rush in at the first sound**
> **Never wake a sleeping baby (except newborns born early)**

Extreme Fussiness/Colic (20 Percent): High Risk for Sleep Problems After Four Months

Consider our original group of 100 babies. Out of the original 20 babies with extreme fussiness/colic, a minority of only 5 or **25 percent** is at risk for developing sleep problems at four months. However, at four months, of the 9 babies with a Difficult temperament, 5 babies or a majority of 56 percent (5 of the 9) had extreme fussiness/colic when younger. So most babies with extreme fussiness do not develop sleep problems later, but by four months of age, extremely fussy/colicky babies are overrepresented in the group at high risk for developing sleep problems. Another way to look at this is that only 9 out of the original

100 babies, a tiny group, or **9 percent** of all babies develop a Difficult temperament and subsequent sleep problems because:

Parents are likely to be stressed during the first four months.
Infant is likely to be overtired.
Infant is likely to be only parent-soothed.
At night, fragmented sleep (night waking) persists.
During the day, irregular and brief naps persist.
If sleep problems exist, "let cry" solutions might be necessary.

Out of 100 babies, 20 have extreme fussiness/colic and of these, 5 might require "let cry" sleep solutions. Also, 80 have common fussiness and of these, 4 might require "let cry" sleep solutions.

I believe that it is in this small percentage of babies that you have the most severe and hard-to-solve sleep problems. There are two reasons for this. The first is that the biologic factors that led to extreme fussiness/colic in the first place in 5 of the 9 babies might persist and frustrate parents' best efforts to solve sleep problems. The second is that the social or family factors that led to parents' distress and difficulty in soothing for 4 of the 9 babies who had common fussiness might persist and interfere with establishing healthy sleep habits. These social or family issues, of course, might also be a factor for those babies with extreme fussiness/colic, either caused by the extreme fussiness or independent of the extreme fussiness/colic.

Breast-feeding these babies may be difficult because everyone is tired. As the biological need for an earlier bedtime develops, the best strategy is to temporarily try to do whatever it takes to maximize sleep and minimize crying. The plan is to keep your child as well rested as possible in order to buy time for the development of more mature sleep/wake rhythms. Once these rhythms are developed, they may be used as an aid to help your child sleep better. For example, the breast-feeding mother might have to take her baby into her bed and nurse her to sleep at the earlier bedtime. However, real-life events, such as returning to work or caring for other family members, might not give you the luxury of always sleeping with your baby whenever she appears to be sleepy.

You may have wanted to practice "attachment parenting" and spent much of the first four months soothing your baby, but now she is heavy when you carry her all day. More importantly, she is more alert and curious and able to resist sleep for the pleasure of your company even when she needs to sleep. This natural desire for social contact may interfere with the equally natural development of healthy sleep habits. It is difficult to have clarity of thought and purpose when everyone is tired. What really is "natural" or "unnatural"?

It is "natural" for all babies to fuss or cry, for all mothers to want to soothe their babies and to be distressed by their baby's fussiness or crying. It is "natural" that more fussiness/crying for the baby means less sleep for the mother, that mother's distress increases with her own sleep loss. It is "natural" that other people are available to help care for the baby in tribal cultures. It is "natural" to breast feed, to change your baby when soiled, to feed your baby when hungry, to soothe your baby when fussy, to sleep your baby when tired. And it is "natural" to sleep with your baby and to carry your baby everywhere in most, but not all, tribal cultures. In some tribal cultures, mothers leave their baby totally alone all day while they work.

It is "unnatural" to have urban stimulation (noises, voices, shopping trips, errands), day care (naps not occurring when sleepy, too late a bedtime at night), mother working outside the home (returning late causing a late bedtime), or social isolation (mother is alone and becomes exhausted with too many things to do). It is "unnatural" to deliberately wake your baby and remove your breast before putting your baby down to sleep "awake." It is "unnatural" to try to force-feed your baby at night to try to make him sleep better. It is "unnatural" to not breast-feed your baby. Is all this brand-new? Probably not. We know that during the Egyptian and Roman Empires, wealthy women did not breast feed their babies but instead they hired wet nurses.

Can you change your lifestyle so that your child will receive all the soothing to sleep she wants at those times when she needs to sleep? Can you prevent too much social stimulation from interfering with sleep at those precise times when she needs to sleep even if it means ignoring your child's crying? These are difficult questions that many families never have to confront. Many popular books on children's sleep give simple answers or easy solutions that often fail in this group of 9 percent of infants.

Gradual Approach

I would like to describe a gradual approach to be tried in infants three, four, or five months old, right after the extreme fussiness/colic seems to have eased.

These are sensitive months in the development of a baby's crying and sleep patterns. In infants under three or four months, crying comes directly out of biological needs—for food and fluid, dry skin, contact and comfort, and, in the case of extreme fussiness/colic, relief from the unknown causes. Babies under three to four months *cannot* be spoiled or taught bad habits by your response to their crying. Infants over four to six months old, by contrast, can indeed learn to cry in order to get their parents to do certain things. Older infants may learn to cry for attention. And older infants may learn how to keep themselves from falling asleep. Remember that parents should be teachers!

Basically, you will gradually decrease the amount of soothing you do when you put your baby to sleep. The goal is to let him develop internal resources to fall asleep, called self-soothing skills. At the same time, you will be teaching yourself how to be the parent of a baby who does not always need your immediate attention for soothing. Each family is different. Babies become ready at different ages. Please think of these suggestions as general principles rather than rigid rules. But do try to understand

the basic theory: gradually, consistently cut back on the elabo-
rate procedure you go through to get your child to sleep, until
he is "weaned" a little from your soothing efforts and can do
some of it on his own. This is called a "fade procedure."

Step 1: Do Not Pick Him Up

Your baby is now around three to four months old. His extreme fussiness is not as bad as it once was, but he still awakens
frequently at night. Begin by figuring out how often your baby
is truly hungry at night. Ask yourself how often he really sucks
with enthusiasm. Listen to the quality of the crying—true
hunger crying in the older infant has a sound all its own. Cal-
culate how much time has passed since last feeing: if it is less
than two hours, your baby is almost certainly not hungry.

Now that you have decided how often you should feed your
baby at night, pick him up and feed him at those times, but
do not pick him up at any other times. This is the first step: Do
not pick the baby up unless you are going to feed him.

Do you just ignore his cries? No. Go into his room and sit
beside him. Pat him, stroke him, or hold his hand. Let him see
you, and let him see you looking at him. Talk or sing. Keep it
calm and gentle. Stay beside him as long as necessary, even
until he falls asleep. Respond promptly each time he cries—
but do not pick him up unless it is time for feeding.

If your baby persists with inconsolable screaming despite
your soothing efforts, stop. Go back to what method(s) you
were using before. Try this suggestion again in a few weeks.
Once you are able to calm him down and pick him up only for
feeding, move on to Step 2.

Step 2: Cut Back on Your Responses

Begin to cut back on what you do as you sit beside your baby.
You might give up the eye contact first, keeping the room dark
and staying out of view. Later, stop rocking the crib or stroking
your baby. Go slowly and see what works. The goal after a week
or two is to reach the stage where you are merely resting your
hand on the baby's back or quietly holding his hand. You still

respond promptly and take as much time as necessary to lull him into a deep sleep. Pay attention to how much time this usually takes, and proceed to Step 3.

Step 3: Spend Less Time

Try to reduce, by a minute or two at a time, the amount of time you sit with your baby. Respond promptly, but slip away a little sooner. If you find that he startles and cries when you leave, go right back. After several days or a few weeks, you may find that just putting your hand on this tummy or back for a few minutes magically induces sleep. That will be a good accomplishment. You will have loosened the connection your baby used to make between long, complex social interactions and falling asleep. Now he may do it with only a quick reassurance of your presence.

Step 4: Wait a While

Now, for the first time, wait a bit before you go to the baby. Give him a chance to settle down by himself. Do not wait so long that a full crying storm develops, because then he will need lengthy calming. Wait two or three minutes to start; wait longer when you feel you can. Learn to recognize the drowsy, testing cries and wait them out. Remember, babies make a lot of noises when they sleep. Your reward will come on those nights when you hear a call, some whimpering, a faint cry, and then silence.

Will It Work?

You need not take all these steps. If, for example, you had success with Steps 1, 2, and 3, but find that your baby always develops crying fits when you try Step 4, stop where you are. You have already made fine progress. Live with those brief nighttime visits a few more months until the child outgrows this dependence on your presence. (Sometimes this procedure works only when the father, not the mother, responds to the night awakenings.)

Be patient.

If this plan does not work at all for you, make sure you and your husband, and whoever else might tend to the baby at night, are all being consistent. You should always know how you plan to deal with the baby at night, and you should not give in and pick him up "just this once." It is also possible that your child is not ready; try again in a few weeks. I cannot predict whether this "fade procedure" will work for a particular family, but it is based on tested principles and I feel certain it is worth a serious try.

Focus on the Morning Nap

When your formerly extremely fussy/colicky baby is 4 months of age or older, try to establish a morning nap. The reason that you should focus on the morning nap is because a regular and long morning nap develops before an afternoon nap. Also, you are more likely to be successful with the morning nap because your baby is more rested in the morning following a night's sleep.

First, keep the entire wakeful period from the end of the night to the beginning of the nap to *no more than one hour*. This ultrashort period of wakefulness helps prevent the overtired state. Declare when you think the night's sleep has ended: 5, 6, or 7 A.M., and then look at your watch. This is the "wake-up" time or the "start of day" time. Within one hour clean, change, and feed your baby, then attempt to soothe him back to sleep. This means that there is really no time or little time for playing. Exposing him to bright natural light during this one-hour wakeful period might help, as morning light seems to help set biological rhythms and help regulate sleeping patterns.

Second, soothe for only several minutes. Soothing here may include breast-feeding or bottle feeding. Then put your child down in his crib or lie down with him in your bed. At this particular moment, he may be asleep, awake, or in an in-between state. You do not care; you put him down or lie down with him. Your custom in the past may have been to always hold him until he was in a deep state because you observed that if you put him down awake or in a twilight state he always cried hard.

Now that he is about four months old his sleep rhythms are more developed.

> **You can use his natural or internal sleep rhythms as an aid to help him fall asleep.**

This occurs if and only if you are synchronizing putting the baby down to sleep with the time when drowsiness is surfacing. If available, fathers should help

> **Be consistent.**

soothe, bottle-feed, or lie down with their baby. Fathers can also be involved even if the mother is breast-feeding. The mother can breast-feed or use the breast to soothe, then pass the baby to the father, who soothes and puts the baby down or lies down with the baby.

Putting the baby down or lying down with the baby after soothing but when the baby is not in a deep sleep state is the beginning of allowing your baby to develop some self-soothing skills. You are beginning to wean him from the expectation that you will always lull him into a deep sleep state.

Third, when you put him down or lie down with your baby, if he cries, ignore the crying for five to ten minutes—maybe a little less, maybe a little more, depending on the type of cry. The point is, you do not immediately pick up and soothe your baby when he cries. If, after crying, you do pick him up or soothe him, then you have two choices: (1) the crying may have been so stressful to you that you go out with your baby for a walk to relax, calm down, and try it again the next morning, and (2) your baby is now falling asleep in your arms or at your breast because you have picked him up and soothed him at the breast, so you decide to repeat the process to see if he will stay asleep.

The One- to Two-Hour Window of Wakefulness

Once the morning nap is established, try this procedure for subsequent naps. Keep the interval of wakefulness between the naps to a maximum of two hours. Within one to two hours, babies quickly become overtired, and then it is difficult for them to fall asleep. The reason that the overtired state interferes with good sleeping is that when you are overtired, the body's adaptive biological response to fight the fatigue is to produce stimulating chemicals. This "second wind" was important for early humans' survival—it allowed them to continue the hunt, to fight, or to flee—but this "second wind" interferes with the ability to fall asleep and stay asleep. I do not mean that you should put your child on a two-hour sleep schedule. The correct idea is to watch for drowsy cues developing within one to two hours after awakening and then to quickly begin your soothing-to-sleep efforts. If you do not see drowsy cues, try to soothe your child to sleep anyway after one to two hours of wakefulness.

In these older babies, the quality of sleep is probably better if it is motionless. The movement in strollers, swings, and cars might prevent them from getting the full restorative power of long, deep sleep. By about four months of age, a commonly fussy baby will be taking a morning nap that starts between 9:00 and 10:00 A.M. and an afternoon nap that starts between 12 noon and 2:00 P.M. Each nap will last about one or two hours. This pattern may emerge much later in extremely fussy/colicky babies.

Do I Have to Put My Baby Down While She Is Still Awake?

It is *not* necessary to put the baby down awake. Consistency in your style of soothing to sleep is what is important so that your child associates certain behaviors on your part with falling asleep. Extremely fussy/colicky newborns often settle down and drift off to sleep best when sucking at the breast or bottle. In my practice, most mothers do not deliberately attempt to put their child down to sleep when awake, and most babies in my practice sleep well.

There are two common methods of soothing styles for lulling your child asleep. Method A is soothing for several minutes only, soothing may include feeding, then put your baby down whether he is or is not yet asleep. This rarely works for extremely fussy/colic babies under three to four months of age. Method B is soothing as long as is required for the new-born to drift into a deep sleep state and soothing usually in-cludes feeding. This is the method used by most parents of extremely fussy/colicky babies. Method A and Method B are used to put your baby asleep for daytime sleep or naps. After four months of age, try to be consistent during the day and al-ways use either Method A or Method B. At night, do whatever bedtime routine seems to work best, but be consistent and do it early before your baby becomes overtired.

A totally separate issue is what to do when you hear your baby cry in the middle of night. Around four months of age, extreme fussiness decreases and your baby is more able to sleep at night. Let's consider two approaches for these older infants.

Bottle-feeding and Crib

At night, if your baby is in a bassinet or crib, plan to feed your baby once or twice, but not more than two times. The first is in the middle of the night and the second is early in the morning. You might even bring your baby into your bed for the first or second feeding. It is your choice. If you go more often, if you assume every sleepy sound is a hunger cry, then you will create a night waking habit. The night waking habit emerges because of the stimulation to wakefulness that occurs when you move him about in order to bottle-feed him. By ignoring sleepy sounds and other cries, your baby will learn to return to sleep unassisted by you. By indiscriminately responding to all these cries, this learning process does not occur. The soothing style you use to put your child down to sleep at naps and the bed-time routine at the beginning of night sleep has nothing to do with how well he sleeps at night. How well he sleeps at night depends on how well you can tell the difference between his need to be fed, which you always respond to, and other vocal-izations, which you ignore.

At night, try to have a soothing to sleep or bedtime routine that is consistent. But this nighttime routine may be different from Method A or Method B.

Breast-feeding and Family Bed

At night, if you are sleeping with your baby and breast-feeding, then you might feed much more often throughout the night and never create a night waking habit. This is because your baby is barely awake at the time when you nurse. The mother's sleeping brain is exquisitely sensitive to her baby's sounds.

So requesting that mothers put their child down to sleep when their baby is awake not only does not make sense, it is contrary to what most mothers instinctively feel is right.

AS EXTREME FUSSINESS ENDS

1. **Keep the intervals of wakefulness brief; no more than 2 hours.**
2. **Use motionless sleep.**
3. **Be consistent in soothing style.**

The Treatment of Trained Night Crying

Let the Baby Alone

The best way to manage trained night crying in a formerly extremely fussy/colicky infant, who is bottle fed and in a crib, over four or five months of age, is to feed him only once or twice and all other times to consistently leave him alone at night, even if he cries. This always works if and only if the bedtime is reasonably early and naps are developing. Within a few days you will see a reduction in the frequency and duration of nighttime crying spells. Before long your baby will learn to sleep through the night with one or two awakenings for feeding.

Learn to Be Consistent

Consistency is the key to breaking this habit. Parents who have been through the ups and down and twists and turns of extreme fussiness/colic may find this a big change. For as long as you have known your baby, you have had to be flexible; now you must make an about-face and be consistent. Please believe that your baby is ready for a routine, even if he has never been in the past. Realize that you have a few habits of your own to change: you will have to stop letting the baby "call the tune." You will now set the schedule, and let the baby cry until he sleeps. You will have to harden your heart a tiny bit, after months of flooding your baby with sympathy and prompt attention. Once you and he make the transition your life will be easier and more predictable and, believe me, your baby will be happier too. But you are going to have to teach yourselves a new pattern of parenting.

Reduce External Stimulation

For the child who had extreme fussiness/colic and/or is very stimulus-sensitive, then reducing the amount of external stimulation might help your baby sleep.

Begin by modifying the child's bedroom. To get the room completely dark, mount opaque blackout shades outside the molding of the window and hold them in place with curtains or tape. Obviously, there should be no night-light, and the door should be almost completely closed. If you need to cool the room with a window air-conditioner, run it before the infant goes to bed and turn it off while he sleeps. Keep the windows closed to eliminate street noises. You might cover central air ducts to reduce the noise of the heating or air-conditioning system. A steady background noise from a vaporizer, humidifier, or white-noise machine might help drown out intermittent sounds. Of course, you should not run the garbage disposal, dishwasher, or vacuum cleaner during naptime. If possible, turn the telephone ringer off and lower the volume on your answering machine. Do not go into the baby's room or even open his door to peek in. Crib toys and stuffed animals should be removed except for one special blanket or doll. The bedroom is a place to sleep; it is not a playground.

Making your child's room pitch dark and quiet should be thought of as only a temporary measure. You do not want to make your child permanently dependent upon these conditions in order to sleep. In the future, you want to be able to have dinner parties and go on vacations and have your child sleep. A remarkable change occurs when your baby sleeps well for several weeks or months in a peaceful environment. Gradually, the child appears less jumpy, less irritable, less restless, and more able to attend to one thing at a time. This overall decreased behavioral responsiveness suggests a decrease in the state of arousal, which probably results from the change to better-quality sleep or sleep that is uninterrupted and prolonged. Now that the child is better rested, he is less likely to fight going to sleep and he is less likely to be thoroughly awakened when the telephone rings or the garage door opens. He still may be a light sleeper compared to other children, but he will not behave as if his nervous system was always excitable.

Begin with Bedtime

Maintain a fairly regular sleep schedule, with an early bedtime and wake-up time at about the same hour every day. An exception is to move the bedtime much earlier if your child has overly brief naps during the day. Establish nighttime rituals and stick to them. Fathers should be involved in these rituals and should sometimes place the child in bed after the mother has nursed. Read a book or sing the same medley of songs every night. Make bedtime a happy time; do not act as though you expect a struggle, and do not make going to bed seem like a punishment. The earlier the bedtime the better in order to avoid the overtired state.

Children will learn to fall asleep (or fall back asleep if they wake later) because it is dark, quiet, and boring in the bedroom alone. Once you start leaving the child alone at night, do not relent. The goal is to teach her that she will get no further companionship from you until morning.

Parents: No Excuses!

It is difficult to say that it is all right to leave a baby alone and let her cry. Sometimes a father who is the sole wage earner demands that the mother quiet the child so that he can get his rest. Mothers also worry about disturbing other people: children, resident in-laws, or neighbors.

Sometimes parents are afraid of hurting their baby's feelings or making him angry. They are supported in this fear by a number of popular infant-care books that say leaving a child to cry will make him feel abandoned, give him a complex, and cause him to resent you forever. In my opinion, it is absurd to believe that a few hours of crying will undo the thousands of hours of love, tenderness, and security that you give your baby. Children are very resilient; their psyches are tough, they appear to forget quickly, and they do not carry grudges. I guarantee that even when it has taken your little guy hours to cry himself to sleep, he will be cheerful, affectionate, and glad to see you in the morning. Anyway, this may be the first occasion in your child's life that you will have to do something for his good health that might seem to make him unhappy at the time, but it certainly will not be the last.

Prolonged uninterrupted sleep that is occurring on the right schedule is a health habit. You can teach good sleep habits just as you would teach other important health habits such as hand washing, regular exercise, teeth brushing, good nutrition, buckling up in cars, wearing a helmet when on a bike, and sun safety.

Occasionally parents have hidden conflicts that get in the way of their resolve. Perhaps a mother simultaneously wants to stay at home and nurse her baby but also wants to return to work. Depending on how she is feeling at any given time, she may leave the child alone or she may rush to his side. This inconsistent behavior encourages the night awakening and crying.

Some parents cannot let their child cry because they imagine some illness is causing the night awakening. They may exaggerate minor common colds or rashes. One family decided that their fourteen-month-old child was awakening early every morning because of a gastrointestinal problem. Undigested vegetable matter in the child's stools "proved" this. I examined the stools, reassured the mother that many healthy children have frequent loose stools, and told her that these same children often have no sleep problems. When the family realized that the child would outgrow this diarrhea and that it did not mean he had a disease, they focused their efforts on behaviorally managing the sleep problem by letting the child get himself back to sleep.

Another family blamed all nighttime problems on teething. From the age of six months on, the child was imagined to be constantly suffering from some painful tooth eruption. But surprise—letting this baby cry at night cured the teething pain for good.

Make the Decision

Helping your child break a bad sleep habit is a major task. It is usually quickly accomplished, but it will be hard on you. It might be worth waiting until you can take time off from work. You may be up all night or get only fragments of sleep, and working during this time could be difficult, if not dangerous.

Be sure to discuss your plans with your other children. Explain to them that the baby will be crying at night because you are breaking a bad habit. Make sure your older children know that you are not punishing the baby and that he's not suffering. Let the older children temporarily "camp out" in your bedroom at night if the baby's crying bothers them or disturbs their sleep.

Warn your neighbors if they are within earshot. Explain that the treatment will last only a few nights and will put an end to the nighttime crying, which has probably been bothering them, too.

And Then Do It

Don't be surprised when your baby cries for a long time and with great gusto the first couple of nights. She wants a return of the old style of parental attention and will put forth extra energy to that end. Remember that your baby will not hurt her lungs or vocal cords, choke, suffocate, or anything else. Do not become alarmed. Do not weaken. Do not peek into the bedroom; this will only recharge your baby's battery.

During the few days of sleep training, there will be more crying per day than ever before. But—and this is a very important point—if you allow an overtired state to develop and persist, there will be much more total crying spread out over months or years. Parents naturally tend to worry too much about the possible harmful effects of a few days of crying and fail to see the long-term damaging effects of a stressed family living with a chronically overtired child, then toddler, then adolescent.

When your baby cries and cries the first night, the mother should wear earplugs, take long showers, go into the basement, or go for a walk—anything to get away from the crying! It will tear at your heart. Let your husband sit outside the door of the infant's room. Use your ingenuity: One family lived in a small house with no place to escape from the baby's crying. The father borrowed a friend's camper-van and parked it in the driveway at night. On alternate nights the parents took turns sleeping in the van so that one parent was always rested. Another family found that only if both parents stayed together could they give each other the strength to resist the temptation to rush to the baby's side. Do what works for you.

The typical sequence is for the baby to cry for a few hours the first night and to awaken frequently throughout the night. Often the second night is worse, as your baby tries even harder to get back to the old pattern of enjoying the company of parents at night. Or during the second night there might be a briefer initial crying period and fewer, briefer night awakenings. The parents usually note that the morning after the second night the child awakens later than usual. He is probably tired from two nights of strenuous crying. By the third night, there is substantially less crying. Many parents report that for the first time the child appears tired around the bedtime hour. Usually there are few to no awakenings by the fourth or fifth night.

If It Doesn't Work

If you let your baby cry according to these suggestions and you see no improvement after a few days, perhaps the child is too young. If you see no improvement after four days, revert back to whatever strategy worked best to maximize sleeping and minimize crying. I have seen this plan fail (though rarely) in babies five and six months of age. However, by eight or nine months, when the parents try it again, it always works. I believe this four-day treatment is worth trying every four weeks from six months on.

Improvement

When the parents succeed in encouraging regular sleep habits, the child becomes much easier to live with. The increased rest for both child and parents makes a world of difference. After several months without night awakenings, the parents can relax the strict routine somewhat. They can take trips with the child, cope with an illness (such as an ear infection) that interrupts sleep, and be less rigid in maintaining the sleep schedule when social activities occur. Once the special event or ear infection is over, the parents should resume their consistent regular handling and the child will again start sleeping through the night.

Drugs to Make Your Baby Sleep

I have saved discussion of sedative drugs for last because I do not believe they can solve behavioral problems. It has been my experience that parents view drugs as a quick fix and make no effort to change their behavior. Therefore, despite a few days of improvement, the problems continue. I don't think drugs have any role in the management of trained night crying. One popular book emphasizes unrestricted breast-feeding and the family bed as the solution to all sleep problems, but then the author states that if problems still occur, use chloral hydrate to knock out the baby! This is wrong and only reflects on the author's misunderstanding of what sleep is all about. No melatonin, no progesterone, no tryptophan, no drugs.

Not All Night Waking Is a Problem

I want to emphasize that this approach—letting the overtired older baby cry as long as necessary—is appropriate only in the case of trained night crying. If your baby awakens at night only occasionally, if his fussiness comes from a verified fever or ear infection pain, or if he seems to need comfort when there has been a change in his life, then by all means comfort him. He will not develop a bad habit if you go to him a few nights out of the month. Just be sure you are not using teething or what happened during the day as an excuse night after night.

As Dr. Illingworth, the dean of infant crying research, wrote: "No baby should ever be left crying for prolonged periods—except when one is breaking a habit produced by mismanagement."

Mothers Talk About Their Experiences

The cycle of exhaustion, fussiness, poor sleep habits, and sleep deprivation is a baffling one to families in the midst of it. On the surface, nothing seems terribly amiss, yet everything is wrong. Baby and parents reinforce each other's bizarre schedules. Other problems are blamed. Where there once was extreme fussiness, parents assume it mutated into new and equally distressing forms.

Following are accounts by some of the mothers who have consulted me for their children's sleep problems. All of these babies once had extreme fussiness/colic. I have quoted at length in order to convey the relentless, unpredictable nature of trained night crying. Some of these stories are bound to make any mother feel lucky by comparison. While they show how a sleep problem can get out of hand and how it can masquerade as something else, they also show how easily it can be corrected once it is identified.

First is a thirty-two-year-old mother with professional training. You will notice that despite the professionals she consulted and all of the approaches she tried, no one addressed the issue of sleep, the most obvious problem.

Looking back, my concern for Joel started in the hospital. The nurses said that he cried all the time in the nursery and would bring him to me for feeding and comforting—often at hourly intervals. I left the hospital exhausted. Since Joel is my only child, and I am an only child, I had little to compare him with. The first three months home were brutal and, although I suspected as much, I didn't admit until he was almost four months old that his behavior wasn't normal. I guess that is something no parent ever wants to see or believe.

Life with Joel during those months was disruptive and draining. He had no schedule, slept very little (maybe eight hours in a twenty-four-hour period, in one-to-three-hour blocks), and cried a good deal of the time. Meeting Joel's needs filled my day; besides feeding him and changing him, the major task was keeping him quiet. Several things worked at different times: walking him in his infant seat, especially outside, while singing; car rides; visiting anywhere; carriage rides. We became vagabonds. Often a day would include several carriage rides, some lasting up to ninety minutes; a trip to the store; and a visit with a friend. After only five hours of interrupted sleep each night, I found it hard to get back to sleep. I'd be exhausted. But I couldn't stop moving.

Bedtime for Joel was usually 10:00 P.M. We couldn't just put him in his crib. I had to rock him, walk him, nurse him, and lay him down ever so gently. He would usually wake up once during the process and we'd have to begin again. The process in total generally took an hour. I'd then fall into bed hoping I could un-wind and get to sleep quickly, knowing that I'd be up two to three times that night and up for good at 5:00 to 5:30 A.M.

I waited as patiently as I could for Joel to get his act together. I'd heard that at three to four months colicky fussy babies miracu-lously became settled and slept through the night. At three months Joel did sleep through the night for approximately six days. A start, we thought, but it quickly ended.

By Joel's four-month checkup, I was completely demoralized. I prayed he had an ear infection to explain his irritability and lack of sleep. When he was given a clean bill of health, I cried. The pe-diatrician suggested a sedative. When I filled the prescription the pharmacist told me that the medication was an antihistamine, one sometimes used to make a fussy baby go to sleep.

I decided then to get a second opinion. Joel could get to sleep—he just needed help staying asleep. I put the medication aside and headed for the telephone. Although I felt physically drained myself—hanging on by my fingertips, having to go on despite my physical exhaustion—my greatest anxiety was reserved for Joel. I wanted to help him. He was in discomfort, and the world must have seemed a terrible place to him. I felt so responsi-ble, yet unable to reckon with what I needed to do, and no one to tell me. He wasn't a colicky baby anymore, but he cried a lot and couldn't be comforted. It was obvious that he wanted to sleep, but couldn't. I felt so helpless.

The new pediatrician was supportive but gave few answers. Joel seemed healthy. We did detect a hip problem—though nothing painful enough to explain the poor sleeping pattern.

During this time, I also contacted the local Birth to Three pro-gram for help. The child development specialist there felt that Joel was hypersensitive and irritable, lacked bilateral integration, and showed an uncharacteristic-for-his-age strong preference for his right side. She agreed that Joel was different from other babies and might need a different approach. She gave recommendations for dealing with the motor delays but seemed cool to the idea of letting Joel cry. Joel also saw a physical therapist from Birth to Three who confirmed what the child development specialist saw. He suggested that the cause could be just a developmental delay, a nervous system that wasn't quite ready to stabilize, or a mild brain injury that might or might not repair itself with time.

Now I was busy with exercises for Joel's hip that the physical therapist recommended as well as other activities suggested by the Birth to Three specialists to help improve Joel's left side functioning and bilateral integration. No one addressed the issue of sleep. By the time Joel was eight months old, his irritability had decreased some but his sleep patterns had not improved. On the days he was rested, he was charming. In fact, even when he wasn't rested he could appear jovial and content—as long as we kept moving. At this time I issued an edict: no more night feeding. I'd feed Joel at 9:30 P.M., his bedtime, and at 5:00 A.M., his waking time, but not in between. I felt he was ready for this.

My husband became Joel's "walker." Once or twice a night, he'd go to Joel and walk him back to sleep. The first few months of Joel's life had been mine; these next few were his father's. In the early months, it was "Joel must be hungry" or "I have to go to work," so Mother dealt with Joel. Now Mother bowed out and Dad finally began to believe that maybe something really was wrong with Joel. Mother didn't actually sleep more, but at least I spent more time in bed!

Our marriage was really strained during Joel's first year. We couldn't take out our frustrations on Joel, so we took them out on each other. Looking back, some of my behavior was hysterical and irrational. My husband seemed to do a lot of denying. We both realized our behavior was related to physical exhaustion, but we seemed unable to reverse the direction.

I saw an announcement in a local paper about an infant sleep disorder center. They sent me a questionnaire; I filled it out immediately. The questions make me think perhaps there were other children like Joel.

At the center Dr. Weissbluth agreed that Joel was healthy. Joel, he said, just needed some sleep, and so did his parents. The fact that the doctor had seen other children like Joel and that they had improved was reassuring. The doctor's confidence in his procedure was encouraging, but did he really know Joel? I was hooked by the doctor's promise to follow up by phone to check Joel's progress during the course of the treatment to get Joel to sleep. I could scream at him if it didn't work and he could share in the frustration.

Something inside told me that at nine and a half months Joel was ready and I was ready too. I liked the doctor's picture of my assuming a parenting role with Joel—not letting him cry but teaching him to sleep, letting him become independent and learning to get to sleep on his own.

Anyway, we all were ready. And, with a few setbacks, it worked in two days. I believe it worked because Joel's system had matured. Could it have worked sooner? Maybe he was ready a month earlier, but earlier than that, I'm not sure.

It helped us not only to be given permission to let Joel get himself to sleep in his own crib, but in fact to be told it was a parental responsibility. With a baby who slept through the night and napped twice a day, our lives not so much improved as began again. I feel we're normal now.

The distressing sequence of events is not uncommon. Nor is it uncommon that the mother tried everything, took all advice, drove herself frantic, even believed for a time that her son had a brain injury, when all they needed was sleep.

Another mother, a twenty-seven-year-old homemaker with a partial college education, described her experiences ("our ten-month ordeal") with her first daughter as follows:

My husband, Kevin, and I were blessed with a beautiful baby girl on June 13, 1981. We were so happy, but it was definitely a change in the household. I started breast-feeding and I wasn't very successful, so after two weeks Melissa was put on formula. I really don't think it was easy for Melissa to settle in. Two weeks after she was born we moved from an apartment into a house. It was a really chaotic time for all of us.

After a month or so in the house we all felt better being settled in, but we became sure of one thing—Melissa had extreme fussiness. She was not on any kind of schedule and the most she slept was about four hours at one time. This was not always consistent either. At this time we didn't consider her not sleeping too much of a problem. Being new parents, we weren't exactly sure how things were supposed to be or what we should do.

After the colic stage was supposed to have ended we started worrying because Melissa still was not sleeping. Consulting her pediatrician on many occasions, we tried everything: different formulas, Donnatal, chamomile tea, warm clothes on her tummy, Tylenol. We even tried the Rail Runner, a train put on the rail of her crib that played music and moved back and forth very slowly. Within fifteen minutes Melissa was supposed to be sound asleep. No luck.

For ten months, nothing we did worked. During this time everyone had advice to give us. Some of the comments were: "Maybe you just have a baby that won't sleep." "You are spoiling her by holding her all the time so she will sleep." "Just leave her in the crib and let her scream." "When she's ready she'll fall into a schedule." I was so confused! Kevin and I would talk about the situation and our worry was that something was wrong with Melissa, even though she appeared to be a totally healthy baby.

We loved her so much that we worked our schedules around Melissa. We both were like walking zombies. I would hold Melissa and give her a bottle so she might get an hour or two of sleep. As soon as I laid her in the crib she would start crying. At times I was so tired I would lay her next to me on our bed and pray for one hour of sleep. I would spend all day in my pajamas tending to Melissa. Since Kevin's sleep was more important due to a full-time job, I would sleep for two to three hours when he got home from work and the rest of the time I would catnap when Melissa did. The longest period of time I was up without sleep was seventy-two hours. I had to call Kevin home from work because I couldn't stand up anymore.

It was a physically and emotionally trying time for Kevin and myself. We argued a lot and we really weren't communicating with each other. We were both just too tired to even talk sometimes. We didn't have much of a love life, but it was our strong love for each other that held all three of us together. I would cry a lot and pray that soon Melissa would sleep.

Melissa was so happy and good under the circumstances. I would look at her while she was awake and be amazed. How can she be so playful and alert? She's not getting enough sleep! She even had dark circles under her eyes.

Well, after ten months Kevin saw an excerpt on the news about sleep problems in children. We decided to get more information. I called and we were sent a questionnaire to fill out. Kevin and I felt this was our last hope.

We talked with Dr. Weissbluth about Melissa and he checked her over. After our discussion he said that we had to put Melissa on a regular schedule. Even if she cried we had to leave her in the crib during naps and nighttime. We could use music and a fan but had to make sure almost everything was out of her crib and the room was dark. He told us this procedure should show results in about seven days. I remember crying all the way home, but Kevin reassured me that it was for Melissa's own good as well as ours.

We started on a Friday night. Kevin stayed with Melissa and I went to stay at my mom's. I knew if I stayed home I would be in tears all the time and we probably wouldn't have gone through with it.

It wasn't as bad as I had imagined. Kevin told me that Melissa cried for about forty-five minutes and then fell asleep. She also got up in the night and cried, but not for very long. He left her in the crib no matter what.

After the first night she adapted very well. It was harder trying to get her to take a nap, but after about two to three weeks of constant reinforcement we had a baby who enjoyed sleeping. We would put her down for the night at 7:30 P.M., and she would sleep until 7:00 A.M. the next morning. Her naps would range from two to four hours, one nap a day. Believe me, we had a lot to celebrate on Melissa's first birthday!

Now Melissa is sixteen months old. She cries in her sleep from time to time, due to teething or illness, but at least we know what is wrong and we can help her. We have a beautiful daughter whom we love very much. Kevin and I can now enjoy a good night's sleep and peace of mind.

Another sensitive, intelligent thirty-eight-year-old mother went through a seventeen-month-long series of explanations for her son's problem before discovering it was a sleep disturbance.

As you will see, she blamed hunger, the food she was eating, the medicine she was taking, the makeup she was wearing, flu, hyperactivity, teething, Tylenol, etc. Time and again she believed she had solved the problem, only to have it recur. Let me assure you, as the doctor who examined David, that despite the mother's harrowing descriptions of bloody stools, throwing up, bulging eyes, etc., there was never anything physically wrong with David. Please consider reading this account twice, first paying attention to how the baby behaved, and then focusing on how the mother behaved.

David is seventeen months old and for the first time I can honestly say I enjoy him and being a mother. With him sleeping through the night, I see a tremendous personality change. He has suddenly come alive and has taken a greater interest in his environment. He explores the outside rather than asking to be carried. He is no longer terrified of new situations and is beginning to interact with other children. He actually sits down and plays with his toys. Most important, he is now a happy, affectionate baby.

I feel a very large load has been taken off me. I know now it was David's extreme fussiness and lack of sleep that affected his behavior, not my mothering. Up until now, no matter how I tried to convince myself otherwise, I was certain it was my fault.

Why? Our first pediatrician considered David to be a "well baby." He was the type of doctor who believed a baby wasn't ill unless he had a terrible disease like cystic fibrosis. He never even suggested we might have a baby with extreme fussiness. Through the first five miserable months, he repeatedly told us there was nothing wrong with David; he was gaining weight, therefore he was healthy.

All I had to do was compare David with other babies his age and I knew there was something wrong. I assumed that it had to be my mothering. He was not comfortable enough to sleep during the day, sit in an infant seat or ride in a buggy without crying. He was up three times a night, each time for at least forty-five minutes. When he was up he wanted to be held.

He was so hungry that initially he rejected nursing. It took too long and he found it too difficult to suck. I remember feeling personally rejected when he refused to nurse, but I wanted to badly and continued to try. It took three weeks to get him to nurse without giving him a short drink from the bottle first. During that time he would scream before a feeding, drink for a short period, then scream again and double up with stomach cramps. I hung on, hoping the nursing would get better.

The only information I had about nursing and a mother's diet during nursing was from books. Our pediatrician never offered any information or reasons for my child's behavior.

When David was one month old, the flu bouts started. I began to have flu-like symptoms, diarrhea and severe cramps. The next day David would begin throwing up, having diarrhea with mucus and severe cramps. My flu lasted a few days each episode; his lasted exactly ten days. This occurred five different times before his three-month checkup. Each time, we called the pediatrician and he reassured us. As long as David wasn't dehydrated and had gained weight at his last checkup, the doctor said we shouldn't worry.

I finally realized every time I ate chop suey, it seemed to make both of us sick. I had never reacted to Chinese food before but it seemed like the pregnancy and delivery changed my system. The MSG must have had a violent effect on both of us!

During this time, I was becoming increasingly depressed. I was making my baby sick and feeling incredibly guilty about it. Many well-meaning friends and relatives urged me to stop nursing. I was hearing terrific comments like "There must be something wrong with your milk" or "What have you been eating to make David sick again?"

After David's three-month checkup, he began having screaming bouts that were so severe his eyes bulged. There was no way to comfort him. Also during this time, David's stools changed to dark green with mucus and traces of blood.

Bill and I were very worried. We were tired of the platitudes from our pediatrician. When we pushed him for more help, he suggested we take David in for an upper and lower GI series.

It was obviously time to find a new doctor. A friend referred Dr. K.

In my first telephone conversation with the new doctor, he asked me more questions than my first pediatrician did during the entire time he was treating David.

We focused on my diet. I eliminated milk products and slowly stopped those foods I was eating on a daily basis that might affect David. Nothing seemed to help.

Then the pediatrician questioned me about medication I might be using. I was taking an antihistamine for allergies. He suggested I stop for a few days because of the yellow dye. I seemed to have a new baby. His stools changed from green to yellow. He stopped screaming. He was calmer and happier. We were ecstatic. I very much wanted to believe everything would be fine.

I started a new antihistamine with a green dye. David reacted again, but this time worse than ever. I tried several white allergy medications until I found one that didn't make either one of us sick.

At this point, my pediatrician suggested we read a book on hyperactive children. We didn't want to read it, but then David had a reaction to the dyes in children's Tylenol. When he was six months old, we gave him Tylenol for what we thought was teething pain. The pain got worse and we gave him more Tylenol. This continued until I realized his reactions were too severe to be teething-related. I couldn't hold him. He never stopped moving. He'd crawl down my leg, continuously squirm in my arms, bang his head against objects, and grab at our faces and scream. As bad as his sleeping was before, it was now much worse. There were some nights when he was up for hours either staring into space or constantly moving.

Bill and I read Feingold and were convinced he was writing about our baby. We tried to reassure ourselves that David wasn't seriously ill, but in our guts I don't think it really helped. Our kid was hyperactive. We were in too much pain to question the book or ask for another opinion.

Since David was nursing exclusively, I went on the Feingold diet and eliminated foods with dyes and chemicals in them. Just to play it safe, I also eliminated milk and egg products in case David was allergic to them. There were days he seemed improved but would then have another reaction. I would play detective and frantically search for the cause of his reactions. I even stopped using toothpaste and wearing lipstick.

When David was seven months old, I couldn't stand nursing anymore. I was convinced I was poisoning my baby. I hired a nurse for a week to relieve me and to help me wean him. David screamed for ten hours straight while the nurse held him and offered him a bottle. He wouldn't even close his mouth on the nipple. Bill became concerned that the weaning by a stranger was traumatic for David and he wanted it stopped. By that time, I couldn't listen to the baby scream anymore. So I continued to nurse.

Shortly after we tried to wean, Bill went out of the country for ten days. I was in terrible shape. It was bad enough trying to cope with David with Bill's help, but alone it seemed impossible. Because I was in such bad shape emotionally, Dr. K suggested I wean him cold turkey; that is, we'd leave David with a nurse for the weekend and he'd be weaned when we returned.

I must have been a wreck to even consider it. When Bill came home, I pushed him to do it. He was rightfully concerned about the traumatic effect this would have on David. Bill asked the advice of a psychiatrist regarding weaning in this manner and was told to avoid it if possible. During this meeting, the psychiatrist gave Bill more insight into the difficult time I was going through. This helped tremendously. With his added emotional support, I dropped the idea of weaning and was able to pull myself together enough to avoid a breakdown.

Having a baby can put a strain on a marriage. Having one with extreme fussiness can push the strongest marriages to the point of divorce. When there's an infant who's miserable for months, the parents' anger has to go someplace, and it's usually toward each other. Bill hated coming home. I counted the minutes till he got there, then raged at him when he arrived. It was fortunate that we had a strong marriage to begin with and Bill had the maturity to handle a wife who was an emotional wreck.

During the winter, I was too depressed to take David out very much. To get dressed and take him for a short walk in the buggy took all my strength. Even during those short walks, I'd be terribly tense, waiting for him to start screaming. Unfortunately for us, the relatives and friends who could have helped me the most in caring for David live out of town. This was an added burden and made the winter endless.

David's teething was also a complicating factor in this health. From the time he was six months until he was ten and a half months old he had from four to ten bowel movements a day. Each time he cut a tooth he would begin vomiting a week before and continued until he had the dry heaves on the day the tooth was cut. I can remember changing my clothes several times a day and holding him constantly.

At ten and a half months, after David finally cut his eighth tooth, we saw a tremendous change in him. He soon began crawling (he never could before) and then at twelve months he began walking. He was so proud of himself and happy. For the first time, I could begin taking him out and enjoy it.

A few days after he cut his teeth, he began eating solids—everything. This turned out to be a mixed blessing. It appeared that his stomach wasn't quite ready for them. At night and during his nap, he developed severe gas pains. He'd awaken every one and a half to two hours screaming. We could hear and smell the gas as he doubled up in pain. Sometimes it would take forty-five minutes to an hour to get him back to sleep. During the day, except for naps, he had much less gas. He probably walked it off. He was in constant motion.

Obviously, waking up every two hours was incredibly difficult on me, but initially I didn't mind it much. At least I had a happy baby during the day. A happy baby! I began to think I was an okay mother after all.

David quickly caught up to other babies his age in many areas and I hoped would soon catch up in all others. He was very shy and needed more socialization since he had been in the house so much when he was younger.

David was still waking up every few hours. The lack of sleep was taking its toll on all of us. I continued blaming his teeth. I thought his molars might be coming in and upsetting his stomach. I convinced myself that once his teeth came in everything would be fine.

In the meantime, I was still nursing him to sleep and nursing him every time he woke up. Bill and I almost never went out. My daytime schedule depended on when and if David was ready to nap. There were days he never did.

What I didn't notice were the subtle and gradual changes in David. He was becoming more and more grouchy. He was especially miserable in the morning, and grew more frightened in social situations.

When he was fifteen months old, David ran a high fever for several days from a viral infection. A week later he ran a high fever again as a reaction to the measles vaccine. We had to hold him and carry him a great deal. When he got well, all he wanted to do was to be carried. He had no interest in going outside or playing. He just wanted me to read to him.

I took David to play group the week after his illnesses. We hadn't been with the group for a month because of his nap schedule. He screamed the entire time.

I was appalled when I compared him with the other babies. They were younger than David but were far ahead of him developmentally. What was most upsetting was watching those babies sit, concentrate, and play with toys. David never played with toys; he was constantly moving.

I felt like I'd been kicked in the gut again. There was still something wrong with my baby. Was he hyperactive despite the Feingold diet? Was his behavior due to my mothering?

Dr. K suggested the Sleep Disorders Center when David was about thirteen months old, but it took me a few months to face the fact that I needed to call. I knew the clinic dealt with parent and child interaction as well as physical disorders, and I was too afraid of being criticized. I had convinced myself that David would get better on his own. Bill was afraid the clinic would discover some serious neurological disorder, so he was also reluctant to go.

We were incredibly fortunate that we finally went. First and foremost, we learned we had a normal baby whose past behavior and lack of social development was due to sleep deprivation, not hyperactivity. Second, we learned we were not alone in our responses to David. Many parents of babies who had extreme fussiness continue to respond to them as if they were still ill and tend to foster the poor sleep patterns.

We learned that we had to let David cry it out so he could get the sleep he desperately needed. This turned out to be easier than either Bill or I anticipated. But we needed to retrain ourselves before we could retrain David. The doctor gave instructions on every possible contingency, including what to do if David threw up.

Armed with our instructions, double scotches, frozen pizzas, Häagen-Dazs chocolate ice cream, and a few chocolate bars—we were ready for a long night—we put David in bed while he was still awake. Fifteen minutes later, he was asleep! He was only up twice that night for approximately five minutes each time. This was the baby who previously had been up every one and a half hours! David's sleep patterns have backslid occasionally if he is teething or ill, but his normal pattern now is to sleep through the night, and to take one nap a day.

Now that David sleeps through the night, we have a rested, happy baby and also a rested, happy mother. Not until I was sleeping through the night did I realize what a toll the sleep deprivation had taken on myself as well as David. We are really a happy family for the first time.

If the change in David's behavior seems unbelievable, remember that this is a mother prone to dramatization. I can attest, however, that trained night crying can sometimes be stopped almost overnight, as it was in this case. Perhaps the child senses in the parents' calm resolve that they really mean business.

The following description from a thirty-three-year-old housewife was given to me six months after a single visit. She describes many of the changes in parental behavior that David's family found useful.

When Dan was born, we knew he was someone very special. From the moment of birth I felt he was quite different from his older brother, Brian. I had hoped one of these differences would be his sleep behavior since Brian slept at least four to six hours less per day than any of his peers. Well, his sleep patterns were different from Brian's, all right. Unfortunately, they were worse.

We noticed from the beginning that Dan had always been a very light sleeper, especially for an infant. He would awaken at the slightest sound or disruption. Dan slept through the night (ten hours) for the first time at about one and a half months old. I was thrilled, but I knew, based on experience with our first son, that this could be a fluke. It was. That was the only night he did it until he was over eleven months old! From then on, Dan got up every one to three hours each night.

For the first several months, I nursed him each time he woke, thinking he might be hungry since he refused solids. Then we tried other responses: my husband going to him, walking with him, rocking him, even letting him cry. We set up the playpen in our bedroom and put Dan there because he was waking his brother, but Dan invariably awoke when my husband and I came to bed. So we moved his playpen to the family room (farthest from Brian's and our bedrooms). Some nights I would put him in his crib, and other nights, when we decided to let him cry, he would go back to his playpen. We were concerned that Dan would wake Brian or vice versa.

Needless to say, this was wreaking havoc with our lives. I was getting up as many as four to five times per night with Dan. John would get up with Brian if he awoke. On a number of occasions he also got up with Dan. We would both have to be up for the day after 6:00 A.M., when my husband went to work. My fatigue was intensified since I was breast-feeding.

John and I were always tired. We very often retired as early as 8:00 or 8:30 P.M. to try to catch up on sleep. It didn't help much since we still weren't getting a long stretch of uninterrupted sleep. One advantage John had over me is that he could immediately fall back to sleep during the night. Most times it took me a good half hour or more to get back to sleep. This really was frustrating and gave me even less sleep.

John and I grew more and more irritable with each other and the children due to fatigue, little or no relaxed time together, and frustration at not being able to solve Dan's problem. Dan was also showing ill effects of his sleep pattern. We knew we had to do something.

At every baby checkup I mentioned to his doctor that he wasn't sleeping well. At first we discussed it rather casually. I implied that it was not a serious problem. I tend to let things go almost too long before I complain. Then we got to the point where Dan's doctor felt that something should be done. Dan was nearly eight months old, and our doctor was getting concerned not only for Dan but also for me. I had to avoid getting too run-down, especially since I had two small children to take care of.

Dr. H first prescribed Benadryl, an antihistamine, at bedtime. He said this should make Dan drowsy and better able to fall asleep. Nothing changed. We continued this for about a week. Dan has always been, and still is, most difficult when it comes to trying to get medicine, or even food, into him. Unless he can feed himself, he wants no part of it. It was a struggle every night, especially since I wasn't really comfortable giving my child medication when he wasn't sick.

I called Dr. H again. He felt it was time to use a mild sedative but wanted to consult with a pediatrician. The pediatrician concurred with Dr. H's decision, which made me frightened and very upset. Dr. H prescribed Noctec [chloryl hydrate] at bedtime and during the night if Dan awakened. Both doctors insisted that this drug was not habit-forming. The idea was to get him into a deep enough sleep so that he would not wake as easily during the night.

I was very uncomfortable with the situation, but that night we tried to get the dosage into Dan. He took about half of it. He did fall asleep quicker, but four hours later he woke and continued his pattern of waking every one or two hours through the rest of the night.

The next day Dan caught a cold. It was my excuse to take him to see Dr. H in person again. He checked Dan out for any possible problems beyond a mild cold, but Dan seemed fine.

The doctor and I talked over my apprehensions about the sedative. I have always avoided medication or drugs if at all possible. Dr. H had seemed to have the same philosophy. I told the doctor that I felt I was being selfish by drugging my son so that I could get a night's sleep. He reassured me that we were doing this for Dan, that he needed sleep as much as I did. The doctor convinced me—sort of.

For the next week or so we went back to giving Dan Benadryl in a normal dosage for his cold. As soon as we was healthy again we resumed using the Noctec. It still did no good. Dan would sort of pass out right after he took the medication but then revert to his old pattern after four hours or so. At this nine-month checkup, Dr. H doubled the dosage. We continued this for ten days and then gave up. We were about to schedule an appointment with a pediatric neurologist when a close friend saw a special report on the evening news about children's sleeping problems. From the information I received on the phone and the questionnaire I received, I felt that this, rather than the pediatric neurologist, was the correct next step for Dan.

Dan was over eleven months old when my husband and I took him to see Dr. Weissbluth. We were very nervous about what he would find, but deep inside I knew there was nothing really wrong with Dan, that he really was normal. When the doctor arrived, Dan seemed content, so we went over our questionnaire and answered further questions while Dr. W observed Dan.

The doctor examined him and told us that there was nothing wrong with Dan. Naturally, our response was, "Great, but why won't he sleep normally? Does he just require very little sleep?" We were told that a child Dan's age needs ten to twelve hours of sleep at night plus one to four hours during the day.

Dr. W said that Dan seemed to be extremely sensitive to all stimuli and suggested we do the following: take Brian out of the room (his tossing and even his breathing were probably disturbing Dan), keep Dan's room as dark as possible (take out the nightlight, use a room-darkening shade, and of course keep the door closed), take all toys out of his bed, have Dan sleep in a sleeper so that only his hands and head were exposed to rubbing against the sheets, and do no noisy cleaning and turn off the phones while Dan slept.

If Dan still woke up during the night, we were not to go to him. I was concerned that maybe Dan was waking due to hunger. Dr. W. said that Dan was the correct height and weight for his age and was not waking because of hunger.

He warned us that Dan could possibly cry as long as five and a half hours for the first night. Before I could verbalize my thoughts, Dr. W stated them for me. He said that since I wouldn't be able to sleep anyway, I should get up and do something, such as take a ride, read a book, watch TV, whatever. Let my husband handle the situation. This crying would stop within five to seven days.

Fortunately, we did not need to experience any of this trauma. We did all that Dr. W suggested to minimize any stimuli for Dan during the night. We had only two bedrooms, so poor Brian was put to bed in our room and moved to a sofa bed in the family room when we retired. The situation was obviously far from ideal, but it worked.

Dan slept ten and a half hours straight that first night. I was so exhausted that I slept through also. When I woke at 5:00 A.M., I wanted to run in and see if Dan was still alive!

It has been almost six months since then, and Dan has slept through every night. Occasionally he will wake during the night and cry or call out, but we don't go to him and he goes back to sleep shortly.

After about two months we decided we should try putting Brian back in his own room. Poor Brian had gone through a lot because of Dan's problems; not only was he expected to keep very quiet when Dan was napping, but he couldn't even sleep in his own bed!

The problem was that Dan needed complete darkness with the door closed, while Brian required a night-light and the door open. It took a while, but they both got used to having the door open with the night-light in the bathroom out of Dan's view. Dan was in relative darkness but Brian could see some light from his bed. We put Dan to bed with the door closed. Brian goes to bed after Dan falls asleep, and after that the door stays open for the night.

Dan has his toys back in his bed since he's older and will now play with them for a while in the morning. He's still a very light sleeper and we've had to adjust, but things are very good around here now. We haven't had a group of people over after Dan's bedtime, and we don't keep Dan out past 7:30 or 8:00 P.M. because we want him to fall asleep in his bed for the night. We used to be able to put Brian to sleep at someone else's house and just take him home to his own bed relatively undisturbed. That would be impossible for Dan. We don't leave the house if it's close to naptime, and we get home quickly if we are already out.

All of these changes have been inconvenient but well worth the trouble. Things will get even better than they already are. We're having a couple of bedrooms put in upstairs, so this will remove Dan further from the first-floor commotion.

It's amazing what a sleep problem can do to a family. Dan's problem seemed to totally consume our lives. Besides the physical effects of the fatigue on us all, it took its toll on our social life as well. We rarely went out in the evening or had people over to our home. We seldom had time to just spend with each other. We were preoccupied and too darned tired. We were lucky to make it through the day!

Needless to say, our lives have improved dramatically. We are especially happy that it took no drugs or medication and that nothing is wrong with our son.

I personally received an added good feeling from all of this. I belong to a parenting support group and the word got out rather quickly that one of my children had a sleep problem that was solved. I have received many calls from mothers who are experiencing trouble with their child's sleep pattern, and now I can confidently steer them in the right direction to get help.

Another mother of a very stimulus-sensitive baby was told by her pediatrician to make her baby's bedroom "like a cave." Unfortunately he provided no specific information on how to do this.

The comments of the next mother, a thirty-year-old artist, wondered if he meant she was supposed to paint stalactites, stalagmites, and bats on the walls! Her comments, below, illustrate how dramatic improvement can occur rapidly, and how important it is for both parents to make careful plans about letting baby alone.

Everywhere I went people smiled at my baby, Jackie, because she lights up for everyone. People were amazed at how happy she always appeared and how well she behaved. I'd graciously acknowledge their praise but at the same time I'd think to myself: "Yeah, but if she would only sleep through the night, or even a little during the day!"

As an infant, Jackie was breast-fed, adapted well to any schedule, and to my amazement slept through the night. In fact, I remember bragging about it to all my friends who were new mothers and walked around like zombies from exhaustion. Well, my sleep-filled nights were short-lived.

When Jackie was three months old her sleep habits turned into a nightmare. During the day she took two or three naps that lasted about fifteen minutes apiece. She would stay up until 10:30 P.M., then wake up five to eight times during the night for a bottle or a diaper change or a half hour of attention. Usually she would go right back to sleep and get up for good at 6:00 or 7:00.

We were so desperate that we took any advice that was offered. We added cereal to her formula, started early on solids, fed her chamomile tea, eliminated naps in the afternoon, bathed her at night for an hour, gave her massages, took her swimming, and then tried the most painful experiment of all: letting her cry for half-hour periods at night before giving her a bottle. We did this for eight straight days with no results. Then for the next two days we let her cry for forty-five minutes at a time. We gave up.

I hired someone to live in and help me attend to Jackie at night since after two months of interrupted sleep I was unable to function. When Jackie turned eight months old, my pediatrician recommended that she take an amino acid with dinner that would act as a sedative. This made me stop and think. I opted for a consultation with Dr. Weissbluth.

While I was talking with him, Jackie performed one of her fifteen-minute naps in her stroller. It was apparent to Dr. Weissbluth that when she awoke she was still very tired. She was living on nervous energy, he said. He pointed out that all babies need about fourteen hours of sleep, so my conclusion that Jackie just didn't need that much sleep was false.

I mentioned that her father would come home late from work and tiptoe into her room, and she would snap out of her sleep immediately to play with him. Jackie always seemed sensitive to noise. A moderately loud sound would make her jump, and if she was sleeping, the slightest sound would wake her up.

Dr. Weissbluth suggested that Jackie's sensitivity to stimuli was the root of her sleeping problems. He said she should sleep in a pitch-dark, quiet atmosphere. He said I shouldn't respond to her crying for attention at night as long as she was healthy. He also said I would most likely be up all night the first night and that after three nights it would definitely subside. He said my husband would have to support me in carrying out this plan; that was my main worry.

When I got home I immediately took Jackie's crib into our den, which has no windows. I put her down for a nap and within minutes she was sound asleep! She slept for two hours! I was sure the covers were over her head and she was suffocating to death, or that she had fallen out of her crib and was unconscious on the floor, but I didn't dare go peek. Jackie woke up smiling, ready to play. I couldn't believe it.

I explained everything to my husband. He wasn't very convinced that we should just let her cry. I called up a friend of a friend who had had a similar problem with her baby and was claiming that Dr. W's treatment worked. I wanted her to tell my husband of her great results. That finally sold him, so we got set to try it.

My husband slept at the new house we were building, my housekeeper locked herself in her bedroom, and I sat up working in the kitchen, prepared to be up all night.

We put Jackie down to sleep in the den at 8:00 P.M. She cried for forty minutes and then went to sleep. I worked in the kitchen until 1:30, when it dawned on me that maybe she wasn't going to be up crying all night after all. I heard her whine a few times, but she didn't cry until 8:45 the next morning. Three days later she was sleeping through the night from 8:00 P.M. until 7:00 A.M. and took two naps, one from 10:00 to 11:30 A.M. and another from 1:30 to 2:00 P.M. We've all been celebrating ever since.

As these testimonies indicate, older children who do not sleep through the night grind their parents down. It's a long nightmare. These cures may sound miraculous, but I assure you, when the baby and the parents are really ready, their joint bad habit can be broken just this quickly. So please, do not be afraid to leave your children alone at night. You are teaching a health habit: prolonged and uninterrupted sleep . . . for your child and yourselves!

What Should I Do?

Dear parents, when your baby is crying, do nothing. But do nothing deliberately, quietly, gently, confidently, and firmly. In other words, please try to develop an attitude of:

Purposeful inattention
Studied inattentiveness
Gentle firmness
Constructive resignation
Expectant observation
Watchful waiting

Be attentive to your baby's behavior at night, but try to cultivate a detached and relaxed attitude. As you have read, it does work!

CHAPTER 6

Love Your Baby

Every baby is a unique person. Even identical twins have subtle differences. But all babies have certain instincts such as the rooting reflex, which might have survival value. Fussing/crying might also be based on a survival reflex: a signal system based on sometimes being apart from mother, a separation signal. The signal communicates to the mother, "Come to me, pick me up, feed me." But the signaling system may be imperfectly attuned to the reality that the baby is in fact held in the mother's arms or at the breast, the baby might have some expectation of being inside the womb. It is a little like saying the system was designed for a twelve-month gestation and has difficulty coping with the bombardment of extra external stimulation resulting from being born at nine months gestation. You can see how confusing this would be for a newborn!

There is no reason to introduce psychological terms such as *fear*, *loneliness*, *tension*, or *anxiety*. These terms simply cause us to feel that we are bad parents if our child cries because we then believe that our baby has unmet psychological needs.

If your newborn fusses or cries despite your best efforts, always remember:

IT'S NOT YOUR FAULT

Some newborns cry a little, some cry a lot. Each day may be different for each baby. During the first few months, nothing about your baby—including crying—will be predictable. At times you may feel thoroughly bewildered.

Relax. After three or four months, things usually calm down. You have read about babies who created havoc in their parents' lives and then developed into sweet little four-month-olds. If you accept your fussy baby as a dear, wonderful child who will outgrow the fussing/crying phase, you will be more relaxed and better prepared to cope with the challenges each day brings.

If your very young baby cries more than three hours most days, if you don't seem to be able to console him, and if this has been going on for several weeks, it may help you to think of him as having a very common, blessedly short-lived condition called extreme fussiness/colic. I hope you understand more about extreme fussiness/colic after reading this book.

Do not expect that finding a name for your child's behavior will end your bewilderment. Extreme fussiness/colic changes from day to day. During the time they suffer from spells of extreme fussiness/colic, infants may also be erratic in sleeping patterns, irregular in the degree to which they can be consoled, and highly variable in how much they cry. Parents tend to think of extreme fussiness/colic as a constant state, but I think that in retrospect they focus on the worst nights and let everything blur together. Extreme fussiness/colic is not as regular or relentless as it may seem.

It will help you and your baby if you can emphasize the good, quiet, calm times. Do not let the 10 percent or 25 percent of your baby's day when she is extremely fussy overshadow the rest.

You may assume, like many people, that your own anxieties are transmitted to your infant and cause him to cry or fuss or sleep poorly. I urge you to put this idea out of your mind. Researchers now know that powerful and complex biological forces contribute to each baby's behavior, including his fussing, crying, and sleeping patterns. There are many factors that neither you nor your pediatrician can influence. So the best advice may be as simple as this: Be *patient* and *loving* during the many difficult hours of the first few months, and do not be afraid to try a few of the techniques that have proven effective for others. It is especially important for fathers to get involved as early as possible.

Remember that unexplained crying occurs in all infants during the first few months of life. In only about 20 percent does it become severe enough to be called extreme fussiness/colic. Despite much conjecture, there has been a striking failure to discover any definite gastrointestinal, allergic, or maternally provoked causes of extreme fussiness. It may be set off instead by one or more biological disturbances.

What these biological causes might be is a question for further study. As I have suggested, they might include disordered regulation of breathing, sleeping patterns that are out of sync with other body rhythms, or abnormal levels of naturally occurring hormones.

There is a great deal that we do not know about a baby's hormones and chemicals, the developing brain, the effects of low birth weight, the control over vital functions during sleep, and the biological basis for rhythmic patterns. Associations among measurable temperament, sleep patterns, breathing during sleep, and crying suggest that extreme fussiness may be related to all four. Most likely, extreme fussiness is the result of several related or unrelated disturbances.

Throughout this book I have emphasized that gradations occur in all our measurements: duration of crying spells, sleep durations, temperament ratings, melatonin and progesterone levels and respiratory pauses during sleep. Is it really necessary to impose labels like "extreme fussiness/colic" and "difficult temperament"? It is mostly researchers who divide behavior into categories like normal and abnormal, easy and difficult, or extreme fussiness and common fussiness. You as parents should always be thinking of that little person—not a condition, a ranking, or a label.

When your baby cries at night, remember the smiling, cheerful moments. Focus on everything lovely about her while you help her work out her difficulties.

Hugs, Kisses, and Love Help Your Baby Grow

After a few months of age, after the fussiness quiets down, helping your baby learn to sleep is very important. Regularity of handling, feeding, and sleeping calms down the storm of newborn fussiness. Do not become a slave to your baby's sleep schedule; instead, respect his need to have good-quality sleep in the same way you are sensitive to good-quality nutrition. Try to distinguish between routine days and exceptional days. On routine days, somewhat organize your activities around naps and an early bedtime. On exceptional days, sleep may suffer because of special events.

Since my firstborn son's extremely fussy days (and nights), researchers have learned much about infant behaviors. Would I handle my first son, who had extreme fussiness, or my second, third, or fourth sons, who did not have extreme fussiness, any differently now? Absolutely not. The natural course of parenting has not changed significantly because of scientific endeavors. I play with my children and grandchildren and I am tickled when they laugh. I smile when they giggle and I am distressed when they cry. I feel how my children feel and I share their joys and sorrows. I want to love, hug, kiss, caress, tease, and wrestle with my children and grandchildren. Loving hugs and kisses still are the best treatment for developing an affectionate, giving personality.

Your baby is very special. Each baby is a miracle. Accept and love your bundle of joy with all your heart and all your soul, and be assured that soon your newborn will become that what we all hope for, a sweet baby.

CHAPTER 7

Summary and Action Plans for Exhausted Parents

Fussiness often leads to crying if parents do not soothe their baby. Soothing prevents most, but not all, fussiness from escalating into crying. Some babies require very little soothing and some babies require a lot. Parents who spend a total of more than three hours a day soothing their baby to prevent distress or crying, for more than three days a week, and for more than three weeks are dealing with *extreme fussiness*, which is also called colic.

All Healthy Babies Fuss and Cry

Because of all this soothing effort, there may be very little or no crying, or despite all this soothing effort, your baby might still cry a lot. The more skillful you become, the more effort you are able to put forth, and the earlier you start to soothe your baby, the less likely it is that fussiness will escalate into crying. Skillful soothing of fussiness may prevent most crying.

All babies become fussy a few days after they are born, or a few days after the expected date of delivery if they are born early. The fussing and crying behavior will increase and peak at about six weeks; then, it will be mainly in the evening. After six weeks, the fussing and

The Fussiness and Crying May Last Three to Four Months

crying will decrease but it may last for three or four months. About 20 percent of babies will develop extreme fussiness. When babies fuss or cry, they do not sleep. When they do not sleep, mothers do not sleep. Mind-numbing fatigue from no sleep is the main enemy!

IMPORTANT POINTS

Know Your Enemy: Sleep Deprivation
Parents Do *Not* Cause the Fussy Behavior
The Exact Cause Is Not Known
You Cannot Spoil Your Baby
The Fussiness and Crying Will Not Last Forever

The following are *not* the cause of fussiness:

- **Age of the mother**
- **Educational status of the mother**
- **Parity of the mother (how many children she has had before)**
- **Maternal illness during pregnancy**
- **Maternal anxiety**
- **Maternal intelligence**
- **Father's occupation**
- **Family history of allergy**
- **Family tension**
- **Allergy in the infant during the first six months**
- **Sex of the baby**
- **Birth weight of the baby**
- **Birth order of the baby**
- **Weight gain of the baby**
- **Number of feedings per day**
- **Breast versus formula feeding**
- **Duration of each feeding**
- **Type of formula**
- **Amount of spitting or vomiting**

- **Number of stools per day**
- **Constipation**
- **Gastroesophageal reflux**

ALWAYS REMEMBER

Parents Do *Not* Cause the Fussy Behavior

For soothing, match your parenting decisions to yourself and your family's resources. Consider a balance between your baby's disposition to express distress and your ability to soothe your baby. Not only do babies vary in their expression of distress, but parents also vary in their ability to soothe. The resources for parents' ability to soothe fussiness and crying and promote sleep in their baby include the following items.

**RESOURCES FOR
PARENTS' ABILITY TO SOOTHE**

- **Father involvement**
- **Agreements between mother and father regarding child rearing, such as breast-feeding versus bottle-feeding or crib versus family bed**
- **Absence of marital discord between wife and husband**
- **Absence of baby blues or postpartum depression**
- **Absence of other children requiring attention**
- **Ease in breast-feeding**
- **Absence of medical problems in child, mother, father, or other children**
- **Number of bedrooms in home**
- **Presence of relatives, friends, or neighbors to help out**
- **Ability to afford housekeeping help**
- **Ability to afford child-care help**
- **Absence of financial or psychological pressures such as mother having to return to work soon**

Your ability to soothe your baby depends on innate factors within your baby and on the resources you have to assist you. Try to identify areas of support or difficulty for you and your family.

Birth to Four Months: How to Soothe and Help Your Baby Learn to Sleep	***Birth to Four Months*** • **Encourage sucking; do not worry if your baby falls asleep while sucking** • **Rhythmic rocking motions** • **Swaddling** • **Massage** • **Lullabies, voices; sounds of waves, wind, or birds**

   • **Sleep associations: create a habit**

FOR SUCCESSFUL SOOTHING TO PREVENT CRYING AND PROMOTE SLEEPING

1. **Involve fathers**
2. **Start sleep training early: sleep time routines, short intervals of wakefulness, watch for drowsy signs**

---

1. **Fathers should become involved in helping care for their baby!**
   • **Start early; become involved right away, as soon as the baby is born.**
   • **Plan to come home early from work or take a few days off when your baby is six weeks of age (or, for a baby born early, six weeks old counting from the expected date of delivery). Why? Your wife will be more exhausted then, because six weeks is when your baby will be most fussy and wakeful. She needs your help. Take your baby for a long car ride to give your wife a break.**
   • **As soon as your baby comes home from the hospital, become involved in putting your baby to sleep.**
   • **Spend lots of time soothing your baby; learn infant massage or lullabies.**

- Help feed your baby so that you can help out when your baby is fussy, or in the middle of the night when your wife needs some extra sleep. Gently try not to let your wife become a "gatekeeper" whereby she creates a rigid separation between her role as a mother/caregiver and your role as father/worker.
- Tell your wife that she should put your child to sleep at night when she is tired even if you have not yet returned to work. You do not want to sleep starve your baby by forcing your wife to delay night sleep.
- If the father is not available to provide help, try to get relatives and friends lined up to assist you, especially in the evening hours and at any time when your baby is six weeks old.

2. **Start sleep training early**

Sleep Time Routines

Before sleep times, decrease the amount of stimulation: reduce noise, light, handling, playing activity. Choose the items you feel work best for your baby, and consistently try to do all of them in the same order.

- Room should be quiet, dark (use room-darkening shades), and warm, but not too warm
- Bathe
- Dress for sleep
- Gentle rhythmic rocking, swinging in arms
- Swaddle if it comforts and relaxes your baby; use warm blanket from clothes dryer
- Feed
- Lullaby, quiet singing, or humming; be consistent
- Favorite words, sounds, or phrases; be consistent
- Put down drowsy but awake, if possible (usually does not work for extreme fussy/colicky babies, and may not work for common fussy babies around six weeks old)
- Massage after bath; smooth and gentle movements

- Do not deliberately awaken before sleeping
- Do not rush in at the first sound your baby makes
- Never wake a sleeping baby (except newborns born premature)

Short Intervals of Wakefulness

Respect your baby's need to sleep: the one-to-two-hour window. Think and plan *how* you want to soothe your baby, but *when* you soothe your baby is more important.

- Babies quickly become overtired after only one or two hours of wakefulness. During the day, note the time when your baby wakes up and try to help your baby nap by soothing within the next one or two hours as she moves into the sleep zone before she becomes overtired. Try to keep the intervals of wakefulness brief. Learn to recognize drowsy cues. See page 83.
- Babies less than six weeks old fall asleep at night very late and do not sleep very long, day or night. Try to soothe your baby to sleep during the day, before she becomes overtired. Always respond to your baby. Avoid the overtired state.
- Eighty percent of babies more than six weeks old become more settled at night, sleep a little longer at night, and begin to become drowsy for night sleep at an earlier hour. Try to soothe your baby to sleep at an earlier hour if she shows signs of drowsiness earlier. Do not let the baby cry.
- Twenty percent of babies more than six weeks old do not appear to become more settled at night, do not appear to sleep longer at night, and do not become drowsy at an earlier hour. Nevertheless, try to soothe your baby to sleep at an earlier hour even if she does not show signs of drowsiness. Spend extra time soothing; prolonged swinging, long luxurious baths, and never-ending car rides. Fathers should put forth extra effort to help out. Do not let her cry.

Watch for Drowsy Signs
Sleep Training
Summary

Sleep training involves several general principles that use the natural development of sleep/wake rhythms to help your child learn to sleep. For 80 percent of babies, sleep training will *prevent* sleep problems.

- Respect your baby's need to sleep; avoid the overtired state.
- Start early to anticipate when your baby will need to sleep, similar to anticipating when your baby will need to feed.
- Maintain brief intervals (one to two hours) of wakefulness. This is the one- to two-hour window.
- Learn to recognize drowsy cues. Drowsy cues may be absent in 20 percent of all or in extremely fussy/colicky babies. Drowsy cues or sleep signs tell you that your baby is becoming sleepy, and this is when you begin your soothing efforts.
- When you put your baby down or lie down with your

SLEEPY SIGNS, SLEEPY SIGNALS, OR DROWSY CUES:

Moving into the sleep zone
Becoming Drowsy
Decreased activity
Slower motions
Less vocal
Sucking is weaker or slower
Quieting
Appearing uninterested in surroundings, calmer
Eyes are less focused
Eyelids drooping
Yawning

FATIGUE SIGNS:

Entering overtired zone
Becoming Overtired
Fussiness
Rubbing eyes
Irritability
Crankiness

baby, she may be drowsy, awake, or in a deep sleep. Any way works if you have good timing.

The key is matching the time when you soothe your baby to sleep to the time when your baby naturally needs to sleep. For 80 percent of common fussy babies, perfect timing produces no crying.

- **During the first several weeks, many babies fall asleep while feeding or sucking to soothe, even if not hungry. This is natural. It is not necessary to deliberately wake your baby at this time before you put him down to sleep or lie down with him in your bed. Later, your older baby may or may not momentarily and partially awaken as you remove your breast or bottle before he falls asleep. Do not force him to a wakeful state before attempting to put him to sleep.**
- **Use consistent soothing styles for naps.**

For common fussy babies (80 percent), use method A for naps: After several minutes of soothing (which may include breast-feeding) place your baby in the crib or lie down with your baby whether or not he is awake.

For extremely fussy/colicky babies (20 percent), use method B for naps: Always soothe as long as needed, until your baby is in a deep sleep.

- **After a few weeks of age, put the baby to sleep in a quiet and dark place.**
- **Do not rush in if your baby makes quiet sounds or whimpers.**
- **After a few weeks of age, stationary sleep is better than sleeping in a moving swing or stroller.**
- **At six weeks of age, watch for signs of an earlier bedtime in common fussy babies. Extremely fussy/colicky babies may show an earlier bedtime when older.**
- **At four months of age, your baby will have longer peri-**

ods of wakefulness. But still synchronize the beginning of your soothing efforts with the beginning of your baby's drowsiness. For common fussy babies, this may appear to be highly predictable. For extremely fussy babies, they may appear to have predictable and regular sleep times only when much older.

- After four months of age, cry it out (ignoring or extinction), check and console, or graduated extinction (controlled crying) might be needed for a once extremely fussy/colicky baby. Rarely, this might be done for a younger baby.

Plan Ahead for Your Baby's Tendency to Fuss/Cry and Your Baby's Temperament at Four Months of Age.

Four Months of Age

At four months of age, babies who become overtired appear to develop features of a *difficult temperament*, defined as more intense (lots of energy in their emotional expressions), more slowly adaptable (difficulty accepting changes in routines), more negative in mood (more fussiness/crying and less smiling/laughing), more withdrawing (initial reaction to novelty is objecting, rejecting, or turning away) and irregular in biologic functions (less of a pattern regarding when he is hungry or sleepy, or how much he eats or sleeps). The opposite of a difficult temperament is an *easy temperament* and many babies are an *intermediate temperament*, in between. The more your baby has the tendency to have extreme fussiness/colic during the first few months, the more likely he will appear to have a difficult temperament at four months. This knowledge will help you plan to increase your resources for soothing and make decisions regarding sleeping arrangements and breast-feeding.

For 100 Babies
- **At birth, 80 percent of babies have common fussiness. Of these 80 babies,**
- **49 percent (39 babies) will become EASY**
- **46 percent (37 babies) will become INTERMEDIATE**
- **5 percent (4 babies) will become DIFFICULT**
- **At birth, 20 percent of babies have extreme fussiness/ colic. Of these 20 babies,**
- **14 percent (3 babies) will become EASY**
- **59 percent (12 babies) will become INTERMEDIATE**
- **27 percent (5 babies) will become DIFFICULT**

Match Your Parenting Decisions to Your Baby's Evolving Temperament

---

Family bed: All the time, part-time, never, with or without co-sleeper.

For about 80 percent of babies, those who have common fussiness, an early commitment to a family bed usually works well. Sleep problems later are unlikely.

For about 20 percent of babies, those with extreme fussiness, an early commitment to a family bed may be associated with sleep-deprived parents for several weeks, but the strong soothing power of bodily warmth, close physical contact, sounds of breathing, hearing the heartbeat when sucking at the breast, or the smell of breast milk may make the effort worth it. Sleep problems might occur later when about four months old if the child is allowed to stay up too late.

During the day, some parents with extremely fussy/colicky or common fussy babies are overwhelmed because they may have limited resources for soothing. For babies whose parents did not initially want to have a family bed but later made that decision because of its soothing power, sleep problems are more likely to occur. The sleep problems are more likely to occur and persist not because of the family bed, but because of the continuation of limited resources for soothing.

Breast-feed: All the time, part-time (expressed breast milk or formula), never.

For about 80 percent of babies, the common fussy babies, mothers are better rested and feeding is mostly for nutrition. Breast-feeding is usually easy.

For about 20 percent of babies, those with extreme fussiness/ colic, mothers are fatigued from sleep deprivation. The stress from loss of sleep might inhibit lactation. Breast-feeding may be difficult because it is used for both nutrition and soothing. Nursing more frequently and for longer durations might cause discomfort or pain if the skin of the breast becomes cracked or dry. The mother might worry that there is not enough breast milk or that her diet is causing the breast milk to upset her baby. Consider a single bottle of expressed breast milk given once per 24 hours by someone else.

> **Only a Few Children Are at a High Risk for Sleep Problems after Four Months of Age**

- **49 percent of babies have an intermediate temperament at four months of age (37 had common fussiness and 12 had extreme fussiness/colic when younger). Their temperament may resemble that of an easy or a difficult temperament.**
- **42 percent of babies have an easy temperament at four months of age (39 had common fussiness and 3 had extreme fussiness/colic when younger).**
  Parents are not likely to be stressed.
  Infant is likely to be well rested.
  Infant is likely to be able to self-soothe.
  At night, consolidated sleep (long sleep duration) develops early.
  During the day, regular and long naps naturally develop early, without parental scheduling.
  If sleep problems exist, "no cry" solutions usually work.
- **9 percent of babies have a difficult temperament (4 had common fussiness and 5 had extreme fussiness/colic).**
  Parents are likely to be stressed.
  Infant is likely to be overtired.
  Infant is likely to be only parent-soothed.

At night, fragmented sleep (night waking) persists.
If sleep problems exist, "let cry" solutions might be necessary.

At Four Months of Age, Different Sleep Solutions Work Better for Different Temperaments

---

What will work for one family may not work for you and your baby. Think of caring for your baby in the context of your resources for soothing and your decisions regarding breast feeding and the family bed, not of finding a cure for extreme fussiness/colic.

After Four Months of Age.

1. Watch for the development of an *earlier sleep time at night* by watching for *drowsy signs* and soothe your baby to sleep early before they change into *irritable signs*. Use *sleep time routines. Fathers* should be involved.
    a. For the family bed, lie down in your bed and use a safe nest in your bed, or a co-sleeper. Or use a crib only for sleep onset at the earlier bedtime.
    b. If you use a crib, *fathers can help* put their baby to sleep and at the first night feeding return her to her crib, or bring her to your bed for the remainder of the night.

If you cannot put your child to sleep at an early time because of day care, long commutes, or other real-life circumstances, do the best you can. The earlier, the better.

---

2. If you use a crib, try to feed your baby no more than two times at night; otherwise, you might create a *night waking habit.*

    a. For the family bed, breast-feed as often as you wish.
3. The *morning nap develops first, around 9:00–10:00 A.M.* Use this nap rhythm as an aid to help your baby fall asleep. Naps occurring in synch with the internal biological nap rhythm are more restorative and better in quality than naps occurring at other times.

    a. Extremely fussy/colicky infants might have to go down for their first nap after only *one hour of wakefulness. Focus on the morning nap* (see page 180).
4. The *afternoon nap develops when the baby is older and occurs around 12:00–2:00 P.M.*

    a. Extremely fussy/colicky infants might still have to be put down to sleep after *one to two hours of wakefulness* following their morning nap.

    b. Switching from "sleepy signs" to sleeping "by the clock" may occur in common fussy babies who are temperamentally very regular at three to four months of age.
5. For extremely fussy/colic infants, the development of nap rhythms and long naps occurs when they are older.

    a. Try the "fade procedure" at four months, as described on page 177.

    b. Try to "focus on the morning nap" at four months, as described on page 180.

    c. Plan to switch from "sleepy signs" to "by the clock" only when much older.

Different families will want to try different methods to help their child sleep better at night. Here is a description of several different ways to encourage night sleep at or after four months of age.

> **IMPORTANT POINT**
>
> **Be Patient**
> **Be Consistent**

1. *Extinction:* **Let Cry**
    Let your child cry at night with no time limit.
2. *Graduated Extinction (Controlled Crying):* **Let Cry**
    Let your child cry with time limits. When your

child cries at night, you delay for five to ten minutes your response for soothing. The delay is gradually increased by five additional minutes either on the same night or on subsequent nights. You soothe your child until she is drowsy or until she is in a deep sleep. The expectation is that your baby will fall asleep during one of the crying spells.

3. *Check and Console:* Maybe Cry

Respond to your child promptly. Repeat as often as needed. You attempt to do the least amount of soothing required until he is drowsy or until he is in a deep sleep. Gently, quietly soothe in darkness by trying not to pick her up (rub her tummy, stroke her hair, gently rock the crib). If needed, pick her up and do the least amount of rocking, singing, or nursing to soothe her back to a calm state. Leave the room but return again when she cries, and repeat the process.

4. *Family Bed:* No Cry

Respond to your child promptly. Repeat as often as needed. Soothe until he is in a deep sleep.

**Different Children Require Different Sleep Solutions
and
Different Families Have Different Resources for Soothing**

If your baby has common fussiness and he *is* well rested, usually anything will work. At six weeks of age, "check and console" may stimulate more than soothe some of these babies.

If your baby has common fussiness and he is *not* well rested, "check and console" may be more stimulating than soothing at any age. Graduated extinction might wear you down because your baby's crying outlasts your patience or resolve, especially at six weeks of age.

If your baby has extreme fussiness/colic, "check and console" may be more stimulating than soothing, or it simply appears never to work. Graduated extinction, and extinction or let cry, may fail because the intensity and duration of crying is too much for a parent to accept.

If your baby cries loudly with intensity and persistence and you do not want to let your baby cry:

Bring your baby to your bed for soothing and use your breast to soothe, walk with your baby, go for a car ride, try a swing, and let your baby fall asleep on your chest on the sofa, or try to repeat other soothing maneuvers.

If you cannot tolerate your child's crying and you are becoming angry with your baby for crying too much, and you do not want to sleep with your baby, it is far better to let your baby cry rather than harming or injuring your child.

Changes of routine such as holiday trips or special events such as birthdays may cause your child to become very overtired, and you may also be overtired and *not* patient or consistent. "Check and console" and "graduated extinction" may go on and on. The total amount of crying with "extinction" may be less than "graduated extinction." Disruptions of routine may occur repeatedly and "extinction" (no parent soothing) may allow the child to regain self-soothing *faster* than "graduated extinction" (some parent soothing). This may be important for parents who do not have extensive resources for prolonged nighttime soothing.

Graduated extinction requires a plan for each night, and some parents have difficulty being patient and consistent at night. Extinction is a simpler method that does not require keeping a record of how long to delay the response. However, extinction appears harsher: "Check and console" and "graduated extinction" appear gentler. Do what works for your baby, and do what your soothing resource support system allows you to do. The family bed may be parents' first choice from the beginning or a reaction to extreme fussiness/colic. Perhaps the family bed is the best strategy for soothing for a family with limited resources.

REMEMBER

Parents Do Not Cause Extreme Fussiness/Colic

Extreme Fussiness/Colic Will End

Overtiredness Is Part of Extreme Fussiness/Colic

Do What Works Best For Your Baby and Your Family to Soothe Your Baby

Parents Need to Take Care of Themselves to Be Better Able to Soothe Their Baby

Index

—A—
abuse, 30, 131
activity, as temperament
    characteristic, 120
adaptability, as temperament
    characteristic, 121–25
Aeneid (Virgil), 79
Ainsworth, Mary, 3–5
air, fresh, 37
air swallowing, 18
allergies, 32–34, 43, 45–47,
    115
American Academy of
    Pediatrics, 89
animals, studies of, 60
anxiety, maternal, 30–31, 49,
    52–54, 62, 141
approach/withdrawal, as
    temperament
    characteristic, 120
"attachment parenting," 169,
    176

—B—
"baby brain," xvii
bed, family, 88–89, 105, 172,
    173, 184, 191, 226, 228,
    229, 231
bedtime routines, 174, 186,
    221–22
behavioral research, extreme
    fussiness/colic and, 26–27
Bell, Silvia, 3–5
biology, 7, 9, 40–41, 61, 62,
    118, 135–36, 141, 146–17,
    148, 160, 175, 214–15
Blake, William, 67
Boke of Chyldren, The (1553),
    23, 31
bottle feeding, 74, 86, 103,
    105, 170–71, 183
Boulton, T. C., 36
boys vs. girls, extreme
    fussiness/colic and, 37
Brazelton Neonatal
    Assessment Scale, 130
Brazelton, T. Berry, 8, 9, 10,
    14, 50, 52, 62, 118–19,
    141, 152
breast-feeding, 7–8, 34–36,
    73–74, 96, 177
    babies awakening more often
        and, 162
    bottle-feeding vs., 105,
        170–71
    breast engorgement and,
        112

breast-feeding (*cont'd*)
    common fussy babies and, 103
    extreme fussiness/colic and,
        104–10
    family bed and, 184
    foremilk and, 114
    the fussy baby, 111–17
    hindmilk and, 114
    inverted nipples and, 112
    lactose overload and, 114
    let-down reflex and, 114
    low milk supply and, 111
    poor positioning and, 112
    sleep and, 175–76, 191, 224,
        226–27, 229
    vs. formula feeding, 86–88
breathing, 139–40, 153
Brennemann, Joseph, xxi
Burrell, Toria, 78

—C—
caffeine, 34–35
Carey Infant Temperament
    Questionnaire, 130
Carey, W. B., 119, 131–32, 145,
    146
"check and console" method,
    171–72, 229–31
Chess, Stella, 119, 128
Children's Memorial Hospital
    (Chicago), 57, 133, 135,
    140, 146
China, 136
Chinese, 23, 131
chloral hydrate, 191, 206
circadian pattern, 141, 144
"Colic as the Sole Symptom of
    Urinary Tract Infection in
    Infants,", 54

colic, defined, 16–17, 19, 46
colon, 31
consistency, 185, 187
coping, extreme fussiness/colic,
    69–70
cribs, 88, 103, 171, 183, 228
crying
    biologically driven, 7, 9
    causes of, 3, 6–8
    controlled, 171–72, 229–31
    cultural differences and, 7,
        10, 88
    daily average of, 8–9
    decreasing of, 9
    defined, 19
    frequency of, 5, 7
    fussing vs., 18–19
    gradual approach and,
        177–80
    graduated extinction for,
        231
    inconsolable, 21
    meaning of, 2–3
    night, 9, 163, 184–91, 192
    "no cry" vs. "let cry," 92, 98
    normal vs. extreme
        fussiness/colic, 10–14
    parents' response to, 3–5, 10,
        212
    peaking of, 9, 10, 70
    persistent, 19
    personality and, 14–15
    sleep and, 9, 92, 98, 168–69,
        173, 177, 184–91, 192,
        227, 228, 229–31
    soothing responses to, 181,
        217
    studies on, 5–14, 66–67
    sucking behavior and, 152
    as survival mechanism, 2

temperament and, 128–29
unknown reasons for, 6, 7, 8,
    215
"Crying in Infants and
    Children" (Illingworth),
    14
cuddling, 63, 116
cultural differences, 7, 10, 23,
    36, 136, 176–77
"cures," 24–25

—D—

Darwin, Charles, 140
Davis, Adelle, 85
day sleep organization, 135
diagnoses, 25
dicyclomine, 147–48
disease, fussiness and, 22
distractibility, as temperament
    characteristic, 127
doctors, 25–26
    See also pediatricians
drowsy cues, 83–84, 90, 103,
    223–24, 228
drugs. *See* medications
"Drugs During Labor May
    Disturb Normal
    Behavioral Development"
    (Thomas), 54

—E—
"early co-sleepers," 88
education, of mothers, 37
Emde, Robert, 143
England, 136
epidural anesthesia, 54–55
ethnic groups, 131

*Expression of the Emotions of Men
    and Animals* (Darwin), 140
exterogestation, 59–60
extreme fussiness/colic
    See also fussiness
    common fussiness vs., 10–14,
        17–18, 99, 134
    commonness of, 22–23
    defined, 17, 20–22, 46, 48
    factors not influencing, 45,
        47, 49–50, 134
    history of, 24–29
    important things to
        remember about, 24
Eysenk Personality Inventory,
    52

—F—
"fade procedure," 178, 180
fathers, xvii, 66, 70–72, 80,
    105, 109–10, 148, 181,
    186, 214, 220–21, 228
fatigue, 83, 142, 165–66, 182,
    223
feeding problems, 11
feeding, under/over, 43
firstborn children, 36–37, 62,
    154–56
flexibility. *See* adaptability, as
    temperament
    characteristic
foremilk, 114
France, 162
fussiness
    common vs. extreme, 10–14,
        17–18, 99, 134
    defined, xvii–xix, 18–19
    what are not causes of,
        218–19

—G—
gassiness, 18, 31–32, 113
gastroesophageal reflux, 55, 113
gastrointestinal problems, 31, 44
"graduated extinction." *See* "check and console" method

—H—
Harvard University, 9
hindmilk, 114
history, of extreme fussiness/colic, 24–29
hospitalization, 68–69
human growth hormone, 141
hydrocortisone ointment, 107, 108
hyperactivity, 120
hypertonic, baby as, 18

—I—
Illingworth, R. S., 3, 14, 16–17, 25, 31, 42–45, 47, 49, 191
Infant Massage: A Handbook for Loving Parents (McClure), 81
intelligence, 37
intensity, as temperament characteristic, 126
internal timing system, xxii–xxiii
International Association of Infant Massage, 81

International Board Certified Lactation Consultant (IBCLC), 117
International Board of Lactation Consultant Examiners (IBLCE), 117

—J—
Jessop Hospital for Women (Sheffield, England), 42
jet lag syndrome, 141
Johns Hopkins University, 3
Jorup, S., 44, 119

—K—
!Kung San babies, 7, 9, 10, 36

—L—
labor, drugs during, 54–55
lactation consultant, 111, 112, 113, 117
lactose intolerance, 33–34
lactose overload, 114
Let's Have Healthy Children (Davis), 85
Liebman, William, 33
lullabies, 78–79

—M—
massage, 80–81
Massage for Healthier Children (Sinclair), 81
Mayo Clinic study, 6, 8
McClure, Vimala, 81
McDevitt, S. C., 119

medications, 27–28, 46–47, 54–55, 147–48, 190–91, 193, 200, 206–7, 209
melatonin, 57, 58, 59, 141, 191
melt down, xviii, 1·
milk, cow's, 32–34, 115
Minnesota Multiphasic Personality Inventory (MMPI), 48–49
mood, as temperament characteristic, 126
mothers
 anxiety of, 30–31, 49, 52–54, 62, 141
 blaming, 27
 descriptions of babies at four months, 150–54
 education of, 37
 experienced mothers and extremely fussy/colicky babies, 158–59
 experienced vs. new, 89–90
 on experiences with sleep problems, 191–211
 fathers helping, 70–72, 105
 on first-born babies, 154–56
 health of, 66, 116
 massage and, 80
 older vs. younger, 90
 personality/emotional state of, 52–54
 on personality of, 47–50
 resting/taking breaks, 66–68
 on second-born infants, 157–58
 sleep deprivation of, 104–5
 social class of, 38
 support groups for new, 116
 work, returning to, 91

muscle paralysis, 142–43
music, 77, 78–79, 81
myths, about extreme fussiness/colic, 29–39

—N—
naps, 95–96, 135, 165, 172, 173, 180–82, 183, 186, 224–25, 227, 229
Nelson, Nancy, 111, 117
neurological immaturity, 4, 5, 145
"night air," 37
night crying, 9, 163, 184–91, 192
night-lights, 86
night sleep organization, 185
night waking, 146, 162–65, 171, 172, 183, 228
"nipple confusion," 73–74, 105
nursing. *See* breast-feeding

—P—
pacifiers, 73–75, 116
 See also thumbsucking
Paradise, Jack L., 47–50, 49–50
parental behavior, 65, 67–68, 145, 147–48, 150, 163
parent-child relationship, 64–65
parents' health, 65–67
paroxysmal fussing, 18, 45, 46, 140
"Paroxysmal Fussing in Infancy, Sometimes Called 'Colic'" (Wessel), 46
paroxysms, 16, 17

pediatricians, 28–29, 69
    See also doctors
persistence, as temperament
    characteristic, 126–27
personality, 47–50, 52–54, 118,
    128, 130
physiological disturbances,
    60–61
physiological research, 40–42
placebo effects, 85
postpartum depression, 148
progesterone, 56–57, 191
prostaglandins, 55–56
"proximity-promoting
    behaviors," 60

—Q—
quantitative research, 41

—R—
rapid eye movement (REM),
    136–39, 142–44
"reactive co-sleepers," 88
rhythmicity, as temperament
    characteristic, 120
rhythmic motions, 59, 64,
    75–76, 220, 221
Rochester (Minnesota) Child
    Health Services, 48
Royal Children's Hospital
    Clinic (Parkville,
    Australia), 52

—S—
Samaritan Children's Hospital
    (Stockholm), 44
Schnall, R., 52

second-born infants, 157–58
"second wind," 182
sensitivity. *See* threshold, as
    temperament
    characteristic
separation signal, 213
serotonin, 58, 148, 168
serum cortisol, 141
Shakespeare, William, 23
Shaver, Benjamin, 53–54
SIDS. *See* sudden infant death
    syndrome (SIDS)
Sinclair, Marybetts, 81
six-week peak, 9, 11–12, 70
sleep, 133–50
    See also bed, family; cribs;
        naps; sleep training;
        soothing
    "acted-out" REM and,
        142–44
    after extreme fussiness/colic
        ends, 159–66
    "ambiguous," 143
    arrangements, 88–89
    associations, 81–82
    awake and sleep patterns of,
        145
    baby's need to, 82–83
    back vs. side sleeping, 64
    bedtime routines and, 174,
        221–22
    biology and, 135–36, 141,
        160, 175
    breast-feeding and,
        175–76, 191, 224, 226–27,
        229
    breast-feeding vs. bottle-
        feeding and, 170–71
    breathing rhythms and,
        139–40

changes in patterns from 0–3
months, 138
circadian pattern and, 141,
144
crying and, 9, 92, 98,
168–69, 173, 177, 184–91,
192, 227, 228, 229–31
cues, 83
day sleep organization, 135
day vs. night, 137–38
drowsiness cues, 83–84, 90,
103, 223–24, 228
durations, 135, 145, 148,
161–62, 165
erratic patterns of, 214
factors not influencing
extreme fussiness/colic,
184
"fade procedure" and, 178,
180
fatigue and, 83, 142,
165–66, 182, 223
gradual approach and,
177–80
habits, 122–25, 165
hormone rhythms and,
140–42
immature development and,
168
motionless, 93, 182
muscle paralysis and,
142–43
"natural" vs. "unnatural"
and, 176–77
newborn patterns of,
135–36, 137, 161
night sleep organization, 135
night waking, 146, 162–65,
171, 172, 183, 228
organization, 138–39

positions, 89, 136
problems after four months,
167–68, 174–75
process of falling asleep,
149–50
quality vs. quantity, 138,
160
quiet (non-REM), 136–39,
143, 162–63
REM (rapid eye movement),
136–39, 142–44
restorative power of, 160
"second wind" and, 182
signals, 83
solid foods and, 162
state control, 144
states, 136, 137, 139
study of patterns of, 190–91
temperament and, 144–47,
167–68, 169, 173, 175,
225–27, 228
temperature and, 140–42
timing, 165
sleep training, 84, 92–98,
223–32
babies a few weeks old and,
94
mistaken ideas about, 98
newborns and, 93–94
"no cry" vs. "let cry," 92, 98
preventing sleep problems
with, 93
problems in older babies,
97–98
six-week-old and older
babies and, 95–97
soothing and, 94
smiling, social, 4, 83
snuggling, 63
social class, of mothers, 37

soothing, 101, 149, 169,
    170, 176–77, 177–78,
    180–81, 182–83, 184,
    219–20, 222, 224, 226,
    228, 231
  breast-feeding in the family
    bed and, 105
  crying and, 98–99, 217
  defined, 63–64
  fathers and, 70–72
  lullabies, 78–79
  massage, 80–81
  music, 77
  "nestling" as, 89
  night-lights, 86
  other methods for, 84–85
  pacifiers, 73–75
  resources for parents' ability
    to provide, 219–20
  rhythmic motions, 75–76
  sleep training and, 94
  sound machines, 77–78
  sucking as, 72–75
  swaddling, 76–77
  swings as, 75
  temperament and, 98–100,
    102
  useless remedies for, 85
  voices, 77
sound machines, 77–78
spoiling, 3–5, 44, 177
Stewart, A. H., 50–52
"stimulus-overload extreme
    fussiness," 50
stimulus-sensitivity, of infants,
    18, 209
St. James-Roberts, Ian,
    18–20
sucking, 11, 60, 64, 72–75,
    152, 220

sudden infant death syndrome
    (SIDS), 59, 86, 89, 136,
    140
support groups, new mothers,
    116
survival reflex, 213
swaddling, 59, 76–77, 116,
    220, 221
*Sweet Baby Lullabies to Soothe
    Your Newborn* (CD), 78

—T—
teething, 188
temperament, 99, 100, 101,
    102, 128–29, 145, 147,
    148, 149
  breathing and, 140
  characteristics, 119–27
  crying and, 128–29
  defined, 119
  extreme fussiness/colic and,
    131–32
  at four months, 118–32
  parent-response
    questionnaire, 119, 127,
    130–31, 140, 145, 150
  personality and, 130
  profile, 127, 129–30, 131,
    131–32
  sleep and, 144–47, 167–68,
    169, 173, 175, 225–27,
    228
  soothing and, 98–100, 102
  study of, 99–102
tension, 50–52
Thomas, Alexander, 119, 128
Thomas, David, 54–55
"Three Months' Colic"
    (Illingworth), 42

threshold, as temperament
characteristic, 127, 145–46
thumbsucking, 152
See also pacifiers
trained night crying, 163
treatment, 25, 27–28, 69,
147–48
tryptophan, 191
Twain, Mark, 91
twins, 91

—U—
United States Consumer Product
Safety Commission, 89
University of Adelaide, 36
University of California School
of Medicine, 33
University of Colorado
Medical Center, 143
urinary tract infections, 54

—V—
Vietnamese, 23
Virgil, 79
voices, 77

—W—
weight loss, xviii
Weissbluth, Jed, 79
Weissbluth, Linda, 31, 57,
58
Wessel, Morris A., 17, 18,
45–47, 49, 153
"wind colic," 37
work, returning to, 91

—Y—
Yale University School of
Medicine, 45
yeast infections, 115

About the Author

A pediatrician for thirty years, MARC WEISSBLUTH, M.D., is also a leading researcher on sleep and children. He founded the original Sleep Disorders Center at Chicago's Children's Memorial Hospital in 1985 and is a Professor of Clinical Pediatrics at Northwestern University School of Medicine. Dr. Weissbluth discovered that sleep is linked to temperament and that sleeping problems are related to infant colic. His landmark seven-year study on the development and disappearance of naps highlighted the importance of daytime sleep. In addition to his own research, he has written chapters on sleep problems in textbooks for pediatricians, lectured extensively to parent groups, and appeared on *Oprah*. Dr. Weissbluth has been married for thirty-eight years to Linda, and she has provided both inspiration and original ideas for this book. Dr. Weissbluth is the father of four sons, two grandsons, and, thankfully, one granddaughter—and they are all good sleepers.

Look for this completely revised and expanded version of a classic!

In this new edition, Dr. Marc Weissbluth, one of the country's leading pediatricians, updates his groundbreaking approach to solving and preventing your children's sleep problems. He explains with authority and reassurance his step-by-step regime for instituting beneficial habits within the framework of your child's natural sleep cycles. This valuable sourcebook contains the following new material:

• How to handle "nap-resistant" kids and when to start sleep-training
• Help for working moms and children with sleep issues
• Expanded discussion on the father's role in comforting children
• Key studies on how early sleep troubles can lead to later problems
• The benefits and drawbacks of allowing kids to sleep in "the family bed"

Rest is vital to your child's health, growth, and development. *Healthy Sleep Habits, Happy Child* outlines proven strategies that ensure good, healthy sleep for every age.

Published by Ballantine Books
Available wherever books are sold

About the Author

A pediatrician for thirty years, MARC WEISSBLUTH, M.D., is also a leading researcher on sleep and children. He founded the original Sleep Disorders Center at Chicago's Children's Memorial Hospital in 1985 and is a Professor of Clinical Pediatrics at Northwestern University School of Medicine. Dr. Weissbluth discovered that sleep is linked to temperament and that sleeping problems are related to infant colic. His landmark seven-year study on the development and disappearance of naps highlighted the importance of daytime sleep. In addition to his own research, he has written chapters on sleep problems in textbooks for pediatricians, lectured extensively to parent groups, and appeared on *Oprah*. Dr. Weissbluth has been married for thirty-eight years to Linda, and she has provided both inspiration and original ideas for this book. Dr. Weissbluth is the father of four sons, two grandsons, and, thankfully, one granddaughter—and they are all good sleepers.

Look for this completely revised and expanded version of a classic!

HEALTHY
SLEEP
HABITS,
HAPPY
CHILD

3rd Edition
Completely
Revised and
Expanded!

A
step-by-step
program for a
good night's
sleep

"I love Dr. Weissbluth's philosophy that
the most important thing to have is a well-
rested family. And fortunately, thanks to
this book, most days (and nights) we do!"
—From the foreword by
CINDY CRAWFORD

Marc
Weissbluth, M.D.
Author of *Your Fussy Baby*

In this new edition, Dr. Marc Weissbluth, one of the country's leading pediatricians, updates his groundbreaking approach to solving and preventing your children's sleep problems. He explains with authority and reassurance his step-by-step regime for instituting beneficial habits within the framework of your child's natural sleep cycles. This valuable sourcebook contains the following new material:

- How to handle "nap-resistant" kids and when to start sleep-training
- Help for working moms and children with sleep issues
- Expanded discussion on the father's role in comforting children
- Key studies on how early sleep troubles can lead to later problems
- The benefits and drawbacks of allowing kids to sleep in "the family bed"

Rest is vital to your child's health, growth, and development. *Healthy Sleep Habits, Happy Child* outlines proven strategies that ensure good, healthy sleep for every age.